CLAUSEWITZ ON SMALL WAR

Clausewitz on Small War

CARL VON CLAUSEWITZ

Edited and Translated
by
CHRISTOPHER DAASE AND
JAMES W. DAVIS
With an Introductory Essay by
JAMES W. DAVIS

OXFORD
UNIVERSITY PRESS

OXFORD

UNIVERSITY PRESS

Great Clarendon Street, Oxford, OX2 6DP,
United Kingdom

Oxford University Press is a department of the University of Oxford.
It furthers the University's objective of excellence in research, scholarship,
and education by publishing worldwide. Oxford is a registered trade mark of
Oxford University Press in the UK and in certain other countries

First Edition published in 2015

Published in the United States of America by Oxford University Press
198 Madison Avenue, New York, NY 10016, United States of America

British Library Cataloguing in Publication Data
Data available

Library of Congress Control Number: 2015938216

ISBN 978–0–19–873713–1

Acknowledgments

In preparing this volume we have benefitted from the assistance and counsel of many colleagues and friends. Preliminary drafts of the translations were presented to a group of eminent Clausewitz scholars at a workshop convened at the Nitze School of Advanced International Studies in Washington, DC, and revised to address critical feedback. And while we no doubt have failed to redress every shortcoming identified, we are deeply indebted to Christopher Bassford, Eliot Cohen, Antulio Echevarria, Andreas Herberg-Rothe, Terence Holmes, Jan Willem Honig, Timothy Hoyt, Brad Lee, Jack Levy, Thomas Mahnken, and John Sumida for their constructive criticism. We wish to extend special thanks to Thomas Mahnken and his colleagues in the Philip Merrill Center for Strategic Studies at the Nitze School for hosting the workshop.

Over the course of the translations, we also benefitted from discussions with General Klaus Naumann, Sebastian Schindler, Peter Platzgummer, Marc DeVore, Rolf Sieferle, and Dirk Ippen.

Alexander Graef, Karl Hampel, and Sebastian Plappert provided invaluable assistance preparing the manuscript for publication and creating the bibliography.

Finally, we gladly acknowledge the financial support we enjoyed from the Smith-Richardson Foundation without which this project would not have been possible. In particular, we thank Nadia Schadlow who not only saw merit in the project but also stuck with us during eventual delays in its completion.

Christopher Daase and James W. Davis

Contents

List of illustrations

1

Introduction to Clausewitz on Small War

James W. Davis

Ongoing and lively debates over the continuing relevance of Clausewitz in an era in which the incidence of interstate warfare pales in comparison to that of civil and ethnic conflict, transnational terrorism, and other forms of asymmetric violence, attest to his enduring status as a giant in the study of war. In the English-speaking world, that status results largely, perhaps even exclusively, from the prominence accorded his major work, *On War*, in universities, think tanks, and military academies. Engagement with the ideas developed in *On War* is facilitated by the fact that the first edition, published in 1832, now is available in numerous English-language translations.[1]

The corpus of Clausewitz's writings on the topic of warfare, however, is far greater. The military historian Werner Hahlweg, long-time curator of Clausewitz's papers at the University of Münster, eventually edited and published two collections of his articles, studies, lectures, and letters, that together amount to over two thousand pages.[2] With few exceptions, most of these texts are inaccessible to scholars and military analysts who do not read German. They simply have never been translated. The current volume represents an effort to begin to redress this unfortunate state of affairs.

Persuaded that many arguments over Clausewitz's general theory of warfare and its relevance for contemporary developments could benefit from a more thorough knowledge of the evolution of his thinking on the subject, as well as a better appreciation of the specific political context within which many of the ideas emerged, we have translated what we regard to be Clausewitz's most important writings on the subject of "Small War." For most of what is included here, no other English translation is available. The goal is not to

---

[1] See, for example, Clausewitz (1835), which originally appeared in *The Metropolitan Magazine* (London), 13 (May and June 1835), 64–71, 166–76; also Clausewitz (1873, 1908, 1909, 1943, 1984). Unless otherwise indicated, subsequent English language quotations from *On War* and the relevant page references refer to the 1984 volume.

[2] See Hahlweg (1966–90).

offer a particular interpretation of Clausewitz's writings, although some of the ongoing controversies are engaged in this introductory essay. Rather, the intention is to stimulate additional scholarship and debate: both over the proper interpretation and the relevance of his analyses for understanding various forms of warfare.

Our approach to translation is not different from that adopted by Michael Howard and Peter Paret in their widely acclaimed and cited translation of *On War* (Clausewitz 1984: xi): "We have attempted to present Clausewitz's ideas as accurately as possible, while remaining as close to his style and vocabulary as modern English usage would permit. But we have not hesitated to translate the same term in different ways if the context seemed to demand it." Because the meaning of many German terms has evolved since the time of Clausewitz, we consulted sources from the period as well as the works of military historians in an effort to ensure their proper translation. For many terms, the German is included in parenthesis for the benefit of those with knowledge of the language. When confronted with awkward or overly complex formulations, we chose to simplify them, preferring to sacrifice nineteenth-century style for clearer meaning.

We have translated the original texts as they appear in the Hahlweg volumes and added some annotations, but we have not included the marginalia contained in the original lecture notes or the extensive annotations, historical references, and comments provided by Hahlweg. Diagrams found in the original lecture notes, which are accessible to scholars in the *Universitäts- und Landesbibliothek Münster*, have been photographically reproduced and integrated into the text with explanatory captions provided by Daase and Davis. However, we chose to omit some additional material that Clausewitz apparently used to provide historical examples of general points. And whereas Hahlweg provided precise transcriptions of original texts, reproducing errors in spelling or numeration, in most cases we have corrected errors in spelling, used contemporary spellings for names and places as well as German-language terms, and provided consistent numerations in the various lists that appear throughout the manuscript. To foster easier comparison with the Hahlweg transcriptions, we have not corrected for Clausewitz's inconsistent numbering of paragraphs in the "Lectures on Small War," but have included the bracketed corrections made by Hahlweg. Because Clausewitz circulated them among fellow reform-minded soldiers, the original lecture notes also comprise numerous comments of uncertain provenance written in the margins of the main text. Hahlweg went to great lengths to try to establish the identity of the authors of the marginalia, but we have restricted our translations to those parts of the text that are clearly written by Clausewitz himself. Footnotes that are original to Clausewitz are indicated by a cue system that follows the pattern: *, †, ‡, §, ¶. Annotations and references from the editors of this volume are footnoted with Arabic numerals. Finally, we have chosen to identify sections in the texts that Clausewitz underscored, presumably for emphasis, with bold font.

We chose four texts for this collection. In the "Lectures on Small War" held at the Prussian War College in 1810 and 1811, Clausewitz analyzed small-unit warfare by studying the rebellion in the Vendée (1793–8), the Tyrolean uprising of 1809, and most prominently, the then ongoing Spanish insurrection in the Peninsular War against Napoleonic France. In the *Bekenntnisdenkschrift*, or testimonial, of 1812, Clausewitz calls for a "Spanish civil war in Germany" and develops a political argument and military strategy for a popular insurgency against the French occupation of Prussia. In the short text, "On the political advantages and disadvantages of the Prussian institution of the *Landwehr*," from 1819, Clausewitz discusses the specific organizational form of the Prussian citizen militia that was improvised in 1813, officially established in the Defense Act of 1814, but ultimately subordinated to the regular army in 1819 as a result of the fear and resentment it inspired among aristocratic officers and an alleged history of poor performance.[3] For Clausewitz, the military effectiveness of the *Landwehr*, especially in strategic defense, was a proven fact. Hence he devotes the text—which he sent to his fellow military reformer, Field Marshal Neidhardt von Gneisenau, as well as the Prussian Chancellor and political reformer Karl August von Hardenberg—to a political defense of a citizens' militia in an era of revolution.[4] Finally, we provide a new translation of a short chapter from *On War*. In Chapter 26 of Book VI—entitled *Volksbewaffnung* or "The arming of the people"—Clausewitz addresses the practical as well as theoretical aspects of popular uprising and guerrilla warfare. Placed in the context of the "Lectures on Small War" and the *Bekenntnisdenkschrift*, it seems safe to argue that biographically and intellectually "The arming of the people" reflects some of Clausewitz's earliest thinking about warfare.

CLAUSEWITZ ON WAR

Widely recognized as one of the most influential theorists of war, if not the greatest of all time, Carl von Clausewitz is nonetheless more often cited than read. Frequently taken out of context, his thoughts have been used to support a stunning range of contradictory claims by journalists, businessmen, scholars, soldiers, and politicians. But even serious scholars and military students of Clausewitz disagree on the precise meaning of key tenets of his thought and interpret central arguments in rather different ways.

[3] See Showalter (1971).   [4] See Moran (1989).

Thus, Clausewitz is variously criticized as the *spiritus rector* of Prussian militarism and championed as an advocate for the subordination of the military to civilian political authority.[5] Some criticize him for an excessive level of abstraction bordering on the metaphysical.[6] For others, his analysis stands out for its "jargon-free language" and the successful combination of abstract theory and historical practice.[7]

By no means the product of intellectual dilettantism, the origins of these ongoing debates are at least twofold. Most fundamental is the fact that Clausewitz's magnum opus, *On War*, is an unfinished work, published posthumously by his widow. Clausewitz was aware of the ambiguities and imperfections in the manuscript, and in a note dated July 10, 1827 (four years prior to his death) admitted: "I regard the first six books, which are already in a clean copy, merely as a rather formless mass that must be thoroughly reworked once more." In 1830 he wrote: "The manuscript on the conduct of major operations that will be found after my death can, in its present state, be regarded as nothing but a collection of materials from which a theory of war was to have been distilled."[8] Prior to his death on November 16, 1831, the great theorist of war had completed revisions on only the first of the eight books comprising *On War*.

Exacerbating the confusion created by the ambiguities of the original text are disputes arising from its translation. Many scholars of war and the history of ideas cannot read German, and hence their understanding of Clausewitz is strongly influenced by the way individual translations cope with ambiguities in the original text as well as with concepts for which there may be multiple meanings. The problem is central to English-language debates, where scholars working from translations of *On War* in which key concepts as well as important analytical and theoretical devices have been translated in different ways reach very different interpretations of central claims as well as of the work as a whole.

Take, for example, what is certainly Clausewitz's most famous dictum: *"Der Krieg ist eine bloße Fortsetzung der Politik mit anderen Mitteln."* For translators the rather short sentence poses a daunting challenge, owing to the fact that the German word *"Politik"* can take on at least three meanings for which

---

[5] For the former claim, see Mertsalov (2004). Additional examples are provided in Strachan (2001: 373–4); B. H. Liddell Hart (1932: 24) attributed the pernicious effects of Clausewitz's writings to an "obscure" style of writing. For claims that Clausewitz provides an intellectual antidote to militarism, see Brodie (1973) and Huntington (1957).

[6] See, for example, Camon (1911: vii), quoted by Rothfels (1943: 93) and Eikmeier (2013).

[7] The former argument was made by Brodie (1984: 45). The latter argument is developed in Sumida (2001: 333–54).

[8] Both notes are reproduced in Clausewitz (1984), the Howard and Paret translation of *On War*, pp. 69–71. There is some debate as to the correct dating of these letters. See Gat (2001: 257–65).

English provides distinct words. If one translates *Politik* with "policy," as do Michael Howard and Peter Paret in what is perhaps the most widely used English language translation of *On War*, one is likely to conclude that Clausewitz is making a normative argument: Because "war is merely the continuation of policy by other means," its conduct should always be governed by an appreciation of the state's ultimate political goals. For many scholars and military analysts, the belief that Clausewitz was a strong proponent of the subordination of military means to political ends then serves as a justification for criticizing historical instances of the militarization of politics.[9]

If, however, one translates *Politik* with "politics" or "political affairs," as suggested by scholars such as Antulio Echevarria, Clausewitz's dictum seems more appropriately understood as a descriptive statement.[10] War *is* merely the continuation of politics by other means.[11] Understanding Clausewitz's dictum as an assertion of fact leads to the conclusion that *On War* is first and foremost an effort to uncover objective knowledge about the phenomenon of war rather than a primer on military, let alone political, strategy.

Although some might argue that good strategy rests on an understanding, if only intuitive, of valid causal regularities, Clausewitz was not so certain. If commanders were to try to master all that can be known of war, they might become bogged down in the trivial details of academic knowledge. "[D]istinguished commanders," Clausewitz (1984: 145) asserted, "have never emerged from the ranks of the most erudite or scholarly officers, but have been for the most part men whose station in life could not have brought them a high degree of education.... Everyone with a grain of common sense realized the vast distance between a genius of the highest order and a learned pedant."[12]

At other points in the text, however, war is analyzed less through the lens of political process or substantive policy objectives and more through that of the formal, structural, or institutional manifestations of politics. Thus, in Book VIII, Chapter 3 B, "On the Magnitude of the Military Purpose and its Corresponding Efforts," Clausewitz (1984: 586) engages in a form of comparative political analysis in which different political systems are held to produce different forms of warfare:

---

[9] This was at least one of the claims made by Harry Summers in his influential critique of the American conduct of the Vietnam War. See Summers (1984: 137). Also see Cohen (2002).

[10] See Echevarria II (2007: 4) and Echevarria II (1996: 76–80).

[11] The dictum appears no less than six times in *On War*. Twice, however, Clausewitz replaces the word *Politik* with the concept "*politischer Verkehr*," which is best translated as "political intercourse" or perhaps "political commerce." Insofar as intercourse and commerce refer to a relationship between two or more political actors, confining the meaning of *Politik* to the policies of one or the other of these seems misplaced. See the discussion in Daase and Schindler (2009: 712).

[12] Sumida (2008: 2) has argued that Clausewitz was interested in developing a theory of the practice and not the phenomenon of war, because "no theory of war as a phenomenon was capable of representing the nature of war as it occurred in reality."

A more general and theoretical treatment of the subject may become feasible if we consider the nature of states and societies as they are determined by their times and prevailing conditions. Let us take a brief look at history.

The semi-barbarous Tartars, the republics of antiquity, the feudal lords and commercial cities of the Middle Ages, kings of the eighteenth century, and finally, princes and peoples of the nineteenth century all waged war in their own way, conducted it differently, with different means, and for different aims.

In the ensuing analysis, Clausewitz (1984: 586) demonstrates how specific historical relationships among rulers, their populations, and military institutions combine to produce distinctive forms of warfare:

The Tartar hordes searched for new land. Setting forth as a nation, with women and children, they outnumbered any other army. Their aim was to subdue their enemies or expel them. If a high degree of civilization could have been combined with such methods, they would have carried all before them.

The republics of antiquity, Rome excepted, were small and their armies smaller still, for the plebs, the mass of the people, was excluded. Being so many and so close together these republics found that the balance that some law of nature will always establish among small and unconnected units formed an obstacle to major enterprises. They therefore limited their wars to plundering the countryside and seizing a few towns, in order to gain a degree of influence over them.

A few paragraphs further Clausewitz (1984: 589) argues:

The Tartar people and army had been one; in the republics of antiquity and during the Middle Ages the people (if we confine the concept to those who had the rights of citizens) had still played a prominent part; but in the circumstances of the eighteenth century the people's part had been extinguished.

Because the outer form of warfare changes in each specific instance owing to differing relationships between peoples, soldiers, political authority, and territory, Clausewitz compares war, the essence of which he seeks to understand, to a chameleon. Although the essential biology of the chameleon remains constant, its appearance changes to match particular circumstances.[13] The same, Clausewitz argues, is true of war.

To account for war's changing appearance despite its enduring constitution, Clausewitz (2010: 46–7) develops and employs the analytic device of the trinity:

War is thus not merely a chameleon, because it changes its nature somewhat in every concrete case. Rather, with respect to the dominant tendencies within, it is in its complete appearance a wondrous trinity, comprised of the primordial violence of its elements, hatred and enmity, which can be seen as a blind natural

---

[13] The irreducibility of an organism's phenotype to its genotype is now widely accepted in the biological sciences.

instinct; of the play of chance and accident, which makes it an affair of the free spirit; and of the subordinated nature of a political instrument that is subject to pure reason.

The first of these facets is allocated primarily to the population, the second more to the commander and his army, the third more to the government. The passions, which should burn in war, must already be inherent in the peoples. The scope that the play of courage and talent will enjoy in the realm of chance and accident depends on the characteristics of the commander and his army, but the political purpose is the propriety of the government alone.

These three tendencies, which thus appear as three different laws, are deeply anchored in the nature of the subject and simultaneously subject to variation in relationship to one another. A theory that ignores one of these facets or wishes to set an arbitrary relationship among them, conflicts with reality to such a degree that it must be disregarded for this reason alone.

Thus the task is to suspend the theory between these three tendencies, as between three points of attraction.[14]

Clausewitz's comparative analysis of different historical manifestations of warfare—e.g. war perpetrated by stateless Tartar hordes, ancient city-states, feudal lords, and the territorial states of the nineteenth century—and the analytic device of the trinity, which draws our attention to the effects of changing relations amongst the constitutive features (hatred and enmity, chance and contingency, subordination to reason) of war, attest to the goal of developing a general theory of warfare, freed from the specifics of time and place. Clausewitz warns against fixing an arbitrary relationship amongst the elements of the trinity. To do so would be to miss the point of the analytic exercise.[15] It is an exercise in which he had engaged at least since 1812, as the following passage from the *Bekenntnisdenkschrift* makes clear:

The war of the current era is a war of all against all. Kings no longer wage war against kings, nor armies against each other, but one nation against the other, the nation encompassing the king and army.

It is unlikely that this character of war will change again, and it truly is not to be wished that the old bloody and the too often boring chess-game of struggling soldiers will ever return.

This is not to say that the national uprising *en Masse*, as we have twice witnessed in great examples (France and Spain), will be the only way in which nations will wage war against each other in the future, heaven help us. This phenomenon belongs alone to the present and its fateful hours.[16]

[14] Translation mine.
Because I find the Howard and Paret translation of this essential passage unsatisfactory and a source for much subsequent confusion, I have chosen to offer my own translation here. Similar efforts (for similar reasons) have been made by Bassford (1999) and Echevarria II (2007: 69).
[15] For an excellent discussion of Clausewitz's method of analysis, see Echevarria II (2007: chs 1 and 2).
[16] See p. 216 of this volume.

Curiously, however, Clausewitz's ideas regularly come up for criticism as time-bound and obsolete. Thus, in the period leading to the First World War, the Prussian officer and military historian Colmar von der Goltz (1887: 114–16) argued that Clausewitz had lost his relevance in an industrial era characterized by ever larger armies with modern arms, complex mobilization schedules, and dramatically increased costs:

> War has not withdrawn itself from the effects of politics; yet its influence is modified in comparison with former times. Clausewitz may talk of wars, such as the wars of coalition, or the Austrian Wars of Succession, when the Allied Powers bound themselves to support one or the other with a definite number of combatants, when operations were undertaken with a part and not the whole of the forces, and policy alone stood in the foreground, but we, in these days, can disregard all this. Such conditions are scarcely conceivable in modern Europe. . . .
> If two European Powers of the first order clash together, their whole organised forces will, from the outset, be set in motion to decide their quarrel. All political considerations, such as attach to the lukewarm half-ness of wars of alliance fall to the ground. . . . In the face of the great weight of warlike events in our modern times, politics retreat more and more into the background, so soon as the cannon thunder."[17]

Goltz may have been correct to note that the specific form of the Wars of the Austrian Succession was different from the likely form of wars to come, but he does not provide sufficient grounds for dismissing the analytic framework of the trinity. The relationship between the increasingly urban and industrial population, a mechanized army, and a semi-constitutional monarchy in Wilhelmine Germany was already quite different from the relationship of the people, army, and government that prevailed in the absolute monarchies of the mid-eighteenth century.[18]

During the Cold War, Goltz's argument, that Clausewitz had become irrelevant because the dynamics of the industrial age removed political constraints on the scope of warfare, was echoed by those who believed that nuclear war would inevitably lead to annihilation. For example, Peter Moody argued that the inherent escalatory dynamics of nuclear war transformed Clausewitz's notion of total war from an ideal type to an empirical form. War, he argued, "is no longer an instrument of state policy, a means whereby those who rule the state achieve their values; instead it is the fact or possibility of total war that determines the values of the state" (Moody 1979: 424).

By contrast, at the start of the twenty-first century, it is his alleged inapplicability to low-intensity, irregular, and asymmetric conflicts that lead many to dismiss Clausewitz as obsolete. Thus, Mary Kaldor (2012: 17) argues that

---

[17] See too the discussion in Howard (1984: 31–3).
[18] Goltz was himself an advocate of uniting the roles of statesman and Commander-in-Chief in the person of the King. See Goltz (1887: 117).

globalization has produced a situation in which "the centralized, territorialized modern state gives way to new types of polity . . . so war, as we presently conceive it, is becoming an anachronism." Because "the type of war that Clausewitz analysed, even though he did devote some writing to small wars, was predominantly war between states for a definable political end, i.e. state interest," Clausewitz is of limited utility when trying to understand contemporary asymmetric conflicts (Kaldor 2012: 17). In a similar vein, Philip Wilkinson (2003: 29) finds that in the current age of low-intensity conflicts, "the European Westphalian state model and Clausewitzian approach to military operations [have] been thoroughly challenged and found wanting." Some have gone so far as to blame the suboptimal outcomes of the US engagements in Iraq and Afghanistan on the undue influence of Clausewitz and his outmoded conception of "monarchical war" (Melton 2009).

The claim that Clausewitz's thought is obsolete is justified not only by a purported exclusive focus on states and state interests at the expense of non-state or sub-state actors, but also an asserted failure to appreciate that some wars are governed by an economic rather than political logic (Kaldor 2010: 271–81). Clearly influenced by the prevalence of ethnic conflicts, civil wars, and conflicts over the control of natural resources in late twentieth and early twenty-first centuries, Kaldor (2010: 274) argues that war is no longer best characterized as a "contests of wills" but rather as a "mutual enterprise" in which "both sides need the other in order to carry on the enterprise of war and therefore war tends to be long and inconclusive." Old wars were about defeating the enemy, whereas in new wars, "[t]he aim is to create a state of war in which particular groups benefit. In new wars, battles are rare and violence is mainly directed against avoidance of direct combat" (Kaldor 2010: 274). "The inner tendency of such wars is not war without limits but war without end. Wars, defined in this way, create shared self-perpetuating interest in war to reproduce political identity and to further economic interest" (Kaldor 2012: 218).

Kaldor is not alone in her dismissal of Clausewitz's relevance for an understanding of contemporary warfare. Herfried Münkler (2008: 37, 2004, 2003: 25), though an admirer of Clausewitz's mode of analysis, nonetheless has argued that the concept of war today needs to be decoupled from that of politics, as warfare is increasingly governed by processes of privatization and their attendant economic logic. Similarly, David Keen (2000: ch. 2) has suggested that in the current age war is rather more the continuation of economics by other means. And the claim that wars driven by ethnic conflict and the politics of identity cannot be accommodated in Clausewitz's framework is echoed by the Tofflers (Toffler and Toffler 1994), Donald Snow (1997), and Monty Marshall (1997: ch. 6).

Martin van Creveld (1991) has repeatedly argued that the trinitarian conception of warfare—understood by him simply in terms of the people, the government, and the army—does not apply to contemporary non-state actors.[19] John Keegan (1994: 58) has dismissed Clausewitz as inapplicable to the sorts of "primitive war" seen in the Balkans and Transcaucasia in the 1990s. These, he argued, were "fed by passions and rancours that do not yield to rational measures of persuasion or control: they are apolitical to a degree for which Clausewitz made little allowance." And writing in the decade prior to the terrorist attacks of September 2001, Edward Luttwak (1995: 115–16) derided an American military mentality that was steeped in outdated Clausewitzian concepts and thus ill-suited to meeting the challenge of "aggressors inflamed by nationalism or religious fanaticism." Leaving aside the problematic interpretation of Clausewitz presented in his analysis, Luttwak seems to have missed the fact that at the time, at least some in the US military were making similar arguments. According to one army officer: "Combating modern terrorism or large drug-dealing enterprises may require nations to mount warlike efforts against amorphous and shadowy transnational networks—an idea rather far removed from the Clausewitzian concept of war between states obliging the clash of opposing field armies" (Shepherd 1990: 86).[20]

The alleged obsolescence of Clausewitz in the early twenty-first century is thus attributed to a time-bound framework of analysis and a failure to anticipate forms of warfare beyond the rather symmetric pitched battlefield exchanges of large regular armies—the "old wars" that are said to have characterized his own times.[21] The problem with such criticisms is that they apply rather more to later interpretations of Clausewitz's writings than to the writings themselves, for Clausewitz did write on the interrelationship of national identity and war, the economic logic of warfare, and also low-intensity and asymmetric conflict.[22] To date, however, the most extensive treatment of these subjects, Clausewitz's "Lectures on Small War" held at the Prussian War College (*Allgemeine Kriegsschule*) in Berlin from 1810–11, have been inaccessible to scholars unable to read the original German. The near exclusive focus of Anglo-Saxon scholars on the unfinished work *On War* obscures the true breadth of Clausewitz's strategic thought, which extends to the prosecution of wars of national liberation, guerrilla-style warfare, light-unit tactics and their relationship to overall strategy, and the political economy of sub-state warfare. Indeed, the development of Clausewitz's thinking on war in general is closely linked to his analysis of Small War. Seen in the context of the evolution of his thinking over time, the political conception of warfare at the center of *On War* is clearly not limited to state actors engaged in pitched battles, but provides an analytic framework with

---

[19] The US version of the book is entitled *Transformation of War*. See too van Creveld (2002: 8).
[20] For an excellent critique of van Creveld's and Luttwak's interpretations of Clausewitz, see Kinross (2004: 35–58).
[21] See Strachan (2011: 113).
[22] For a similar critique see Villacres and Bassford (1995: 10).

which the transformation of political violence can be understood or even explained.[23]

In presenting Clausewitz's most explicit thinking on these topics outside of the rather short discussion in Book VI, Chapter 26 ("The People in Arms") in *On War*, we provide the first full English translation of the lectures on Small War. The concept of Small War and its relationship to Clausewitz's overall approach to understanding war are the topics of the remainder of this introductory essay.

SMALL WAR

In the language of the eighteenth and nineteenth centuries, asymmetric military conflict was routinely referred to as Small War.[24] In French, the appropriate term was "*petite guerre*"; in German, "*kleiner Krieg.*" The Spanish-language term "*guerrilla*" originally referred to the nature of the conflict—Small War—rather than the political aspirations of the combatants. The original *guerrilleros* were reactionary Roman Catholic Bourbon royalists, not supporters of the revolution (Heuser 2010b: 393–4). In his survey of the literature, Martin Rink (2006: 360) identified approximately sixty works published on the topic of Small War in the period between 1750 and 1850. He found the early literature primarily devoted to describing and conceptualizing the phenomenon, a process that stretched at least from the writings of the French officer de la Croix from 1752 to the publication of Scharnhorst's military handbook in 1792. As late as 1864 one author could still criticize what he regarded the "checkered list of items" presented by contemporary analysts of Small War.[25]

Clausewitz thus began his lectures with a definition that was consistent with eighteenth- and early nineteenth-century usage: "We understand Small Wars to be the use of small units in the field. Battles of 20, 50, 100, 300 or 400 soldiers, as long as they are not part of a larger battle, fall under Small War."[26] Similar to that of others in the period, the definition is narrower than later uses of the term, which came to encompass almost any form of asymmetric conflict.[27] Nevertheless, the makeup of units engaged in Small War as defined by Clausewitz and practiced in the eighteenth and nineteenth centuries was

---

[23] For a full development of this argument, see Daase and Schindler (2009).

[24] Beatrice Heuser traces the term's origins to Sebastián de Covarrubias who in his dictionary of 1611 used it to refer to feuds and civil war. See Heuser (2010b: 391).

[25] See Rink (2006), Croix (1759), and Scharnhorst (1980).

[26] See p. 21 of this volume.

[27] See, for example, Jeney (1759: ch. 1), Roche (1770), and Ewald (1774: 74, 1798, 1790: 17–23).

diverse and one should be careful not to impose more conceptual order on Clausewitz's thinking than the texts allow. Indeed, Clausewitz goes on to say that the "definition may seem mechanical and unphilosophical," thus betraying a rejection of absolute definitions that characterizes his approach to the study of warfare in general.[28] In addition to light regular troops, he variously applied the term to units recruited from the ethnic minorities of the Habsburg Empire who were skilled in so-called "Eastern" methods of sabotage and ambush (a practice later emulated in other parts of Europe); specialized units equipped with precision rifles (e.g. the *Tirailleurs* of the French Revolutionary Wars and the *Jäger*, spawned by Prussia's encounter with the Napoleonic forces); as well as irregular troops taken from the ranks of the peasantry. Small units of the sort devoted to specialized operations were referred to as *Partheyen* in German, *parties* in French; their leaders as *Partheygänger* or *partisan* respectively.[29]

Beatrice Heuser maintains that well into the nineteenth century, the term "partisan warfare" was reserved for what we today call special operations: "Until the American War of Independence and then the Napoleonic Wars, partisan warfare was entirely devoid of ideology or other political content, but was professional warfare carried out by professional units specializing not in regular war and pitched battles but in irregular activities" (Heuser 2010b: 391). For example, the Hessian Andreas Emmerich, who led light units during the American War of Independence (1775–83) on the side of the British, referred to his own men as "partisans." Their purpose was to harass the enemy, gather intelligence, and support the efforts of the regulars (Heuser 2010a: 143). But developments during the two revolutionary conflicts led to the expansion of the concept of Small War such that by the time of Clausewitz's writings, it could include ideologically driven "peoples' wars" as well as insurgencies backed by small bands of ideologically motivated fighters supported by the local population (Heuser 2010a: 149–58).

Clausewitz was clearly aware of the use to which General Washington put irregular light units in the American War of Independence, and cites numerous examples from the writings of Emmerich, Scharnhorst, and Johann von Ewald (who was a veteran of the Seven Years' War and also fought on the side of the British in the American War) in the lectures.[30] Nonetheless, he makes no mention of the ideological motivations of the colonists—the desire to shake off the yoke of British rule—in his discussions of the American War. Indeed, the lectures are largely devoid of any discussion of ideology as a motivation for

---

[28] On this point see Paret (2010).
[29] The discussion here follows that found in Rink (2006: 361–5). See too Heuser (2010b: 391–2).
[30] In addition to the works of Scharnhorst and Ewald cited above, see Emmerich (1789).

engaging in Small War, a significant oversight in the opinion of some (Heuser 2010a: 149).

By contrast, the *Bekenntnisdenkschrift*, with its frequent references to the counter-revolutionary and monarchist peasants' uprising in the Vendée (1793–6), and the Tyrolean insurgency against Napoleon's Bavarian allies in 1809, betrays a keen understanding of the martial potential of ideologically motivated irregulars drawn from the population. The discussion of the *Landsturm* (people's militia) is particularly illustrative:

> Very few people have a clear understanding of the full extent of this fearsome, decisive measure, which throws the country into a state of dangerous crisis. They do not understand how individual citizens or communities, united into loose bands, can possess the daring courage to resist a large army or even just to enrage it through inflicting losses on its distant units.
>
> The basic idea is the following. Every able-bodied man from 18 to 60 years, who does not serve in the standing forces, is armed and belongs to the *Landsturm*. Their arms and equipment include nothing more than a musket, if unavailable a pike or a scythe, a pack to carry a few days' worth of foodstuffs and some munition, a cap, outfitted with a straw wreath to protect against blows and on which a sign of the province and the commune is affixed.
>
> This outfitting certainly does not demand too much. The farmers in the Vendée have equipped themselves without any external support even more completely.[31]

For Clausewitz, extraordinary courage and morale would be guaranteed by the fact that the irregulars of the *Landsturm* would be fighting to defend their own homes and villages against a foreign foe.[32]

In separating his discussion of the technical and practical dimensions of small-unit warfare from his thinking on the political purposes toward which Small War could be applied, Clausewitz was not only keeping true to his general approach to scientific analysis but also was quite characteristic of the period. Most writings on the subject of Small War at the time were apolitical, whereas the plans of Prussian patriots to engage in it were revolutionary, both because they were inspired by national ideology and because they proposed the integration of the historically unarmed peasantry into the war effort (Rink 2006: 373).

Together, the "Lectures on Small War" and the *Bekenntnisdenkschrift* provide a more complete picture of Clausewitz's thinking on Small War than either alone. Thus, whereas Heuser is correct to note that he devotes

---

[31] See p. 196 in this volume.
[32] See, for example, pp. 189, 196, and 214 in this volume. Clausewitz betrays similar sentiments in the short analysis, "On the political advantages and disadvantages of the Prussian institution of the *Landwehr*." See pp. 217–20 in this volume. For an analysis of the political and ideological effects of the French Revolution on Small War thinking in Prussia, see Hahlweg (1962: 56).

the bulk of his analysis in the lectures to the ways in which small detachments can be used for special operations in support of the major war effort, the conclusion that Clausewitz understood Small War exclusively as "an auxiliary part of major war . . . a side show to the main confrontations of regular forces" is open to debate (Heuser 2010a: 145). For example, in the lectures, Clausewitz discusses how small forward posts can be used to confuse the enemy and slow his advance. By avoiding direct confrontation of the main enemy formation, small units can contribute to strategic goals by hindering the enemy's ability to conduct reconnaissance, forcing him to disperse his forces, and thereby lengthening his lines of communication.

The potential contribution of the *Landsturm* to the goal of driving French forces from Prussia as discussed in the *Bekenntnisdenkschrift* is far greater than that of auxiliary support for the major war effort: "The first characteristic, if it is to be that which it was for the Austrians in 1809—namely, a rich source for reinforcing the army and a defensive militia for remote spots of the war theater—seems to be inappropriate for our situation, because a large number of our provinces will be cut off from the army."[33] Rather, through raids on convoys and storehouses as well as by ambushing and harassing enemy detachments, irregular forces could play an independent role in the war effort by forcing the French to disperse their forces in an effort to gain control of the countryside:

> If the enemy does not want to accept these disadvantages, if he wants to continue to rule all the distant provinces, he must maintain specific corps therein. It is easy to see that if, from an army of 200,000 men, 50,000 men are used for this purpose, this would already create a significant diversion in the central theater of war, for one must not forget, that from the remaining 150,000 men, according to all historical experience, another 50,000 will be absent, either in the sick bay or left behind as occupying forces. Thus, the *Landsturm* deprives the main theater of war of 1/3 of its armed forces according to simple calculations. Whoever is not able to appreciate this great advantage is lacking in good judgment in this matter. For he knows nothing of how things develop in war.[34]

Clausewitz's thinking here probably reflects the historical origins and development of Small War in eighteenth-century Europe. Rink (2006: 365; 1999: 93–8), for example, points out that attenuated rule along the fluid borders of the European "Wild East" and within the southeastern Slavic territories of the Habsburg Empire and the Ukraine depended on the presence of Cossacks, Hussars, Uhlans, and Pandurs. And it echoes the similar call of Ewald (1798: vol. 1, 106) to remember the experience of the Seven Years' War and allow small and light units to act independently of the army and beyond the main field of battle in the war against the French Republic.

---

[33] See pp. 195–6 of this volume.   [34] See p. 197 of this volume.

The military historian Hew Strachan (2011: 177) maintains that most of Clausewitz's thinking about warfare was devoted to strategy understood rather narrowly as "the use of engagement for the object of the war." In the lectures, Clausewitz states clearly that "the strategy of Small War is a component of tactics . . . the entirety of Small War belongs to tactics" whereas the purpose of Small War is based on the necessities of strategy.[35] In the *Bekenntnisdenkschrift* Clausewitz defines tactics as the "art of battle" whereas the term strategy is reserved for "the art of combining individual battles (for the end of the campaign, of the war) into a whole."[36] Insofar as the *avant-garde* and the forward posts, subjects to which Clausewitz devotes a great deal of attention in the lectures, detect the enemy, try to divine his intentions, and shape the subsequent battle, they are located "on the cusp of strategy and tactics," as Strachan (2011: 109) maintains. In many circumstances, they constitute the first forces to encounter the enemy and engage in combat. Understood in these terms, the question of whether Small War constitutes a "sideshow," as Heuser (2010a: 145) argues, is a function of whether and how it proves crucial to a given strategy.

Many contemporary failures to appreciate the potential that Clausewitz attached to Small War in pursuit of strategic ends probably result from the focus devoted to his discussion of decisive battles and the "center of gravity" in *On War*.[37] Others miss the fact that the ends for which Small War was to bring about its effects were both political and military in nature.[38] But in the discussions of the nature of defensive operations in the *Bekenntnisdenkschrift* and the lectures, Clausewitz makes clear that Small War can serve tactical military, strategic military, and political ends.[39] Political defense consists of the nation fighting for its survival rather than expansion. Strategic (military) defense involves the defense of national territory rather than conquest of foreign lands. Finally, tactical defense requires waiting for the enemy's attack rather than seizing the initiative and striking first.

It is certainly significant that Clausewitz used the *Bekenntnisdenkschrift*— an affirmation of his commitment to Prussian nationalism and call for popular insurgency in defense of the state's territorial integrity—to develop ideas on the relative strength of offense and defense that led to later and more

---

[35] See p. 23 of this volume.   [36] See p. 210 of this volume.

[37] See Clausewitz (1984), Book IV, Chs 9–12, Book VI, Ch. 27, and Book VIII, Ch. 4. There is considerable debate on whether "center of gravity" is the appropriate translation of the German term *"Schwerpunkt"* used by Clausewitz. For useful discussions of the issues involved, see Echevarria II (2004) and Strange and Iron (2004).

[38] See Rink (2006: 385, 1999: 357–9) and Pertz (1865: 106–42). The correspondence of Gneisenau reprinted in the latter volume contains arguments also found in the *Bekenntnisdenkschrift* and betrays the close friendship and frequent exchange of ideas that took place between the representatives of the anti-French faction in Prussian military and political circles.

[39] See pp. 209–16 in this volume.

elaborate expression in Book VI of *On War*. After calling for the arming of the peasants, the employment of bands of 2,000–5,000 men as well as larger formations of the *Landsturm*, Clausewitz turns to arguing that a defensive strategy can be supported through the effects produced by such units employed tactically for offensive ends: "It is self-evident, that the strategic defense does not necessarily imply a tactical defense. Within the theater of war that one has committed to defend, the enemy can be attacked wherever and whenever one pleases. Hence, one thereby has a means to completely destroy an enemy army as good as that offered by any offense: yes, it is easier in our own theater of war for us than for the enemy."[40] As Christopher Daase and Sebastian Schindler have pointed out, this form of "active defense" corresponds to contemporary understandings of guerrilla warfare, which aims to defeat the enemy through exhaustion.[41] Or as Clausewitz puts it in his discussion of the *Landsturm*: "In this way the enemy *corps* will have to overcome the most difficult defense and will lose strength daily in this most unfortunate of all wars."[42]

Thus, while Heuser (2010a: 149) yet again may be correct in pointing out that Clausewitz never focused on counter-insurgency, she distracts from the more interesting point that the writings on Small War comprise a rudimentary theory of insurgency as Werner Hahlweg (1986: 127–33), editor of the most comprehensive compendia of Clausewitz's writings, maintained. The main focus of the discussions of the *Landwehr* and *Landsturm* is directed at the strategic advantages that would accrue to Prussia if it were to move from reliance on a centralized state-controlled army toward a system of defense based on decentralized and relatively independent groups of armed volunteers drawn from the rural population. Indeed, this form of strategic defense is not far removed from guerrilla strategy as understood by Mao (Tse-Tung 1961: 46): "When guerrillas engage a stronger enemy, they withdraw when he advances; harass him when he stops; strike him when he is weary; pursue him when he withdraws. In guerrilla strategy, the enemy's rear, flanks, and other vulnerable spots are his vital points, and there he must be harassed, attacked, dispersed, exhausted and annihilated."

Clausewitz returned to the subject of popular insurrection in the relatively short chapter, "The People in Arms," in Book VI of *On War*. Echoing themes already developed in the *Bekenntnisdenkschrift* he argues that "general insurrection" or "popular uprising" must, with few exceptions, remain a form of strategic rather than tactical defense (Clausewitz 1984: 482). As such, it achieves its aims through a slow process of attrition:

---

[40] See *Bekenntnisdenkschrift*, p. 212 of this volume.
[41] The discussion here follows Daase and Schindler (2009: 705). See too Daase (2007).
[42] See *Bekenntnisdenkschrift*, p. 203 of this volume.

Its effect directs itself, as in the process of evaporation, toward the outer surface. The larger the surface area and the contact between it and the enemy army, that is, the more the latter is diffused, the more effective is the arming of the people. The arming of the people destroys the foundations of the enemy army like quietly smoldering embers.[43]

Because he thought that a very large territory would be a necessary condition for an insurgency by itself to sufficiently weaken the enemy, Clausewitz maintained that in practice, most insurgencies would be conducted in support of regular army operations. Nonetheless, the chapter identifies many of the specific mechanisms by which subsequent insurrections defeated occupying powers.

Moreover, the emergence of popular uprising as a feature of nineteenth-century warfare can be analyzed within the general trinitarian framework. Once again, the chameleon changes its outer form as a result of a shift in the relations amongst its constituent elements. Of particular importance is the fact that insurrection originates with the people rather than the state: "Where the enemy has not yet appeared, courage to get ready for him is not lacking, and bit by bit the bulk of the neighboring population will follow this example. In this way, the flame will spread like a fire in the heath and in the end will reach the territory on which the attacker is based."[44] Whereas in the eighteenth century the king and army could be conceived as independent from the people, in the nineteenth century the relationship was one of "the nation encompassing the king and army."[45] For Clausewitz, the people are the facet of war most characterized by primordial violence and its constituent elements hatred and enmity. Hence, "people's war in general is to be regarded as a consequence of the breaching of old artificial barriers by the warlike element in our times; as an extension and reinforcement of the entire process of fermentation, which we call war.... In most cases, those who resort to people's war in a rational manner will gain relative dominance over those who scorn it."[46]

STILL A CHAMELEON

Augmenting our understanding of Clausewitz with his early writings on Small War leads to the conclusion that asymmetric warfare is not a historical development that can be termed pre- or post-Clausewitzian as many

---

[43] See "The arming of the people," p. 222 of this volume.
[44] See "The arming of the people," p. 223 of this volume.
[45] See *Bekenntnisdenkschrift*, p. 216 of this volume.
[46] See "The arming of the people," pp. 221–2 of this volume.

contemporary scholars of war and military strategy argue. Rather it is an empirical exemplar of the general concept of war that can be analyzed, perhaps even explained, in terms of Clausewitz's general analytic framework. The theory developed in *On War* does not constitute a break with his earlier ideas on Small War; it reflects their further development. Hence, the appropriate test is not whether Clausewitz anticipated the forms of asymmetric or hybrid warfare that have come to characterize much armed conflict in the early part of the twenty-first century, or indeed transnational Islamist terrorism of the sort that has consumed the West in the decade following the attacks of September 2001. Rather, the question is whether the application of the analytic framework he developed leads to novel insights into important interrelationships. Clausewitz's framework directs our focus to changes in the relationship between the identity of warriors, the means of violence employed, and the purposes to which it is put. For these are the outward expressions of an inner change in the interaction among hatred and enmity, the play of chance, and efforts to subordinate violence to reason in pursuit of political objectives.[47]

Ultimately, war is an act of violence (Gewalt) intended to compel the enemy to submit to a foreign will (Clausewitz 1984: 75).[48] A close reading of Clausewitz's writings on Small War leads to the conclusion that he did not have a fixed conception of the political organizations that might adopt violent means or of the form the ensuing clash of wills would take. Rather, it is that which unifies warfare despite the diversity of its empirical forms that interested him.

---

[47] Daase and Schindler (2009: 736, fn. 16) argue that twenty-first-century terrorism shares much in common with insurrection and guerrilla warfare and is thus quite amenable to analysis in Clausewitzian terms. Whereas terrorist groups can pursue offensive or defensive political objectives, militarily they share with guerrilla war the strategic defense.

[48] I believe that "violence" rather than "force" is the more appropriate translation of the term *Gewalt* that appears in the German original.

2

My Lectures on Small War, held at the War College in 1810 and 1811

INTRODUCTION TO MY LECTURES

The topic of my lectures[1] is Small War and the operations of the General Staff. The reason for separating these from the other lectures on war is the intention to differentiate the mechanical from the scholarly. The General Staff's operations are mechanical, or, if you would prefer, technical skills, which relate to general war: reconnoitering, marching orders, etc. Small War, however, is not something mechanical or merely technical, though it depends even more on a certain virtuosity, that is, on the development and training of the natural abilities, whereas in general wars more scholarly and articulate views predominate.

You will certainly understand, that when Major Tiedemann[2] teaches you about the nature of war in its broad outlines, when he develops the general principles of war, and wishes to demonstrate the most important issues, the large battles and the relationship between them for the purpose of war, then he is not able to discuss simultaneously the positioning of pickets, the command of patrols etc. in similar detail, without overstretching the bounds of his lecture.

Therefore, those things are separated from these, which, though not quite so close to the main issue, nevertheless are too important to just to skim over. It has been left to me to analyze these things in detail for you and even more, to train you therein, so that you acquire that certain virtuosity, of which I spoke above.

---

[1] Clausewitz's lecture notes consist of 244 handwritten sheets of paper of varied size. See Clausewitz (1810). The text is not edited and was not intended to be published. Rather, it mirrors the spoken word. The translation is based on Werner Hahlweg's careful edition: *Carl von Clausewitz, Schriften, Aufsätze, Studien, Briefe* (1966–90: 226–449). The translation consists of the actual lectures, but omits the appendix comprising a collection of examples and *collectanea*. We greatly benefitted from Hahlweg's annotations and commentaries. We have inserted bracketed references to figures where useful to the reader.

[2] As Hahlweg notes, Karl Ludwig Heinrich v. Tiedemann (1777–1812) was, like Clausewitz, one of General Scharnhorst's favorite disciples. In November 1810 he was Director of Studies at the *Allgemeine Kriegsschule zu Berlin*.

In order to facilitate a coherent division, the analysis of the whole system of forward posts and other security measures of the army has been left to me, because these are encompassed primarily by Small War.

This will therefore be the first main subject of my lecture.

The second will be wars of smaller parties with offensive aims.

The third the General Staff's operations.

Since the subjects of my lecture are those things that first and foremost concern you, that primarily will determine your effectiveness, and in which you should have a certain competence, I will, therefore, mainly concentrate on giving you assignments and letting you work on these independently. I will do this more than I did last year because this year I have more time for it and also am more convinced of the utility of this method.

You would err if you always were to expect great insights in my lectures. Their subjects simply do not lend themselves thereto. Moreover, I am inclined to view things from the most natural and compelling position, and my entire merit will perhaps be found in the destruction of preconceived notions and the eradication of prejudices, and in this way, to remove every obstacle to such an extent as to allow you a clear view of the issue so that you will soon be in the position to draw your own conclusions, which is always best.

INTRODUCTION TO SMALL WAR

Introduction

What is Small War—what gives its tenets their autonomy—what is its relationship to the other teachings in the Art of War?*

---

* **Note**: As an overview, this is our classification of the Art of War. The entire Art of War is composed of

A. The **Supporting Arts**, which are concerned with the **acquisition** and **preparation** of war materials.
   1. **Acquisition.**—military economy borders on the civil affairs and relations.—Warminister.
   2. **Training of the acquired forces.**
      a. Weaponry Training
         α. Artillery,
         β. Construction of fortresses and Entrenchments.
      b. **The teaching and training of the troops.**—Elementary tactics.
      c. **Knowledge of the theater of war in the widest sense.**
B. **The Art of War Proper, which teaches the employment of the trained forces**
   1. Strategy
   2. Higher tactics. Of which Small War is a separate part.

We understand Small Wars to be the use of small units in the field. Battles of 20, 50, 100, 300 or 400 soldiers, as long as they are not part of a larger battle, fall under Small War.

This definition may seem mechanical and unphilosophical, but it is the true one, if one takes the traditional views of the concepts into consideration. It also may be the only one, but to prove this here would take us too far.

Thus, all warlike acts that are carried out with small units are elements of Small Wars. Of course it is impossible to determine strictly what is understood by **small** and **large** units. Such precision, however, really is not necessary at this point. The fact that there is no **strict** borderline between them, this classification has in common with others, which as a result are neither false nor unfruitful. It is enough, if we provide the grounds for the classification.

Since the boundaries between **Small** and **Large War** (if one allows me the latter expression, which by the way is neither very scholarly nor very abstract), I say, since the boundaries merge into one another, **judgment** and **experience** are of course a precondition for deriving a clear conception of Small War. Whoever lacks these must for the time being take our word for it and later come back to this introduction.

Since the foregoing definition is taken from common usage, it does not yet contain the grounds for the classification according to which war is divided into **large** and **small**, and thus the question is: **is this classification inherent to the Art [of War], does it contribute to the development of the same, and why?**

The answer to this is that the classification is indeed inherent and precisely because the doctrine for Small War is different in several general respects from the remaining doctrines of the Art of War, as we will determine more precisely forthwith.

If what we have just claimed is true, then **particular characteristics** of the use of small units must be found, which are **general**, which means that they can be found in most cases. And these particular characteristics, we believe, are basically the following:

1. Small units can sustain themselves quite easily almost anywhere.

2. They can conceal their presence more easily.

3. They can move faster. Especially for **combat**.

4. New insights suggest the necessity of breaking down armies and larger corps into several separate parts, which is impossible in the case of smaller units.

5. Small units by their very nature lose the advantage of an artful **emplacement** (although the advantage of a good choice [of position] often remains), all the more as size decreases; on the other hand, they gain the ability to move to the right or left during the battle.

6. Nearly all of their engagements are meant to be **supporting**.

7. Their retreat is less difficult and can be conducted on unpaved roads and in opposite directions.

8. Their deployment requires no great preparations.

9. Finally, their purpose is not always defense or offense, which is the case with large units. Rather, they usually have a purpose that is relatively alien to Large Wars, namely **observation** of the enemy.

In addition to these characteristics, several more could be provided. However, to generate such long lists for theory would render them incredibly boring. Perhaps those mentioned above are the **primary** and the **most essential** and this is sufficient.

If we add to these previously mentioned characteristics the one that many of the small detachments have neither a defensive nor offensive purpose, but engage in a **war of observation**—a characteristic that of course is less general than the abovementioned—then this new peculiarity, which is thus added to the tenets of Small War, enhances the difference between it and remaining forms of war.

If the Art of War is divided into **strategy** and **tactics**, that is, if every warlike action must be the subject of the one or the other, then the question follows: is this also the case in **Small Wars?**

To this we answer with the following considerations.

Tactic in our opinion comprises the teachings of the use and command of the **armed forces in** battle; strategy comprises the teachings of the employment and utilization of **the battle.**[†]

Hence, strategy determines for every battle the end and time, place and strength of the forces insofar as these three things have an impact on the aforementioned end; what remains is left to tactics.

It is self-evident that decisions regarding place, time, and strength must also take place with regard to small units; though one can ask whether this is not predetermined by strategy and tactics? Indeed it is. Since the purpose of all actions associated with the Small War is based on the necessities of strategy

---

[†] **Note:** This definition is based on a conceptual development, which would take us too far afield, and of which we only want to mention that we believe that every warlike action is based on a **possible battle**. We deduce this from the fact that one uses armed forces for warlike actions, which would be unnecessary if there were no possibility of battle. We believe, therefore, that the battle is to war what hard cash is for the general trade.

However, we should not be mistaken for having meant that the purpose of all warlike action is the battle. To the contrary, strategy makes use of the battle as a means to reach its purpose.

To determine, that means to define, strategy according to its means instead of its purposes is appropriate because the means (that is the battle), of which it makes use, are singular and cannot be dismissed without destroying the concept of war itself. Potential purposes, by contrast, are manifold and cannot be exhausted.

and tactics—that is on the Large War—it cannot lie within the Small War itself. Most decisions on the strength, place, time, etc. are already determined by this purpose. These decisions usually follow tactical considerations: the security measures, bivouacs, etc..... Thus one can say that the strategy of Small Wars is a component of tactics, and since the tactics of Small Wars certainly must be a component of tactics in general, then the entirety of Small Wars belongs to tactics. That is, it comprises a specific chapter thereof.

ON THE NATURE OF SMALL WAR

So far we have talked about the ends and means of Small Wars. Now a few words on its nature are in order; that is, on the spirit in which it is conducted by the armed forces.

Small Wars display the peculiar characteristic that in addition to the greatest audacity and boldness, a much greater fear of danger exists than is the case in Large Wars. And this characteristic is also evident in the troops who conduct Small Wars. The individual hussar or rifleman has a spirit of initiative, confidence in himself and in his fortune, of which those who always held the line hardly can imagine. It is his experience and habit that make him calm and relaxed while facing the manifold difficult tasks, whereas others would be timorous. Nevertheless, the hussar and rifleman have more respect for the danger inherent in common battles than do soldiers in closed ranks. Where it is not absolutely necessary, he will not engage in battle. He withdraws and looks for cover whenever possible. A single shot of a cannon can keep an army at great distance if it does not itself possess cannons and therefore believes itself to be at a disadvantage. 100 infantrymen can sometimes keep entire cavalry regiments at bay, if they believe the terrain to be advantageous for the infantry and therefore recognized that fortune has not been distributed evenly.

This is an entirely natural characteristic of light units. If this were not the case, how could it be possible that under constant enemy observation they daily engage in battle without being completely destroyed in a single campaign? This is far removed from blaming light units for something that is in their very nature. The greatest audacity must alternate with prudent caution as circumstances require, and every single man must be equally adept therein. One thing is clear: we never have to teach men the fear of danger, therefore the same goes for light units. Natural instinct provides for it. Instinct would so affect the other troops if everything were not done to suppress it. In large battles, one has to face the danger. The individual may not rely on cunning and intelligence. Intelligence and creativity must govern the general war plan and the conduct of its most important aspects, whereas with regard to individual positions, the greatest energy, the most furious defiance of danger, constitutes the highest wisdom.

A battalion will seldom have the opportunity during a battle or any other larger engagement to distinguish itself through wise deployment. It distinguishes itself through its bravery, through its spirited assault, through a steadfast and orderly endurance of lengthy firefights. If, when speaking of a battalion, one says that it has lost half or 2/3 of its men in battle, one has said enough. But this is not the case with regard to light units. In a battle between closed ranks the masses are pushed closer together and for small units there is little opportunity for combination. A battalion that is paying no regard to a neighboring battalion and attacks the enemy in a rash fashion (assuming that a firefight is already underway) could completely ruin itself. However, this danger is hardly comparable to the advantage that could be created. For perhaps from this point the entire battle would take a new turn and thereby, perhaps, the whole campaign could be won. It is impossible to calculate what success could develop out of this and it would be desirable that more battalions would take such risks. In Small Wars such advances by single units can create advantages but they will seldom be crucial and decisive. On the other hand, the dispersal in a larger space during Small Wars creates opportunities for thousands of combinations and the advanced units could easily be destroyed without thereby gaining the prospect of a large success. This free play of the intellect, which takes place in Small Wars, this clever combination of audacity and caution (I wish to say, this lucky admixture of courage and fear), is what makes Small Wars so immensely interesting.

ON THE TACTICS OF SMALL WAR OR BEHAVIOR DURING BATTLE

The use of weaponry in Small Wars is not different from that in Large Wars. The same is true of those things that are taught to soldiers. Flanking (*blänkern*[3]) and sniping (*tiraillieren*) are in Small Wars just the same as in Large Wars. It is thus not necessary to expand here on these issues, which are taught in official instructions and in Major von Tiedemann's lectures.

However, the order of battle in general, as well as the conduct and spirit thereof, are distinguished by peculiarities, which we want to raise here by providing a clear image of the battle in Small Wars.

---

[3] The term "*blänkern*" is generally translated as "flanking" but during the eighteenth century often referred to a tactic employed by mounted Hussars whereby a loosely organized unit briefly appears and engages in rather random shooting only to quickly ride off again. See Adelung et al. (1808: 1042).

Later we will also talk about the defense of small positions and about their attack, when this is linked to specific goals. Often, however, one arrives at a battle without these goals. In this case, only very broad principles, which apply to battles generally, can govern behavior.

1. On Infantry Battle

The characteristics of battles and Small Wars that should be mentioned here are:

1. That one often or even in most cases confronts a superior enemy.
2. That even if one were not weak in relation to the enemy, one is nevertheless so in relation to the region that is to be occupied.
3. That defense seldom requires absolute resistance, but only such of a certain duration. A few observations on this:
   3.1 Absolute resistance is the goal, if a point definitely should not be ceded to the enemy. This is the case for every entrenchment.
   3.2 Relative, that is proportionate, resistance shall only last a certain time, however. It should impede the enemy's advance, not preclude it.
   3.3 In the end, the success of any resistance is uncertain, however designed. And a resistance is only termed absolute if I mobilize all energies, if I invest everything, if I sacrifice everything to reach my goal. The degree of danger to oneself: individual security is no longer an issue, and consequently the retreat is only of secondary importance.
4. That one has greater respect for gunfire in Small Wars because one accepts great losses only in pursuit of great goals; that these seldom are found in Small Wars, and one more often is led into battle by the other side.

Reflecting on all these circumstances, what we perceive to be common to all wars reveals itself as the rule.

§ 1

The infantry in this case is distinguished more through its fire than its thrust and thus fights in a dispersed rather than closed formation.

How could one defend a wide terrain in closed formation?

Against a vastly superior enemy an attack of a small and closed unit is equally ineffective; hence nothing else remains other than to do damage through well-focused gunfire. Resistance with gunfire is admittedly an uncertainty, since those who are to be repelled by fire really are not damaged by it.

The resistance is more moral than physical and therefore it is uncertain. Hence, the defender does not feel completely secure unless he knows that in the most extreme emergency he also can withstand adequately the enemy advance physically.

In Small Wars, however, it is more important to impede the enemy's advance than to preclude it.

Finally, owing to number 4, a line of snipers has a greater effect in Small than in Large Wars.

§ 2

The infantry never completely disbands, but an appropriate component is held together to the rear.

_____

Nearly all books, in particular the Austrian Regulations,[4] prescribe this rule for lines of snipers within the infantry line in Large Wars. It is thus not a particularity to Small Wars, but it is more important to them, because in Small Wars one often only can expect support and reinforcement after a period of some hours, whereas in Large Wars, it is usually within a few hundred to 1000 paces' reach.

Four closely related considerations illustrate the plausibility of this rule:

1. There is a reserve for the protection of the flanks and other unforeseeable situations. **If these men are not grouped**, they would not stand for ready disposition.
2. Men in the sniper lines who **have spent their fire** can be replaced.
3. There is a component to which, in case of calamity, dispersed snipers can reassemble.
4. A coherent component is necessary for the protection of the commanding officer.

§ 3

If circumstances allow, the firing line as discussed in §§ 1 and 2 is intended for a combined assault. One then divides the troops into two parts: the first constitutes the sniper line with auxiliary troops, the other remains concealed for the combined assault.

_____

Very **weak** infantry detachments, for example **to the size of a company**, nearly always have to settle for resistance through mere **gunfire**. **Several** battalions, however, would do wrong if they were to do so. Against a weak enemy they

_____

[4] Clausewitz refers here to Österreich (1816).

can offer absolute resistance; can defeat him. For that, however, assault in closed ranks is necessary. For against a **mere line of fire even the weakest enemy** can approach a single point with superior power.

If the enemy advance is so forceful that an assault is impossible even with the assistance of those components kept to the rear, then **these same components** can be used for replacement and reinforcement of the firing line, and consequently the arrangement has been appropriate for the circumstances.

Which of these two arrangements is appropriate depends not only on the strength but also on the circumstances.

Examples:[5]

[…]

§ 4

Where absolute defense is in order, one must never arrange oneself in a single sniper line but rather must retain most of the troops for combined assault.

The resistance of a firing line is never certain. It is equally unclear what one can achieve through a combined assault. All that is certain is that in this way the troops are animated to the greatest exertion. It is also certain that the assault with closed ranks will have a stronger impact on the enemy than the entire effect of dispersed gunfire. Hand-to-hand fighting is what soldiers fear most. If the defender is unable to resist an attack by way of hand-to-hand fighting, as is the case with a firing line, then the attacker will already have lost all fear.

The advantages of a combined assault, if it is unexpected, are the following:

1. One at least concentrates on one point. It is likely that one will win at this point, and it is very possible that the victory at that point will influence the entire endeavor. It is quite possible that in defeating 1/3 of the enemy force, one wins everything. But it is inconceivable that with 1/3 directed at every point one can successfully resist the entire enemy force.

2. It is easier to respond appropriately to circumstances and one can retreat if one is unwilling to approach, etc.

3. One can throw oneself into the battle and if defeated, it is without doubt honorable, whereas in a firefight, one is more likely to suffer ambiguous judgments.

This does not contradict § 1, for cases where absolute resistance should be exercised in Small Wars are, as we know, few.

---

[5] At various points throughout the lectures we have left out examples or elaborations found in Clausewitz's notes but have indicated their existence with an ellipsis in brackets.

§ 5

During attack, one must keep ready troops in closed ranks wherever one wants to break through.

———————

Although in general, closed ranks seem more natural for attacking, the line of fire is associated with decisive advantages, even when attacking in great battles:

1. It conceals our measures.
2. It often compels the enemy to unfold his own measures and functions generally as a kind of reconnaissance.
3. It distracts his fire.
4. It prevents our closed ranks from becoming involved in a firefight against their will.

These advantages remain the same in Small Wars.

When Should One Start to Fire?

§ 6

Individual riflemen can begin fire at great distance, that is 300 to 400 paces; one thus keeps the enemy at bay. Incidentally, the early commencement of fire as well as its energy should reflect existing stocks of munitions.

But it must also remain the rule that a rifleman should only shoot if he expects an effect.

2. On Cavalry Battle

The cavalry has its flankers as the infantry has its snipers, but admittedly the former have a less important purpose. What they lack is firepower. Their actual engagement is almost without effect, they rather serve to observe the enemy, often also to make some noise through their shooting.

Their actual engagement only becomes effective in combination with the infantry snipers.

From this it follows:

The cavalry flankers only have a secondary purpose; the proper battle is always conducted in closed ranks. They only become important, when a light cavalry through greater agility is able to do harm to a heavy cavalry with flankers.

§ 7

The cavalry commits as many soldiers to flanking as is necessary for the observation and harassment of the enemy or as the strength of the enemy's flankers requires. The actual battle of the cavalry is always united, unless one believes oneself superior to the enemy in individual combat. In this case one allows as many as is possible to flank without too great a danger. But here too, one part must always remain in closed formation.

It is **another question** whether the **combined units should be larger or smaller,** whether one should keep them as one component or divide them into many. We are not speaking here of actually dividing them on the terrain. This will be determined by other objectives. Rather, we are speaking of whether a squadron should act in one or in two separate troops if it is alone; whether two squadrons should act in 1 or 2 units or perhaps in even more.

This leads in a certain way to the determination of the order of battle for the cavalry in general. We cannot address this here. We will assess these only insofar as the peculiarities of Small Wars require special attention.

In Small Wars, where the battle is more of a free play, where it does not depend merely on a determined onslaught, the simple formation in a unit is almost never advisable. One is subject to too many contingencies and doesn't know what to do. Every cavalryman knows that **it is difficult to retreat as a unit.** But in Small Wars it is the case that retreat may at any moment be necessary. In short, effective maneuver is almost impossible as a troop.

§ 8

A cavalry troop, if stronger than 20 men and independent, does not need to stay together, but can divide itself into two parts, which remain close to and support one another.

Whether one should divide larger cavalry units into **more** troops **than 2,** I leave to the gentlemen officers of the cavalry. Here the particular circumstances often will be more decisive than a preconfigured system. But the following principle cannot be disputed.

§ 9

If the light cavalry finds it advantageous in view of the heavy cavalry to divide itself into many troops, then the division and dispersion may only go so far as would still allow them all to take part in one and the same attack.

---

3. Cavalry and Infantry in Combination

Nowhere is this combination closer than in Small Wars and in Small Wars, in turn, nowhere closer than in dispersed battles; and this close combination constitutes the strength of the troop in the Art of Small Wars. Experience has provided the infallible proof; besides, the reasons are so obvious that no further deliberation is necessary.

§ 10

Wherever the terrain allows a horse to scrimmage one can never neglect to support the infantry snipers with cavalry flankers. Their number may be considerably smaller than that of the snipers; yet it should reflect more or less the number of the enemy flankers. They remain more or less far to the rear, depending on the proximity of the enemy sniper line and the roughness of the terrain. They are kept behind for reasons that are easy to comprehend. [. . .]

§ 11

In the same way the cavalry's flankers are supported in the plane (*Ebene*) by individual proficient riflemen of the infantry, provided the danger of losing them is not too great. If the men have grown accustomed to one another they will not act just as machines, but rather with consideration. If the retreat is not too distant, they will seldom be lost. At most, they should be half as many as the cavalrymen. Why half as many?

§ 12

If the riflemen and flankers are linked to each other, so too are their supporting troops. With, however, the following qualifications:

1. In varied terrain, the supporting troops of the cavalry either do not take part in battle, or they are positioned beyond the reach of rifle shots.
2. In the field, the supporting troops of the infantry are located so far to the rear that they are not in danger in the event of sudden retreat.

In both cases the individual combatants of the auxiliary forces are already covered by the individual combatants of the main force and thus require no immediate reinforcement.

The combination of the cavalry and the infantry in closed formations generally has the same tendency as in Large Wars. However, there are two considerations, which are particular to the use of the cavalry in Small Wars.

Thus, the following reflection is necessary.
The cavalry in Large Wars is mainly designed to

1. Make use of the chaos that has resulted among the enemy through the infantry battle and thus further prosecute the ongoing battle.

2. Serve as a reserve for unexpected contingencies.

3. Pursue the enemy in general after he has suffered a defeat.

In general, however, as mentioned earlier, the cavalry in Small Wars has this purpose. It completes what the infantry has started and thus both belong together.

Nonetheless, (and this is the 1st reflection) **the large space**, which one is often compelled to occupy in Small Wars, easily leads to a disconnection of both forces, so that they cannot properly support each other in battle, and hence the purpose of their combination is not achieved.

Examples:

[. . .]

Sometimes one perceives the **necessity** in Small Wars to act in this way. Sometimes it is **merely a misunderstanding of the rule that forces should be used according to the terrain.**

Examples:

[. . .]

§ 13

As long as one can reach one's objective without separating one's forces, one should avoid doing it. For the cavalry is meant to further prosecute the battle initiated by the infantry and to exploit the advantages that the infantry has achieved.

Therefore, the proper location for the cavalry if it is combined with the infantry is either directly behind it or to the side and slightly back, but in any case nearby.

In Small Wars it is not so important whether the cavalry is positioned just behind the infantry or to its side. The first is the natural position. Sometimes, however, the possibility arises to position it completely concealed to the side. In this case, one is not bound by the rule, which is only important for large masses of troops.

[. . .]

The second reflection regarding the use of the cavalry is that the general effect of the cavalry in Small Wars is bigger and its scope more widespread than in Large Wars.

If it is an axiom of Large Wars, as revealed in the history of all campaigns, that the cavalry can achieve nothing against an infantry and artillery that still function and possess ammunition, then this claim requires a large qualification for Small Wars.

Although defending a very weak infantry unit in the field against the cavalry is not impossible and has often occurred, you may not reckon with it. Yet it remains possible that such a unit, if it enjoys no protection from the terrain, will be overrun.

From this it follows that the use of the cavalry and infantry in Small Wars should more often be determined by the nature of the terrain, while their use in Large Wars is more a function of the natural course of battle than it is dependent on the terrain. (Oral elaborations)

Furthermore, it should be noted that in Small Wars, where all battles are intended as supporting measures, time plays a much more decisive role than in Large Wars. But since one often cannot afford to lose any time, one must use the cavalry, which always arrives first, whenever possible.

From all this it follows that the law of using the cavalry only after the infantry has already initiated the success, must be qualified in Small Wars by big and numerous exceptions. The question arises of what sort of rule should be stated. Such a rule is difficult to create and must be judged with hindsight more as a suggestion of what is to be done. With this reservation in mind, I would say the following.

§ 14

Where the terrain provides too many advantages for the infantry and the artillery and no infantry can be employed as quickly and effectively, the cavalry must shoulder the first attack without any concern for the good **condition** of the enemy infantry.

These two §§ (13 and 14), were necessary as a qualifying condition for the battle of closed formations in Small Wars. Moreover, everything that is taught about these issues in Large Wars applies here.

4. Artillery in Combination with Infantry and Cavalry

In Small Wars one usually employs mounted artillery. Why? The cases, for which artillery is provided, are the following:

1. The defense of defiles and other small defensible positions.
2. For reserves, which are intended to reinforce other troops (additional comments on this).
3. For attacking small positions.

The first of these cases, which is most common, leads to the provision of the artillery (though mobile) to the infantry.

This also happens for other reasons. On the one hand it is more natural to keep firearms together. On the other, the cavalry in light wars is usually dispersed in small units and one does not like to entrust a cannon to such a small unit of the cavalry.

Furthermore, both cases—Nos 1 and 2—lead to the much dispersed use of the artillery in Small Wars, so that quite often a cannon becomes isolated from the others and more than 2 or 3 are seldom together.

Only in the third case, in the event of attack, can one exploit the concentrated effect of the artillery.

Yet even in Small Wars, this advantage can be carried too far. The cannon is most essential in the main positions. In minor positions instead of cannons one can provide more infantry instead.

The conditions for the use of cannons in Small Wars will be the following.

§ 15

One must only provide cannons to areas where the infantry cannot achieve the same effect; and above all, the cannon should not be placed in dangerous positions unless there is an urgent need.

§ 16

In every case, a special unit of the detachment must be established to cover the cannon and to move it, because otherwise it will be abandoned in the event of retreat. In skirmishing, this provision is particularly necessary. Here, one of the closed units must be in near proximity to the cannon and direct their attention toward covering it at all times.

5. On the Plan of Battle and the Utilization of the Terrain

A. Defense

The features one seeks in the great battle are the following:

1. Support for flanks.
2. Hindrances in access to the front.
3. Unrestricted view of the front.
4. A varied terrain to the rear, but no real defiles, at least nowhere close by.
5. A concealed positioning of the troops.
6. An advantageous form of posture.

In Smalls Wars one generally has to dispense with **anchoring the flanks.** In the same way, an advantageous **positioning** does not come naturally to small detachments.

The advantages are admittedly not entirely ineffective, however, they are only conceivable in conjunction with a firing line, and then they are not very reliable. [. . .]

What in the end emerges, if one thinks of the tactics of small detachments as scaled-down tactics of larger masses, can be observed in the weak, ineffective, and pitiful defensive postures (*cordon* systems), and in particular the maneuvers.

[. . .]

Whether they enjoy **hindrances in access** to their frontline, a free view, or a varied terrain to their rear, is usually not a matter of their choice. **All these advantages** are for them probably **more essential** than for the army. Because, however, their position usually is a matter of other circumstances, in these respects they are very often in a disadvantageous situation.

The battle of a detachment is different from great battles insofar as **defiles near their rear** are not as dangerous for the detachment as they are for corps or armies. The reason is obvious.

In general, the **retreat** of a detachment is not as easily **cut off** as is that of an army. The former can march faster and more unobservably on all ways. In a mountainous region it nearly always has the opportunity to escape.

The **last advantage** of a position, namely that it is **concealed**, is natural to a small detachment and must be used to compensate for all other disadvantages.

That the firing line of a small detachment urgently demands those features that to some extent secure it from enemy fire and assault is something it shares in common with Large Wars.

Thus:

§ 17

In positioning small units of the troop for the purpose of defense be mindful of:

1. Supporting the flanks.
2. Obstacles to access, which delay the enemy within our range of fire.
3. Unrestricted view of the front and the flanks.
4. Varied terrain to the rear, but above all
5. Means of cover against enemy fire and the 1st assault of the infantry firing line and the cannons. And
6. Concealed positioning.

The more the position resembles an ambush the better.

§ 18

If there are hindrances in access to the front and in addition no means of cover against the assault, one positions the firing line close to the hindrances to access with the exception of the cannons, which are positioned 300–400 paces behind. If there is an additional obstacle, located 100–200 paces behind the defile, then one positions the riflemen in the obstacle, unless the defile is several hundred paces wide.

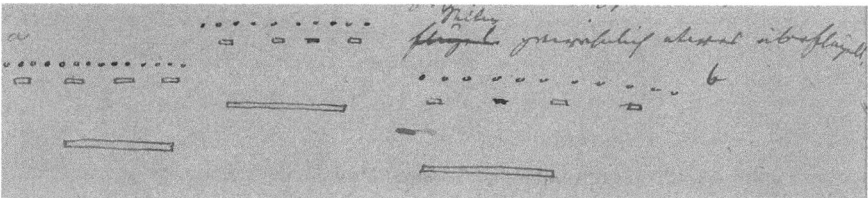

Figure 1. Battalions in Customary Order of Battle.

Source: Clausewitz (1810: 79v.) Copyright © Universitäts- und Landesbibliothek Münster, N. Clausewitz 4,001.

[...]

In contrast to large troop units, **the extension of the front** that is assigned to a detachment organized in a firing line is not determined by the **mere order of battle**. Wherever closed attack is the main objective, the positioning must be shoulder to shoulder. This is the case with large masses of troops. Here, the firing line acquires the extension necessary for its effective use only because it is weaker than the closed ranks and usually can outflank them to some degree.

The figure [see Figure 1] depicts three battalions in customary order of battle, both kept somewhat to the rear of the flanks. Here, the extension of the firing line *a b* is more or less determined by the front of the battalions. The extension of the battalions themselves, insofar as they are parts of a larger whole, is not, however, bigger than the space they themselves occupy.

With regard to weak isolated units of 100–50 men or even smaller units, or even individual battalions, where, as mentioned above, fire is the primary purpose, **this law of positioning does not apply**. The principle of bringing as many combatants as possible into battle at a single location is inappropriate. For if the enemy wants to break through the attack, a firing line will be too weak to withstand.

In this regard the extension cannot be limited easily.

On the other hand, by extending too little, one would subject oneself to unnecessary disadvantages.

If one wished to concentrate 50 riflemen in this or that varied terrain as shown in Figure 1 [see Figure 2A[6]], then the following disadvantages would accrue:

1. The enemy fire would be more effective both frontally and from encirclements.

2. If attacked from encirclements, chaos is more likely to arise.

3. One would defend less terrain than the range of fire would otherwise allow. For the enemy who wished to evade us by few hundred paces, we are nonexistent.

---

[6] In his lecture notes, Clausewitz refers to this figure as Figure 1. It is the second figure to appear in the notes and is here labeled 2A.

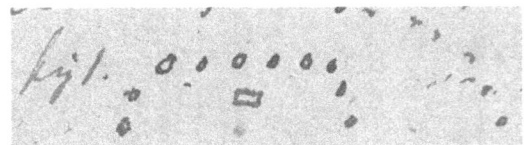

Figure 2A. Positioning of Weak Isolated Units.

Source: Clausewitz (1810: 80v.) Copyright © Universitäts- und Landesbibliothek Münster, N. Clausewitz 4,001.

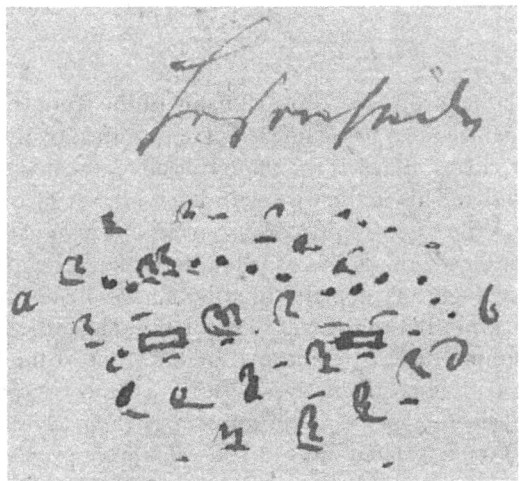

Figure 2B. Extension of Small Detachments.

Source: Clausewitz (1810: 80v.) Copyright © Universitäts- und Landesbibliothek Münster, N. Clausewitz 4,001.

As a rule, small detachments must extend themselves to an extent more than is provided by the order of battle. But what determines the extension?

1. Defense of the terrain

If 100 men are commanded to occupy a wood that has an expanse of 400 paces and is accessible from all sides and defend it against the advance of snipers and weak cavalry detachments, then it is self-evident that those 100 men will draw their firing line from one end to the other with closed troops behind it. In this case, one would still have a relatively strong firing line; if only 1/3 snipers, every 24 paces 2 men [see Figure 2B].

One could if necessary spread throughout the whole wood even if it were the size of 1000 and 1500 paces. This would be impossible if it were a mile long.

At times then, the **extent of the terrain** that is to be occupied is determined by the fact that a certain piece of territory is to be **defended**.

2. Advantages of the terrain

Sometimes supporting positions are determinative.

Sometimes the means of protection, which the terrain offers.

If one finds hedges, trenches, or large groves, etc., then one takes position entirely within them or behind them and unless necessary does not move any elements into the field.

3. Easy command of the whole

Finally, the rule applies that one should not expand unnecessarily more than the maintenance of oversight and command of the whole allow. This rule replaces to a certain extent the rule of victory through closed ranks of large troop masses.

§ 19

Troops intended for the closed assault must be kept together both in Small and Large Wars. But where one wishes to defend through a well-focused rifle fire, the positioning is to be determined according to one or more of the following conditions.

1. According to the expanse of the terrain that one wants to defend.
2. According to the advantages the terrain offers.
3. According to the oversight and ease of command of the whole.

Given the fact that the infantry (according to § 4), when it is a matter of absolute defense, can be effective only through closed assault—and the cavalry never functions any differently—the curious rule emerges **that one** should wherever possible defend oneself offensively; that is, **to lure the enemy into an area and to attack him there from all sides.** This rule is the most important when planning entire defensive battles. It constitutes the capstone.

§ 20

A passive defense is sufficient only for steep passes. In all other cases, one should not count on it too much and wherever the strength of the detachments allows, one should combine offense and defense.

§ 21

This happens:

1. If one awaits the enemy with a sizeable part of one's troops united in a remote terrain while another part takes up extended positions in order to attack unexpectedly the enemy if it believes it has already defeated us.
2. If one assumes forward or sideward a position of ambush in order to attack the enemy from behind.
3. By approaching him head-on and attacking as he marches.
4. By withdrawing without great resistance in the event of the enemy's advance, but immediately thereafter resuming the attack.

§ 22

One should never be misled into developing an artificial and overly complex arrangement, which would subject oneself to too many contingencies.

§ 23

Two rules are to be observed in the event of an assault:

1. That it must be unexpected,
2. That the men be given an assembly point in case of failure.

[. . .]

_____

B. *Offense*

Until now we have spoken about the plan of battle for the case of defense and all that has been mentioned about the offense was related to offensive defense.

The rules for assault remain the same when used in a proper offense and will not be repeated here. But the arrangement of the entire battle in the event of an offensive has some features that are absent in the case of defense and must therefore be dealt with.

The first question is whether and why one also should use a firing line in the offense.

The objectives of the firing line in an offense are the following:

1. To do damage to the enemy through well-focused fire.
2. To lure him into early fire.
3. To cover the closed units against enemy fire.
4. To conceal the movements and strength of the same.
5. To a certain degree to function as a forward post in varied terrain in order to learn about enemy measures.

All these points apply to Small Wars as to Large Wars, but numbers 1 and 5 are the most important. They do not, however, always apply in the same way. Nevertheless, only rarely can one dispense with a firing line entirely, and these cases are: surprises; an all too flat terrain in conjunction with great weakness; and great superiority on our side.

The firing line admittedly is not appropriate for a thrust. Nonetheless, it is not impossible to attack with it, especially when it is more a matter of displacing the enemy than destroying him. Bypassing a line of snipers that enjoys no further cover is usually sufficient to compel it to retreat. This is best accomplished, if one does not wish to endanger oneself too much with one's own line of snipers.

From all this, I draw the following rules.

§ 24

1. In an area that cannot be surveyed, one must not attack the enemy by day without a line of fire.

2. Generally, one must use a line of fire to uncover enemy measures and to weaken his troops, to outflank him, and for mock assault.

3. One must never place trust in the ability of rifle men to break through if the enemy is not simultaneously outflanked.

With respect to the combination of forces one should note that when attacking in Small Wars, one gladly makes use of the cavalry to bypass the enemy. There can be no objection to this, given the greater effectiveness of the cavalry in Small Wars and the necessary speed of maneuver. One should only be careful not to separate both forces too much.

§ 25

One should never use the infantry without the cavalry, except in cases where the terrain is not at all varied (for example in deep forests), for otherwise it is impossible to exploit even the best achievements. An[other] exception to this rule is found in cases where the enemy is defeated and the cavalry is dispatched in pursuit.

§ 26

An especially opportune moment (which one should not miss) to gain the most benefit from the cavalry is the instant when a dispersed infantry abandons its posts in order to withdraw across the field. If it finds no strong support in the field it will seldom be able to reassemble and fall into the hands of our cavalry (as for example the French by Bingen[7]). Eylau after the conquest of Kutschitten.[8]

Finally, it must be mentioned that generally there are two different goals of the offensive, which in Small Wars are even more different than in Large Wars. The first is to inflict a proportionate loss on the enemy. This goal is also found in Large Wars, although today much less often than before, whereas in Small Wars it is more common than the first [goal].

We will talk about the 1st and the rules that are connected to this goal if we deal with offensive undertakings of small detachments. The 2nd is more appropriate here.

---

[7] Clausewitz refers to a situation during the French Revolutionary Wars in which French troops offered a weak defense against Prussian and Hessian troops in Bingen in the Rhine valley.
[8] Battle of Eylau between the Russian Army and Napoleon's Grande Armée in East Prussia on February 8, 1807.

Abandoning a position only becomes necessary if it has lost its nexus; that is, if the flanks have been bypassed, the rear is threatened, and if the frontline has been breached. In Large Wars, one will not have yet reached one's goals by these means in every case. For if the defender has taken adequate measures, especially if his position is deep enough, he will be able to recover from such misfortunes. But in Small Wars where the retreat is so much more essential, these means are even more potent.

§ 27

To displace the enemy from his position, one bypasses him if his flanks are not supported and his front is not too extended. If the latter is the case, one breaks through. That is, one attacks with concentrated strength a single part of his front.

§ 28

When dealing with an inept enemy, one can hazard something. But if the enemy is resourceful, one has to reckon with an active defense and rather more conserve one's strength.

SMALL WAR

First Chapter: Forward Posts	Forward Post System
	Outposts (*Feldwachen*)
	Soutiens[9]
	Chain of Posts[10]
	Mobile Corps
	Patrols
	Reconnaissance
Second Chapter: Small Detachments	Large Patrols
A. Offensive	Reconnaissance
Organization and Conduct during	Observation
Marches	Assaults
Cavalry	Seizure of small posts, Choke points, Villages, Houses, Entrenchments
Infantry	Destruction of depots, bridges, etc.
Artillery	Neutralization of convoys
Joined	————of forages
	————of individual persons
	Collection of intelligence
	Organization of supplies
	foodstuffs
	clothing
	bridging materials

[9] In the original handwritten manuscript, Clausewitz (*c.*1810) crossed out the term *Patrouillen* and substituted it with *soutiens*. The English equivalent is "backup" or "support."

[10] Clausewitz uses the French term *chaine*.

B. Defensive	Defense of post	Accompanying a convoy
Either in a chain of	Choke points	Covering a forage; a depot.
forward posts or alone.		
	Villages and houses	
	Entrenchments	
	Woods	
	Accessible areas	

Third Chapter: Operation of small detachments during skirmishes.

PURPOSE AND ORGANIZATION OF THE FORWARD POSTS OF AN ARMY

1. If an army is encamped or in quarters, or when it marches, a line of light troops is always positioned between it and the enemy. Those are the forward posts.

2. They observe the enemy and at all times provide cover for the army against assault. Depending on the strength provided by the terrain, they sometimes offer resistance against the enemy. They thereby provide time for the army to take up measures which the enemy does not expect.

3. They are comprised of small corps of all service arms, which here will be called brigades. The number of **brigades** corresponds to the number of **divisions** within the **army corps,** so that one **brigade** is attached to each **division** and marches with it, when it is deployed.

4. They occupy all points of access to the army and thereby create a chain of small defensive posts. If possible, the position of this defensive chain of posts should be chosen so as to convey the cover and strength offered by the terrain.

5. A chain of guards is positioned in front of the chain of posts in order to enhance its security. With nothing between them and the enemy, these are called "outposts" (*Feldwachen*). They consist of infantry only in dense forests, otherwise always of light cavalry.

6. Behind these outposts (*Feldwachen*) and between them and the chain of posts, small supporting units are in the field, which are called *soutiens*. They consist of infantry or cavalry; more or less, depending on the lay of the land.

7. Behind the chain of posts of the **brigades** stands a considerable corps for their support. These are the *soutiens* of the forward posts.

8. The *soutiens* of the forward posts and the forward posts themselves together constitute the army *avant-garde*. Together they resist the enemy to the extent afforded by their strength: in the best case compelling the enemy to adopt its measures earlier, thus winning time for our

army to respond accordingly. If the terrain is so accessible [to the enemy] that the resistance of the forward posts is insufficient, then the rear units serve only as accommodation for the forward units.

9. Every **brigade** has its own commander, the whole chain of forward posts a common higher commander; the general of the *avant-garde* exercises total command and is positioned at the *soutienes-corps*.

10. The forward post system thus consists of three main parts:
    10.1 The line of guards and their supporting troops; they are located in the field.
    10.2 The line of actual posts. These are in camps and quarters.
    10.3 The supporting corps.

11. If we do not speak of an army, but rather a *division*, the supporting corps is often lacking, and so is the division with its forward posts.

If we speak only of a **detachment**, the supporting corps and the chain of posts are lacking, and the **detachment** itself takes up the position of the latter and assumes its own guard.

12. Consequently, the first part of the whole forward post system is simultaneously the forward post system of a small detachment.

13. In addition to the forward posts the army deploys field and camp guards in its vicinity. They:
    13.1 Preserve order,
    13.2 Provide greater security,
    13.3 Accommodate the forward posts.

At one point the enemy could break through the chain of forward posts unnoticed and suddenly approach the camp or the quarters. In this case the camp and village guards protect against a regular attack.

14. According to our former rule, they are located close to the camp. During the Prussian War, however, they were positioned approximately a quarter hour's distance forward. Without doubt, they are thus more useful and provide more security. If there is great danger and the current forward post weak, then pickets, who otherwise remain on call, deploy to support the camp and village guards.

15. The strength of the resistance provided by the forward positions varies greatly. For one, this resistance depends on the strength of the forward posts; for another, on the expanse of the terrain which they occupy; and finally, on the size of the obstacles the terrain provides for their protection.

16. The resistance they offer, or more precisely the time lost to the enemy fending them off, always must be sufficient to cover the army against an attack.

17. They achieve this goal mainly through compelling the enemy to advance with caution.

18. But if one can provide them with true defensive strength and if thereby the security and the duration of their resistance increase, then the most important advantages accrue to the army.
    1. Freedom of movement. The army can march wherever other circumstances allow.
    2. It can avoid a battle.
    3. It can defend itself offensively.
    4. It can conceal its measures from the enemy.
    5. It compels the enemy to develop his measures earlier both in time and space.
    6. Because he has to disperse the forward posts the day before and encamp for the night, the enemy usually can only attack with weary troops.
    7. Finally, in many cases the enemy will have come to believe he has survived the greatest difficulties at the moment he encounters the army itself.

Among these advantages, 1 and 2 are of strategic importance for both the offensive and the defensive. The remaining serve only tactical purposes and mainly the defensive.

19. The reason for using light troops mainly for forward posts is found in their composition and training, which is akin to battle in small groups, or at least should be.

20. 1. The systematic composition of the forward posts provides the advantage of simplified service regulations.
    2. The permanent organization has the following advantages.
       2.1 The troops become better acquainted with their duties than if they were to change.
       2.2 There is no need for a new policy whenever a new situation arises.
    3. The reason these posts comprise **brigades** from all service arms is the same as for the arrangement of the army in **divisions**. In rare cases the terrain will make the modification of this composition an urgent necessity. If such cases arise, there is still enough time to take the infantry or cavalry from another post. Moreover, at the time one deploys the forward posts, one never knows enough about the area to arrange the forces according to the terrain. If this is the case, then use all you have.
    4. One needs to have at least as many **brigades** as there are **divisions** of the army. If the terrain is advantageous, one can break up twice as many brigades.

5. Obedience to command is an essential issue. Therefore it is necessary to have one commander for the whole chain of forward posts, who can guarantee the necessary coherence of the whole, since the general of the *avant-garde*, positioned with the *soutien*, is too far away, and when the terrain is very large, one divides the forward posts into districts, putting an officer in charge of each.

More about the composition and efficacy of a chain of forward posts will follow. Beforehand, we will concern ourselves with two specific topics. The first concerns the outposts (*Feldwachen*) and their *soutiens*, the other concerns the small defensive posts. Both can be seen either as parts of the forward posts system, or they can be analyzed separately.

REMARKS ABOUT THE AIM AND NATURE OF THE *AVANT-GARDE*

1. In our introduction we said that an army, in every position and quarter as well as when on the march, is to be cordoned by a chain of light troops against the enemy, which are called forward posts; that these are supported by a corps of troops, which is called the *soutien* of the forward post; and that the entirety is given the name *avant-garde*. However, what we here call an army is either an army of modest strength, which is merely organized into **divisions** (like ours) or a single army corps; but by no means a big army, which consists of several army corps. Because of the large area, which by its nature it needs to occupy, a big army cannot have a unified system of forward posts and in most cases does not have a true corps of the *avant-garde*.

2. The question arises of which concept one commonly associates with *avant-garde*?

It is a corps, which is positioned in front of the army, or when on the march, precedes it in order to impede the advancing enemy, so that the army can implement its measures. This is without a doubt the main idea one associates with it.

In addition thereto, the *avant-garde* should fulfill the following aims,

1. To attack first.
2. To occupy a position faster than the army can reach it.

The first identified aim is evidenced first by the name itself, and second by the fact that this aim is always present. That is, it gives rise to the need for the corps in the first place.

The other two aims are sometimes present and sometimes not, hence other corps may be designated thereto. Furthermore, every corps of the army can fulfill the other two aims just as well as the *avant-garde*. There is, therefore, no need for a specific organization. For the purpose of the forward post, however, it is advantageous to avail oneself of a **specific** organization, namely small **brigades** of light infantry and cavalry troops.

3. It follows then, that the corps that fulfills the first and main aim, namely the forward posts and their support, truly deserve the name *avant-garde*. If in other cases a **division** or a corps of the remaining army proceeds in order to achieve the two additional aims identified, this is not really different from every other particular use and employment of **divisions** and army corps, and the term *avant-garde* is then used quite inappropriately.

4. If one speaks of a **division** or an army corps, then its *avant-garde*, that is its forward posts and their support, can in many if not most cases also fulfill the purpose of an earlier occupation of an area and the initial attack. This is precisely the case when the army is not large, only subdivided into **divisions**, and is concentrated in such a way that the *avant-garde* of their corps or divisions constitutes an entirety.

If, however, the army is divided up into corps, each of these having its own *avant-garde*, then the army is left without a general *avant-garde*. As was mentioned earlier, with regard to security, this also is not necessary.

Consequently, when those secondary aims mentioned above arise, a specific corps has to be designated.

5. If, in what follows, we speak of *avant-garde*, we do so in the first and true sense, and our arguments can only be understood as they apply to this *avant-garde*.

ON THE DUTIES OF THE FORWARD POSTS

§ 1

The surveillance of the enemy and the longest possible defense of their appointed terrain is the purpose of the forward posts and the *avant-garde*.

The commander of the same must at all times keep this purpose in mind and employ all means in his wherewithal to fulfill this aim. This demands constant exertion and attention, that is much more activity than within the army. Hence, the duties of the forward posts are more difficult than any other and their service regulations and procedures more important and consequential than anywhere else.

§ 2

The principal aims, which should be reflected in the specific service regulations include:

1. To provide every commander as fast as possible the necessary overview of the status and conditions of his subordinate troops.

2. To subordinate, to the greatest extent possible, the surveillance and defensive measures to the judgment of the Commander-in-Chief (general of the *avant-garde*).

3. To control the vigilance and operation of the troops.

4. To maintain order and discipline.

5. To assure rapid communication and transmission of commands.

§ 3

Before we turn to the individual provisions, we must determine the chain of subordinate commanders at the forward posts and through which the commands and reports pass.

We have to mention that in general the number of subordinate commanders can just as well ease duties and warfare as it can make them more difficult. In specific cases it is a matter for judgment.

One has to try to manage with as small a number of layers of command as possible. In specific cases, however, one may have to ask oneself if an additional layer will ease the cause.

Consequently, all guards positioned in the forward posts will be placed directly under the command and supervision of the officer, who is in charge of the entire post. Only if this officer finds it necessary to place some guards under the supervision of a specific officer, for example because they are far away and he cannot keep them within his sight, then this additional officer will be appointed and placed between the guards and the post commander.

In normal cases, the post commanders constitute the first line of command. They are followed usually by the commander of the forward post **brigade**. In specific cases, for example, if one part of the brigade is far removed from the other, the commander of the detachment will be placed under the commander of the entire forward post line and thus there is one layer less.

Hence the brigadiers constitute the second layer of command.

The third is the overall commander of the forward post. He exists only when the forward post consists of several brigades. If the army is not large, the strength of the army corps or division consisting only of a forward post brigade, then the respective brigadier is placed directly under the general of the *avant-*

garde. In any case, this general of the *avant-garde* is the last and highest authority, and receives his orders directly from the commanding general.

Hence: The post commander.

The brigadier.

The forward post commander.

The general of the *avant-garde.*

§ 4

The forward post commander is necessary because only he can assure the cohesion of the individual posts of which a chain of forward posts consists. This, however, requires that he visits them frequently. If one were to assign this task to the general of the *avant-garde*, he too often would be absent; orders coming from the main army would not be instantaneously transmitted and in important cases this could lead to dangerous lapses.

The forward post commander is the one who draws together all the bits of intelligence and observation of the enemy that are provided by the forward posts. To this end he must be located within the chain of posts, frequently visit the outposts, and more often approach the enemy in order to verify incoming information. He is the eyes of the army.

The general of the *avant-garde* is granted supreme command over the entire troops of the *avant-garde* and forward posts, he gives the necessary orders, masses the troops, directs marches, etc. For this reason he must be located with the *soutien-corps.*

If the commanding general entrusts the divisions of the *avant-garde* to the most able and determined of his subordinate generals, then the latter shall in the same way choose the most able, agile, and determined of his officers to command all forward posts. There is no more important position in the entire *avant-garde.*

The forward post commander could, by the way, be the commander of a **brigade,** on whose side a deputy commander is assigned to command in his absence. We now turn to the actual service regulations.

§ 5

FIRST REPORTS

As soon as a post commander arrives at his designated station, he regards himself first and foremost as a patrol that has been sent to gather information on the enemy. He will thus send out patrols of appropriate strength, which, assuming one is not trying to remain concealed, move forward to the enemy line in order to determine as precisely as possible where the enemy is located.

Whatever the patrol does not see with its own eyes it will learn from the inhabitants, and regardless how little information it brings back, it nevertheless will on the one hand serve as guidance for the security measures that the posts have to take, and on the other will be highly welcomed by the *avant-garde* and the army. The post commander, as soon as he arrives at the location of his post, immediately sends back a very short message on whether and where he has found the enemy.

§ 6

When the detachment has arrived at its determined post, the commander will survey the area in order to position the guards and *soutiens* in accordance with the terrain, as well as is possible at this early stage. If the patrols have not returned, the posts can be changed later if necessary in accordance with any information they bring back.

Until this preliminary positioning of the guards is in place, the detachment has to remain armed and ready.

If one arrives at night, without knowing the area and the position of the enemy, then one has to settle for the very close placement of guards, in order to assure first the most essential degree of security and thereby double its vigilance.

The initial positioning of the guards will give the officer a first indication of the means at his disposal for the defense of his post, for taking up his forward posts, etc. Subsequently the officer submits his first written report.

He will include therein as many of these circumstances as is possible without delaying its preparation. It will always include:

1. The information that has been gathered about the enemy.
2. The site and location of the post.
3. The guard line.
4. The contact, which does or does not exist to the next post.
5. Comments about the terrain. Whether it is forested or open, cut across by valleys, etc.

This report usually can and must be submitted within the first hour after the arrival of the post. It is to be sent to the brigadier.

The brigadier adds his own report to the incoming reports and sends them all to the commander of the forward post and simultaneously to the general of the *avant-garde*.

In most cases the general of the *avant-garde* will be informed within two to three hours about the status and position of his forward post brigades and will be able to issue a report to the commanding general.

In order for these first reports to arrive as soon as possible, the brigadiers, if absent, have to designate an officer to receive them and once they have all arrived, to pass them on. It might be helpful to designate once and for all a period of time after arrival at the post within which the reports must be sent without consideration for any outstanding information. This creates no disadvantage other than that sometimes the first report will have to be followed immediately by a second, for the fast and precise drafting of the report is of the utmost importance.

§ 7

The overview provided in the initial hours to the general of the *avant-garde* by the reports on the status of his forward post brigades will be supplemented and achieve greater reliability a few hours later by the forward post commander. As soon as he has arrived, he surveys the entire chain of forward posts, makes the necessary changes, and reports either in person or in writing to the general of the *avant-garde*. In most cases it will be helpful to report in person, as then he can discuss any number of issues with the general of the *avant-garde* and immediately receive decisions on his recommendations.

If the general of the *avant-garde* is not held up by important circumstances, he will survey the chain of posts himself, and within a day at the latest, gain rather complete knowledge about the entire line of forward posts, and thus be able to take up position with the *soutien-corps* and take measures appropriate to the specific situation.

To sustain this knowledge of the entire situation, the daily reports of the brigades, which will be discussed below, indicate such changes as have occurred.

This should suffice with regard to the first point raised in § 2.

§ 8

The first report submitted by the post commander probably will not entail the provisions he has made and the description of the post's circumstances. If the forward post remains stationary, he will write a short memorandum on this to the brigadier who in turn will forward it to the commander of the forward posts. The latter will present these reports to the general of the *avant-garde* and further discuss with him the measures taken.

From this, an overall plan emerges, the preparation of which has been ordered by the general of the *avant-garde*. This is communicated in writing to the commanders of the brigades and to the forward post commanders, to the extent deemed necessary for their instruction. He will often keep this or that idea to himself in order not to run the risk of betrayal.

Such provisions will land in the hands of the post commanders by the second or third day at the latest, which in most cases is sufficient, because an army is rarely attacked within the first two days of its arrival.

§ 9

Whatever happens within this time span—or whenever no such provisions have been communicated—must be determined by general procedures that the general of the *avant-garde* has provided to his forward posts. The principles on which these procedures rest are part of the section devoted to the ways in which the forward posts can be effective against the enemy and will be taken up later.

§ 10

As a consequence, it is most unlikely to be the case that an officer without orders and without knowledge of the overall plan will be left to his own devices; in which case he might well act like a sensible man and thereby fulfill his duty, but not always do what is right and best for the situation. Men who are not very determined easily become discouraged and behave irresolutely if it appears that no one cares about them and what they do. By contrast, an officer who knows that he acts in accordance with the thinking of his superiors will fulfill his duties with eagerness and great courage even in difficult situations.

This is what we intended in the second point of § 2.

§ 11

Vigilance is the main attribute of the forward post troops, amongst whom discipline, without which vigilance is almost unthinkable, is most at risk. To secure both through service regulations is therefore truly essential. Although service regulations cannot compensate for deficits in the personal initiative of the commander, they nevertheless serve to support this initiative and to motivate the average man.

The vigilance consists primarily of three things,

the attentiveness of the outposts,
the diligent patrols, and
the readiness of the quarters and camps.

As regards the first two, the post commander can do nothing other than to visit the guards often and at any time without notice. To increase the number of these inspections, the post commander, if not lacking in officers, will appoint one who in addition to himself oversees the vigilance of the forward posts, an adjutant, who assumes responsibility for this matter.

The readiness of quarters and camps is one of degree.

1. At night the troops remain clothed in their quarters. A few men remain awake in every quarter and in every quarter lights are left burning. The cavalry is saddled.

2. When encamped, the troops are housed at night in alarm houses. The cavalry in barns. Bridled.

3. Everything remains under open skies. The cavalry demounted, the infantry bearing their arms.

In most cases the post commander determines the degree of readiness. He will not exhaust his troops without need, but he is responsible for the readiness of his post if the enemy approaches.

The higher officer will determine whether the post's readiness is sufficient or whether he wishes it to be raised. This is especially the case for the forward post commander and the brigadier who remain responsible for accidents which result from negligence.

It is rarely the case that a subordinate officer demands a higher degree of vigilance from his men than his superior. Should this occur, however, the later will be reluctant to change the orders of the former. Rather, if such excesses occur too frequently and the men thus appear too exhausted, he is more likely to try to remove the anxious commander from his position entirely.

Ideally, the forward post commander will be responsible for the vigilance of the aggregate: on the one hand because he has been invested with a special trust; on the other because he is well suited to this task.

The forward post commander will thus precisely monitor the vigilance of the individual posts and in particular their respective commanders, and report back to the general of the *avant-garde*.

§ 12

Since the troops shy away from every exertion and never have a clear understanding of the situation in which they find themselves, nothing is more common than to see them complain about the timidity of their commanders and even to become quite discontented. The older soldiers even tend to cultivate a certain argument in this regard, so that at first glance one might be impressed and inclined to think that one had requested too much and more than is necessary.

Against this one cannot warn enough, especially with regard to our (north German) troops. The officer is in every case better equipped to judge the situation of his troop, and since he is responsible, has a much better standpoint than the private, in any case better than the subordinate who usually only thinks of his own bodily needs. The apparent wisdom and experience with which the subordinates argue in such situations is usually false and upon closer examination the entire argument simple-minded.

One must thus reckon with dissent and discontent and compel oneself from the beginning to a strictness that comes naturally only to a few. As a consequence, if the discontented have come to know the officer as strict and implacable, he now impresses them with that ease with which they earlier tried to control him.

(Comment)

(As a very young officer during a two-year campaign, I had more opportunities to make this observation than any other.[11] Since then I have seen it in the writings of Ewald,[12] Emmerich,[13] and many much-practiced officers and thus conclude that even officers of great experience and reputation have witnessed it.)

If one wants to insist with strictness on the execution of an order, it is of course necessary to thoroughly consider in advance what it is one wishes to command. On the one hand, so as not to demand impossible things, on the other, so as not to waver if one discovers that one has commanded something unnecessary.

There will seldom be a forward post at which one will not be compelled to leave the men dressed in uniform at night. If this order is given, anyone who neglects it must be punished with unwavering strictness, the quarters thus inspected for this purpose.

This, as well as the second degree of readiness, are moreover efforts that can be sustained by the troops for a very long time, because they are not thereby entirely deprived of sleep. Even the second degree of readiness is not an extraordinary sacrifice for a unit that has not marched the previous day, since men can sleep and rest during daytime.

However, if one has completed a long march by day, only arriving in the evening, it is impossible to remain under arms the entire night. In such cases, one settles for a bivouac or leaves one component under arms while the other rests.

§ 13

What one demands from the subordinates one must first perform oneself. In part to provide an example, but even more so because the commanding officer, if he is quick, can issue orders in the first moment whereby everything else is secured.

In most cases it is probably better if the entire assembly of troops lasts five minutes longer than if the commanding officer were to come five minutes late.

---

[11] Hahlweg notes that Clausewitz participated as a Cadet in the ranks of the 34th Prussian Infantry Regiment in 1793–4 in the Rhine Campaign against France.

[12] Johann v. Ewald (1744–1813) was a Military Officer and expert of partisan warfare. As Captain of the Hessian Army, he participated in the American Revolutionary War. Upon his return to Europe, he joined the Danish Army in which he served as Governor General of Holstein during the Napoleonic Wars. Ewald wrote one of the first books on small wars in 1785 (Ewald 1798), and kept a journal during his time in North America (Ewald 1979).

[13] Andreas Emmerich (1737–1809) was a Hessian forester and rifleman. After he had participated in the Seven Years' War, he was sent to North America and led his own unit of light cavalry in the American Revolutionary War. On the basis of his experience, he wrote an influential treatise *The Partisan in War or the Use of a Corps of Light Troops to an Army* (Emmerich 1789), which was translated into German as *Der Partheygänger im Kriege, oder der Nutzen eines Corps leichter Truppen für eine Armee* (Emmerich 1791).

If he is the first to arrive, then the troops immediately can be deployed according to purpose. Alarm and confusion can be avoided, and there will be nowhere a lack of necessary orders.

The vigilance of the commanding officer during the night is thus an essential quality; and whoever is unable to meet the necessary requirements, must not serve as forward post.

This does not mean that a forward post officer has to keep guard regularly during the night. But he must make arrangements so that he is one of the first on the spot and in urgent cases he should keep guard himself. There are enough means available to compensate him for this sacrifice and, in addition to the abovementioned advantages, it produces amongst the soldiers great confidence and great affection when they see that their officer guards them.

§ 14

Just as the tendency towards comfort and sleep at night must be kept in check, so too with absences from quarters and day leave.

Usually the soldier in the field has no other interest in leave than to procure foodstuffs, and this matter captivates him above all others.

However, it is necessary to make arrangements appropriate to the circumstances in order to provide everyone with foodstuffs. If this has been accomplished, then the preferential treatment of individuals is unnecessary and **inconsequential**, even if measures to secure foodstuffs prove inadequate.

Thus, such and indeed every leave of absence from the forward post quarters must be strictly prohibited.

What is said for the private must also apply to the officer.

§ 15

All other aspects of **discipline** are covered by the provisions of the ordinary service **regulations** and thus are not considered further here. We must note, however, that it is impossible to draft a regulation so general as to apply to every single case. The commanding officer thus would be wrong simply to assume that the regulations are effective with his subordinates. Rather he must consider which directives of the internal service could be useful to him and issue such directives.

§ 16

We have already discussed in another place regulations within the quarters, the allocation of duties among the officers, the location of alarm stations, etc. It remains only to recall that when on forward post duty, special vigilance must be directed toward spies. The most general rule is that nobody is to be allowed to pass the *vedettes* and that nobody is tolerated in a forward post quarter who is not a resident of the location. The Magistrate shall be made responsible for suspicious individuals.

§ 17

Generally, reports are distinguished in military terms from messages insofar as the former entail news, whereas the latter notify that nothing has happened. Notwithstanding that the latter seems to be self-evident even if no message arrives, it is nevertheless necessary that one acquires certainty from time to time because a message easily could have been lost.

The common village and camp guards provide their reports in the evening and the morning, as is clear enough from the regulations and duty.

Morning hours are especially important for the forward posts, since most plans are carried out in the morning. Therefore, immediately after sunrise, a report to the posts from which they were sent is quite essential. This report will be forwarded as soon as possible to the headquarters of the *avant-garde* and simultaneously to the commanders of the forward posts. These reports are drawn up on maps.

The latter reports to the general of the *avant-garde*, if possible in person. The brigadiers are unable to do so because it is more important for them to remain at their posts at all times.

In general, orders from headquarters are issued around midday.

Formerly, in our army, officers were sent by their respective corps for this purpose. Today this not possible, because the officers no longer are mounted. The orders, written under seal, are sent to the regiments by couriers, who in and of themselves undoubtedly do not replace the former aide-de-camp (*Ordonanz*) but are much preferable.

The commanding generals, however, often have an interest either in riding to headquarters themselves to conduct necessary discussions or in sending an officer of their general staff. These officers collect the necessary instructions and the requested information about this or that issue from the commanding general and the general staff.

At such occasions supply and other lists, requests, recommendations, etc. are received. The post commander often submits these to the brigadier, and he to the general of the *avant-garde*, so that the same envoy can bring back the order of the day.

A written report on tactics is combined with this submission of lists, etc.

1. Every change of one's own position.
2. Every new observation of the enemy.
3. Any skirmishes that have taken place.
4. The length and manner of supply of troop rations.

If nothing is to be said of these issues, the entire report consists of the phrase:

"nothing has happened at the post (the brigade) NN."

This midday report, which of course often has to be sent several hours earlier, is necessary because one often does not have the time needed to ensure that the first early report is complete.

Only this report is sent to the forward post commander, and indeed early enough so that he can take it with him to headquarters. This officer has nothing to do with the supply lists etc.

Whether an evening report is so important that it cannot be omitted in pursuit of minimizing superfluous communication, I don't want to decide.

But even if it has not been generally implemented, nothing hinders us from ordering it under exceptional circumstances. As a rule, reports would be sent from the forward posts to the headquarters of the *avant-garde* and from there to the general headquarters twice a day.

§ 18

If an army, no matter how small it may be (army corps), is dispersed across many miles in cantonments or encamped, it is quite necessary that the forward post brigades simultaneously dispatch to the headquarters of their corresponding division or brigade all the reports and messages, which they send to the general of the *avant-garde*, for they would otherwise receive such communications only after a long detour, namely from the general headquarters.

§ 19

RAPID TRANSMISSION OF ORDERS AND MESSAGES

The reports and messages that are sent from the small posts and corps to the larger ones are submitted, insofar as individual officers have not been designated for the task, most appropriately through assigned liaisons (*bleibende Ordonanzen*). The persons must be suitable to the task and the horses must receive additional feed. The brigadier has three to four such soldiers, who can also be used for other conveyances.

By contrast, the transmission of difficult commands, which are sent from above, is accomplished most appropriately through couriers, who are sent daily from the individual posts to the brigade quarters. This has the advantage that the individuals know the way to their posts.

§ 20

For long distances, which are common to quarters during winter, one resorts to relays. Small cavalry commandos of three to four men are kept quartered in houses no further than a mile apart; two of these must always be saddled up.[14] If great punctuality is enforced strictly, even on the worst of roads a distance of three miles can be traveled in one-and-a-half hours, which otherwise would be impossible.

The hour of departure is noted on the letters that such couriers transmit, with either "trot" or "walk" added.

§ 21

Very rapid communications are carried out through **signals**.

It would be wrong to neglect them and to only avail oneself of the usual means of notification.

The signals are:

1. Prepared. Beacons, flags, lanterns, etc.
2. Shots. **2.1** cannon shots. **2.2** rifle and pistol shots
3. Drums, horns, and trumpets
4. Bells

ON PICKETS AND THEIR SUPPORTING TROOPS: AS FORWARD POSTS OF SMALL DETACHMENTS

1. Pickets (Explanation)

§ 1

They usually consist of cavalry, more precisely, light cavalry. In rare cases, namely if no cavalry is available, or where dense forests are to be occupied, infantry guards are positioned toward the very front.

§ 2

A picket should never be positioned without a post at its rear to absorb it; or unless a *Piquet* is held in quarters ready for action. Otherwise the picket would be at too great a danger of being neutralized and dispersed.

(This is the forward post system of detachments; in the case of corps and armies this is only a part of the whole.)

§ 3

The strength of the pickets is chiefly a function of the number of forward posts, each consisting of six men, and the number of the forward posts

---

[14] One Prussian mile was the equivalent of 7,532.48 meters.

depends on the terrain, the darkness of the nights, etc. Under adverse conditions one has to calculate one man per 100 paces of the line to be covered.
[…]

§ 4

If possible, the distance between the pickets should not exceed 2500 paces. For in this case, the furthest forward posts are already 1500 paces from the guard and at this distance one can barely hear a pistol shot, which is essential at night. From § 3 and § 4 it follows that the individual pickets will have a strength of 20–30 men; one should not make them weaker without grounds, for stronger pickets can achieve more.

(During daylight hours they can be further apart, and at night one can position intermediate posts if needed.)

§ 5

The distance of pickets from their post is usually 2000–3000 paces; in case of close enemy proximity, shorter.

(We are speaking here about small detachments, which do not need as much time as entire armies. But even in the case of the former, the pickets do not always provide for the necessary security if the quarter is not yet ready, since the enemy usually arrives along with them. If they can be bypassed, safeguard distant pickets with intermediate posts.)

If the picket is positioned 2500 paces from the quarters, then the enemy will be detected by night at a distance of 3000 paces from the quarter. If the enemy covers this distance at a trot, then he will need approximately 10–12 minutes. This provides the security that the quarters gain through the picket. This interval (8 minutes after we deduct the time that has elapsed prior to the alarm) is just enough for the cavalry, which is saddled but not bridled, to mount. This is probably the shortest interval necessary for a troop that is already fielded. An infantry quarter with a strong village guard constitutes an exception.

§ 6

The distance between the forward posts and the picket must be such that they are within sight and earshot of a pistol. If, at night, they are located no further than 500–600 paces from the picket, then one has the advantage that they cannot be neutralized.

Infantry sentinels are positioned at night at least 200 and no more than 400–500 paces from the picket.

§ 7

The positioning of the picket. Close to large paths, yet such that the picket is concealed, or at least cannot be seen from a distance. A picket, which exists for more than 24 hours, should never be positioned at the same place by night as it was during the day.

§ 8

Forward posts are positioned on mountains, in defiles, paths, etc. At night, it is easier to observe higher points from below than vice versa.

　The forward posts also alter their positions at night. In rare cases, a picket can entirely dispense with forward posts to its side and rear.

§ 9

Conduct of Pickets

Before an officer marches, he makes a record of his men, checks whether they have the necessary ammunition, rations, and bread. As far as he himself is concerned, a watch, a quill, ink, paper or maps, a lead pencil, and a telescope are very useful.

§ 10

Familiarity with the area is the most important issue. The officer, if he is unfamiliar with the area, has a man brought to him from the next village, and inquires about the essentials. Above all, he has to take note of:

1. The names of villages to his front and rear.
2. The main roads.
3. The location of bridges and fords.

§ 11

Usually the **forward posts** are positioned by the post commander. If, however, an officer sees a necessity for change, he improves the situation by stationing an additional forward post and notifies the officer who was responsible for the original stations.

§ 12

Everything that approaches the chain of forward posts must come to a stop at a distance. The forward post reports what has appeared through a man sent back to the picket, which then dispatches a troop.

　Emmerich[15] describes a case in which he stood with a commando of Hussars and riflemen in the year 1760 near Northeim. His position was disclosed to the enemy, which wanted to neutralize him. The French attacked

---

[15] See Emmerich (1791: 41–3).

one of his forward posts with the aid of a farmer's wagon, whereby three Frenchmen were soldiers in disguise. In the meantime, Emmerich took note of some noise, hurried back several hundred paces behind the fire only to discover the enemy, who rushed the fire and plundered the knapsacks. He descended upon them and captured nine men.

§ 13

No enemy trumpeter or officer, so desiring, is allowed to be brought directly into the headquarters. He must be taken to the guard blindfolded and wait there until the officer receives orders from headquarters.

(General Ewald[16] provides several examples, where English light troops made use of envoys[17] in order to gain information about the enemy post.)

If, however, the trumpeter or officer brings letters or captives they will be accepted against receipt.

§ 14

Messages

If nothing new has transpired, normal messages are sent to the post commander who established the picket.

Exceptional messages are to be sent to this commander but simultaneously to the commander of the forward posts, if there is one, and if the issue is important, directly to the headquarters. Those posts that are directly affected will be notified at the same time.

§ 15

The format of messages. They must contain:

1. The time.
2. The location of the observation.
3. The name and rank of the reporting officer.
4. Who made the observation.

(This is very important because whoever receives the message can thereby judge its degree of credibility; every message does not deserve the same attention and very many contradict each other.)

5. The **orientation**.
6. The strength, etc.

---

[16] On Ewald see footnote 12. Hahlweg refers to Ewald (1798), where he describes several episodes from the American War of Independence.

[17] Clausewitz uses the French term *Parlementairs*.

§ 16

Passwords[18] and watchwords[19] are sent to the officer under seal. The password is revealed only to the guard officer, the watchword is given to every forward post and sentinel. Every forward post or sentinel will employ the watchword for his own security. The officer discretely retrieves the password from arriving troops by sending a non-commissioned officer to meet them.

(The watchword substitutes to a certain degree for the password, so that the latter is not used too often and too easily betrayed.)

§ 17

Conduct of Forward Posts

(One man is chosen to deliver the message, the other remains at his post during the day for observation.) The men always have to keep their designated position and may not dismount or communicate.

At night: If it is very dark or if the forward post is otherwise not visible from afar, then the men are positioned one behind the other so that they are just within sight of one another. The forward posts have to be addressed loudly so that one can hear from a distance that something is approaching.

As soon as the forward post is suspicious with regard to whatever approaches, it opens fire; one man hurries back to report, the other remains in the vicinity.

If a forward post is rapidly chased back by the enemy, he may not retreat back to the picket. (During daylight hours, the forward posts should take care not to reflect the sunlight with their rifles; during night, they should not draw their caps over their ears.)

§ 18

Vigilance of the Guards Themselves

By day, the pickets dismount; one half feeds the horses, the other has bridled them. The horses are ridden to the watering hole one at a time.

In his treatise on the service of light troops, Ewald provides two examples from the American War in which French officers fell upon pickets by daylight, scattering them and capturing a few.

At night: one half is mounted, the other keeps the horses reined in and in emergency near the enemy. If there is a danger of annihilation, the picket changes its position.

---

[18] Clausewitz uses the term *Feldgeschrei* whereby is meant an agreed-upon verbal signal, usually a first name, which is used to distinguish friend from foe.

[19] Clausewitz uses the term *Losung*. A *Losung* comprises a signal and an agreed-upon response used to distinguish friend from foe.

§ 19

Retreat from the Enemy

Conduct in response to an approaching enemy.

Pickets are intended not to fight but to observe. During the day, this is not difficult, since the picket can observe, communicate, and yet retreat without engaging the enemy. During the night this is more difficult.

If, however, the picket is able to prevent the enemy from advancing too fast by assaulting him, then this is one of its functions. Hence, I believe the following rules to apply:

1. The picket only retreats when faced with a stronger enemy, but tries to lure a weaker enemy into a trap.

2. A picket never retreats during the day so fast as to lose sight of the enemy.

3. If the picket is able to keep the enemy from advancing too rapidly by assaulting him, this must be done with resolve.

4. If the picket retreats by night, it leaves flankers behind who continuously deliver fire.

5. The retreat is accomplished in several squads, which support each other.

6. A detached squad never retreats directly toward the picket or the latter directly toward the *soutiens*, unless the terrain compels it.

§ 20

Retreat under Assault

If an officer is unlucky enough to be assaulted, there is no better choice than to attack the enemy with the few he has with him. If he gains thereby some space, then he wins time for the retreat.

§ 21

Relief: Takes place 2 hours prior to sunrise and the old picket does not depart until complete daylight.

§ 22

Patrols that are sent by the picket can only be weak and cannot cover long distances. They are intended:

1. To prepare the forward posts to guarantee their alertness and at the same time to scan the terrain between them and the guard.

2. To detect the enemy earlier than could the forward posts, that is, to approach him along his expected route.

(Their primary purpose is to gain information from the inhabitants. Since they are weak, they can do little more. Larger patrols are sent by the *soutiens* or the forward posts themselves.)

2. Support Posts of the Pickets

§ 23

They are either already positioned or are kept ready in their quarters for dispatch. Indeed, they deploy throughout the night, in which case they are called *Piquets*.

The purpose of this rear cohort is:

1. To prevent the enemy from too rapid pursuit so that the pickets cannot be annihilated.
2. To secure the pickets from being cut off or to at least to inform them of this. They can just as well be composed of infantry or cavalry; if one has both service arms at one's disposal it is only a function of terrain.

(Infantry in defiles, woods, and in areas which are cut across by hedges. Cavalry in the plain.)

A cannon, light or mounted artillery are very useful.

(A cannon shot usually repels light troops; one always can keep the enemy at bay, which is always an important objective during retreats; one hears the cannon shot in the rear . . . .)

(*Piquets* are less able to accomplish this than trained posts; this is why only very weak detachments resort to *piquets*. If the pickets are very close, a *piquet* is very natural. Concerning the manner in which such weak posts can stall the enemy. Basic principles that follow for the assemblage.)

§ 24

Positioning of the Supporting Posts

If possible:

1. Concealed.
2. To the side of the pickets.
3. At an appropriate distance.

§ 25

Conduct of Supporting Posts

The cavalry is bridled and the horses reined.

For every picket that they are supposed to support, they have a reliable man for information.

They place some posts between themselves and the pickets.
They provide for larger patrols.

§ 26

The manner in which the pickets absorb them.

The infantry tries to keep the pursuing enemy at bay through considered rifle fire.

The cavalry attacks resolutely in the flanks and the rear.

Concluding Remarks

The nature of pickets is twofold: first, one's own security and the observation of the area we hold; second, the defense of this area against enemy patrols and against all too rapid advancement of enemy detachments.

The first objective is achieved by the forward posts, by patrols, by one's own vigilance, and changes in position and *soutiens* as rearguards. On its own, each of these individual measures would not produce any great security. Taken together, however, they are sufficient to defend against too many mishaps.

The second objective is achieved through the deployment of the *soutiens*, the use of the terrain, and a decisive assault in urgent circumstances....

PRELIMINARY REMARKS

On the Defensive

1. If one restricts the concept of the defensive to absolute passivity, complete nonsense would be a likely result. There would be two men fencing, one always striking, the other, only parrying. There would be a kind of war where only one side wages war.

2. Thus it is necessary to broaden the concept. How should we determine its borders?
   No doubt, the defensive must have its own advantages, for otherwise the defensive would not exist; everyone would proceed offensively. Hence, whatever one has said about the superiority of the offensive, there must be some qualities of the defensive to keep it in the balance.
   These can be no other than:
   2.1 That one gains time by awaiting the enemy's actions.
   2.2 That one can fight the enemy in an area one knows well and is in a position to prepare according to one's own aims. With one word, that one enjoys the support of the locality. If these are the main advantages

of the defensive, then one also can regard them as the chief characteristics, according to which the concept is determined in general.

2.3 Thus, it is the defensive when I wait:

2.3.1 For the enemy to approach me; hereby the main purpose of
the defensive is sufficient.

2.3.2 For him to come close enough for me to use the locality to my
advantage. I can fight him here in whatever way pleases me.
The action always is to be called defensive.
The defensive is thus the combating of the enemy in my
theater of war or within my emplacement.

3. If we apply this to small defensive detachments, it then follows that every
type of formation that can be taken up within or behind their positions is
available for use against the enemy.

4. If one were to restrict small defensive posts to the merely passive, one
could indeed give precise reasons for doing so, namely that: (1) these
posts are usually calculated in terms of support; (2) in their area it is not a
matter of absolute resistance, but only of resistance for a certain duration, by which passive defense becomes possible. And in fact, passive
defense appears more often in Small War than in Large War, and even if
in most cases it does not have any great effect, it suffices for its intended
purpose. For very small detachments, however, there is almost never
natural coverage for the flanks and similar things, and nature does not
create small miniature positions for 500 men. Hence, even in Small War,
one has to rely primarily on the active defensive wherever a reasonably
meaningful resistance is desired.

5. Passive defense usually is restricted in Small War to very weak infantry
posts, which by means of their fire are intended to keep the enemy
cavalry at a distance; or which are deployed for the defense of entrenchments, defiles, and if necessary villages; or which are part of a forward
post chain and absorb the retreating pickets, forward posts, etc.

6. If more than a very precarious resistance is desired in situations where
the terrain is not very supportive, nothing remains but the offensive
defense, which in the case of a detachment can only consist of a sort of
ambush. In the case of an entire forward post corps, however, it consists
of combinations very skillfully adapted to the terrain.

7. What we here term defensive detachments or posts are all those detachments that have the aim of fighting the enemy only after he enters
their area, that is, there where he cannot be tolerated. Also included
are those detachments that are only supposed to absorb forward posts,
prevent enemy reconnaissance, etc. By contrast, we will not speak
here about those posts that mainly deal with the art of entrenchment.

This issue is handled in every book and it can be dealt with according to certain rules. Here it will be more important to subject those issues to healthy common sense, that in the absence of great technical reinforcing measures are by virtue of natural circumstances primary and essential.

FOURTH CHAPTER

On Small Defensive Posts, Primarily in Forward Post Warfare

§ 1

The actual forward post chain of an army, that is, those points where the brigades are stationed, is in fact a line of defensive posts, which do not, however, act absolutely defensively but also offensively in order to achieve the purpose of defense. In this regard, even the cavalry is pertinent.

§ 2

Alone the infantry belongs to literal or passive defense. However, the defensive purpose in general also can be achieved by the cavalry, although to a lesser extent. Cavalry is able to absorb the forward posts; cavalry can prevent the advance of enemy patrols and reconnaissance; cavalry can, in emergencies, defend a defile, although here infantry and artillery perform better. In rough but accessible regions, both services combined are most suitable.

§ 3

In addition to the forward post and winter positions, such small defensive posts often are used for other purposes. Where they are not part of an entire chain, but rather isolated, they have to defend a specific location: a bridge, a depot, a mountain pass, etc.

§ 4

Although in the last ten to twenty years one has abandoned *cordon* warfare and many have inveighed against it, there are yet cases where post and *cordon* warfare is unavoidable. Namely:

1. If weak detachments occupy mountains,
2. If two armies want to secure their lines through mountains.

Example: The French Danube Army under Masséna[20] stood with its core positioned on mount Albis behind Zurich and had occupied the river Limmat

---

[20] Clausewitz refers to the Army of the Danube which was a field army of the First French Republic. After its defeat in the battle of Ostrach (March 21, 1799), the Army was reorganized

to the Rhine and the river Aar for a stretch of five miles. In the Frikthal, along the Rhine, one corps was positioned as a link between the core and the left flank. The left flank stood near Basel. The right flank under Lecourbe was spread out four to five miles between Lake Lucerne, Lake Zug, and the river Sill up to mount Albis. For the purpose of linking with Italy, one corps stood in the Valais. The Austrians under Archduke Charles stood opposite to this position equally spread out.

In this type of post chain a large number of defensive posts exist. They do not, however, belong to Small War proper, for the defense of mountains yet could be a matter for Large War. In addition, they differentiate themselves from the defensive positions of forward posts insofar as they aim for absolute defense. Thus, they are covered here only to the extent that what is said about small posts in Small War is applicable.

§ 5

As regards the defensive posts in Small War, one or more of the following goals is present.

1. To hold the position, that is to secure the army's way through it. This applies mainly to bridges and other water crossings.
2. To merely defend the position or to prevent the enemy army from advancing through it, namely:
   2.1 The troops should defend the position until help arrives from the rear.
   2.2 One should defend the position as long as troops are returning from the front.
   2.3 One should defend the position only for as long as is required for the army to gather arms, etc.

Sometimes the nature of the aforementioned goals has some influence on the defensive measures.

§ 6

Regardless of the purpose envisaged, a supportive terrain is almost always necessary. In a completely clear and flat area, one can at most deploy cavalry for these goals, and their actions would be quite simple.

Thus, the terrain must afford some cover or an entrenchment must exist. We will not deal with entrenchments here.

§ 7

On the defense of natural geographic barriers. These are:

and participated under the command of André Masséna (1759–1817) in the Battle of Winterthur and the First and Second Battles of Zurich. The Army was disbanded in November 1799 and its units integrated into other French field armies.

1. Defiles.
   1.1 Rivers and swamps, which are otherwise not passable, across which a bridge or a dam leads.
   1.2 Swamps and rivers, which can be passed without a dam.
   1.3 Mountain defiles.
2. Villages and individual houses.
3. Woods.
4. Other rough but accessible areas.

1. Defiles

§ 8

The defense of defiles is a common task for small defensive posts. The effect can be quite different depending on the circumstances. If the defile cannot be bypassed and is quite large (more than 100 paces), and one has had time to prepare, a few men can achieve quite a lot. If circumstances are different, the post can be lost in the first moment.

§ 9

Two perspectives can and must be considered here. If one is responsible for defending such a position oneself, one should look for opportunities to achieve something extraordinary through determination and appropriate measures, in order to make a name for oneself, even under adverse conditions. History provides many examples of such opportunities.

(Concerning willingness and defiance in war.)

It is different if one has delegated the task to someone else. Then one has to consider the large number of cases in which under the best of circumstances little has been achieved. Among the most dangerous delusions is the belief that, when designing and deploying a forward post system or a defense, a **certain** area is so advantageous that some 100 men can hold up an entire army.

§ 10[21]

Examples: 2nd, 3rd, 4th, 5th from the file.[22]

---

[21] At this point we follow the second numeration of paragraphs found in Clausewitz's lecture notes, which also contain errors of numeration. For example, paragraph 12 is followed by a paragraph numbered 14, with no paragraph 13 appearing in the original text. We have left out some paragraphs that contain cryptic references to historical examples and literature. Presumably Clausewitz spoke from these notes extemporaneously.

[22] Clausewitz maintained a collection of examples and illustrations on issues relating to Small War taken from his readings and experience that are available at the *Universitäts- und Landesbibliothek Münster* (Clausewitz 1810). These were also used by Hahlweg (1966–90: vol. 1, 529–99).

§ 11

Example of Limburg.

§ 12

The means of defending an otherwise inaccessible defile are the following:

1. One tries to adopt measures to close off the defile, as soon as one's troops have passed.
   Barbed Wire
   Barriers
   Wagons
   Pyres
   Planks
   Powder Barrels
   Grenades
2. One lays the path beyond the defile in such a way that the retreat of one's own troops does not lead directly back to it.
   This is always the main difficulty. Sometimes, strong determination can help. Example: Major Ziehen at Bentheim.[23]
3. One places the cannons just behind the defile; or if it is long, also on top of it. If there are no cannons, the infantry has to close off the defile.
4. One places the infantry along the side of the defile and allows them to shoot individually, under cover of terrain.
5. Wherever possible one takes measures for troops and parapets, because otherwise they could be easily dislodged by enemy fire.
6. One places the troops in front of the defile (this is a very dangerous measure, which should only be adopted in cases of urgent need). Such cases can only emerge if the length of the defile and the locality do not allow for its defense from the other side, and one has to accommodate cavalry.

§ 14 [sic!]

In all these cases the cavalry can do nothing other than to deploy in a concealed fashion behind the defile in order to attack the enemy if it passes.

§ 15

The so-called claiming of a defile is quite a different matter.

This mainly occurs if an army or corps wants to make use of the defile and a detachment occupies it as an *av[ante]-g[arde]* so that the enemy cannot contest its passage.

---

[23] Clausewitz's elaboration of the example can be found in Hahlweg (1966–90: vol. 1, 581).

1. If the occupation occurs earlier, then there is no question regarding what is to be done. One entrenches behind it and establishes a sort of bridgehead.

2. If there is not enough time to entrench **and if the terrain beyond is not suitable for defense**, and if the detachment is likely to be attacked, it should occupy the terrain beyond the defile, but position its forward posts far ahead, so as to be informed in a timely fashion of the arrival and strength of the enemy, and if he approaches with decisive superiority, to be able to retreat behind the defile. If the army itself has arrived at the defile, the situation is no longer any different from every other battle. Hence, the detachment, because of the close support can take some risks.

§ 16

If there are several crossings or fords and one is concerned about the flanks, one takes the measures above, but positions, if one is not altogether too weak, part of one's troops concealed to the rear. This is ideally the cavalry.
    Or:
    If one is very weak, one remains hidden with the entire detachment until the decisive moment, in which, through an unexpected action, one achieves more.

§ 17

Example:
The battle near Thein. Example Sheet No. 3.[24]

§ 18

The battle near Audenroy upon the Dommel. File Sheet 2.[25]

MOUNTAIN DEFILES

§ 19

They are as different as River and Morass Defiles. If the face of the mountain is very steep, the defile narrow, and the road wide, then the defile itself must be occupied with troops and artillery; and in case one is weak, one occupies it with all of one's forces. When it comes to ordinary defiles, where the mountains right and left are still passable, the road is very curved, and it is not

---

[24] See Hahlweg (1966–90: vol. 1, 472 ff.).
[25] This must refer to additional lecture notes prepared by Clausewitz. The referenced sheet does not appear in the Hahlweg collection.

possible to man the entire length, then one positions oneself in part or entirely on the most inaccessible heights. Here one is secure from the first assault; one can weaken the enemy through fire and then retreat through the mountain valleys if the danger of being cut off grows too great.

§ 20

Most mountain accesses are extremely difficult to defend. Almost everywhere the enemy is able to circumvent the small established posts, and the posts are seldom able to expand to such an extent as to use a rearguard to circle behind that part of the enemy troops that is circling around it. Therefore it is extremely dangerous to place oneself with the entire detachment in the middle of the defile. In any event, not much is won thereby, because the streets are usually so windy that it makes shooting difficult. At least the Tyroleans do not appear to have done so.[26]

It is more effective to position the entire detachment sidelong on one of the least accessible heights. Then one is secure from being overrun in the first assault, the men are not fearful and one is able for a relatively long period to weaken the enemy by fire. The enemy will try to circumvent us at accessible locations. However, since the danger of being cut off with an infantry in the mountains is not that great, one can wait until the enemy's attempt to circumvent, thereby gaining time. The enemy does not always adopt the quickest and most powerful means. In the beginning he will try to dislodge us by fire and since this will have little effect, will allow his troops to press forward against our mountain ridge. Under such conditions, one can fire about for hours without much effect. The defender is the one who thereby gains time, and when at last he is almost circumvented, he can try to escape through the mountains.

§ 21

It is much easier to be circumvented on the street. As soon as the enemy deploys something right or left of position one has to make a move. Admittedly, one has the advantage that one can retreat faster than the enemy can approach from off road. But, in such areas, the roads are so windy that the danger of being cut off is nevertheless great.

§ 22

The artificial means that are used to enhance such positions are **entrenchments** and **abatises**. If there was time to employ these means, the defense is much stronger. The following points, however, are important:

---

[26] Clausewitz refers to the Tyrolean rebellion in 1809, a peasant uprising led by Andreas Hofer against French and Bavarian troops.

1. Abatises and other obstacles if possible within the range of fire, otherwise they are removed easily.

2. Entrenchments with a steep profile, otherwise they are easily climbed.

3. The entrenchment must defend a considerable span of the road with close fire.

4. It must not be too easy to see.

5. In such a situation, every consideration of retreat must be abandoned and a battle over life and death engaged.

§ 23

We are speaking here about positions that are very small, at most 1000 or 1500 men strong. A larger detachment has other means at its disposal in the disposition and combination of offense and defense, etc. Such detachments, however, no longer belong to Small Wars.

Example:

§ 24

A battalion of riflemen and fusiliers, 500 men strong, has to defend the Engadin Valley in the region of Scamfs.

1. If it only has to accommodate troops that are retreating along this way, one will deploy the battalion in front of Scamfs, positioning them behind the narrowest point, with a number of good shooters to be placed on the knoll to the left along the way.

2. If the battalion is to defend the pass at any price until support arrives; it is better to position oneself in Scamfs or Zulz or in an entrenchment close to the road so as to increase the obstacles to entry as much as possible and to give up every idea of retreat.

(Regarding the Position and Shape of the Entrenchment)

3. The Detachment should defend the position for a certain time, just impeding the enemy's passage. However, since it is uncertain whether it can be reinforced, it must keep open the possibility of retreat. In detachment wars, this is most common in the mountains. Several kinds of formation are possible:

    3.1. Such a position can be taken up along the path where it is most narrow, for example near Capella. The mountain face to the left and the chasm to the right are so steep that no infantryman could climb them, and therefore the battalion would have to be circumvented at great distance. Otherwise the defense would last only a quarter of an hour because the enemy would circumvent us close to the road with a number of snipers who would fire at our rear and attack, and since there would be no room for quick maneuvers here, one probably would be overtaken quickly.

3.2. On the road or close to it in front of Scamfs. This would be the way in which an ordinary infantry battalion would behave.

(Advantages and Disadvantages of Such a Position)

3.3. Finally one positions oneself alongside the road in the least access-ible part of the mountains, for example behind Capella; the precon-dition is that one is without artillery. This is the way the Tyrolean insurgents would do it, and this is without doubt the best one can do. But one has to be close enough to the road to strafe it with effective fire.

If one has cannons, they must remain on the street and consequently a number of troops. In this case, only half or a third of the infantry can be placed on the hillside.

§ 25

The following example demonstrates how little one can count on the difficul-ties nature places before the attacker.[27] In the campaign of 1799 General Loison had to surmount a huge mountain peak covered with 1½ feet of snow with a battalion and then slide down an abyss of more than 100 fathoms on the other side in order to attack the position of Martins Brücke and Finstermüntz from the rear, which was also under attack from General Lecourbe. In this very campaign, a French detachment of Lecourbe's division near Scharl in the Engadin Valley was circumvented by 1½ companies of infantry and a few riflemen by way of an alpine peak, which they could pass only with the aid of climbing irons, after which they fell upon the backside of the French in an avalanche, taking the position.

One sees then that even as nature increases her obstacles, human efforts to overcome them likewise increase.

§ 26

It is true that chains of mountain posts have altogether little effect; almost every general assault destroys their artificial construction, setting back the whole venture. We saw this only recently in the campaign of 1799, where the Austrians and French dislodged each other in the highest mountain ranges of Switzerland without great difficulty. However, this is only true for the entire

---

[27] Clausewitz refers to an incident during the War of the Second Coalition (1798–1802) between revolutionary France and the European monarchies, led by Britain, Austria, and Russia.

chain. With regard to individual positions as long as they are not taken in the rear by columns advancing from left and right, their resistance is strong enough to last for a half or whole day, an effect that is very important for a small detachment. Thus, if one does not improperly use these small defensive positions for great aims, and for example limits their use to forward post chains or wars of small parties, one can be satisfied with what they accomplish and gain great benefits therefrom.

2. Woods

§ 27

Up to now, forests were regarded as natural obstacles that enhance small defensive positions; but we know the danger which they entail. Previously they were treated the same as any river or morass.

§ 28

Advantages which woods offer:

1. If one is positioned on the edge of the woods facing the enemy, one is covered and the enemy is not. He is unaware of our preparations.
2. Through the use of abatises one can now and then gain a measure of security.
3. The battle cannot be decided by the cavalry, and therefore not quickly; and if one is not at all able to hold a position, one nevertheless gains time by retreating slowly.

§ 29

Disadvantages:
By contrast, the danger of being circumvented and of other surprises is greater than in the plain, because one cannot see what is around.

§ 30

In woods, one usually only deploys the infantry. Nevertheless, the following items should be kept in mind:

1. **Chance** can also lead the cavalry into the woods.
2. In a sparsely wooded forest, light cavalry can be used with great success.
3. An infantry post must never be left without some cavalrymen who are indispensable for reporting, reconnaissance, etc.

§ 31

If one is positioned in a wood and does not enjoy the advantages conveyed by barriers to access, one does not position everyone at one point only, but a portion laterally to the rear. Thus, one obtains the means to attack the enemy unexpectedly and to avoid being cut off. (Lake Plötzen example.)[28]

(Some remarks about battle in rough and mountainous terrain. Here it is no longer the bellicose nature of troops or the skill of the commander and the training of the troops that counts.)

§ 32

If in individual battles our troops did not excel, one might forgo looking for woods in which to erect defensive positions. However, one has to occupy them for more important reasons. A forest ahead of the front or on the flank may never go unoccupied. Even if a forward post chain in the woods would be much weaker than on the other side, it must nevertheless be deployed.

For this reason it is often the case. Specifically in forward post wars, small detachments of infantry are very often deployed along the way to man forward positions without any other obstacles of terrain providing for cover. For such cases, the abovementioned rule is important.

3. Small Towns, Villages, and Houses

§ 33a

Sometimes the strength of a locality, its defensibility in connection with its location, is the reason why it is occupied and defended. Sometimes the locality is only chosen for the deployment of a small defensive position because no better barrier of terrain was available. Finally, the location is just a quarter for encampment, in which the occupying troops offer only as much resistance as is necessary to avoid being dispersed by enemy patrols and to accommodate returning forward posts.

These different cases will be considered in what follows.

§ 33b

The difficulties arising from the defense of towns, villages, and houses, etc. are not to be misjudged.

1. If no defile is connected, they easily are circumvented and then any idea of retreat must be abandoned.

---

[28] See Hahlweg (1966–90: vol. 1, 505 ff.).

2. Most localities are much too expansive to be occupied in a proper fashion. Yet, history provides many examples in which under seemingly unfavorable conditions very much was accomplished.

§ 34

1. One should accommodate only the most forward troops and retreat in the face of an overwhelmingly superior enemy.

In this case one should occupy the locality, as long as it is not a defile but can be circumvented, with only one detachment and position oneself to the side or rear.

2. One should hold out until reinforcement arrives.

If the locality is to some degree defensible, if it has walls or trenches etc., then one takes up position, observes the walls by means of sentinels, brings the guns into position at the gates (only in rare cases can the guns be used to fire on the enemy at a distance) and assembles the garrison at one or two points in order to advance against the enemy wherever it attacks.

§ 35

If the locality that is to be defended cannot be held, then one hides in individual buildings, such as churches, palaces, manor houses, etc.

If the locality affords no such positions, nothing else remains than to deploy to cover outside, leaving behind a detachment and waiting for further developments.

§ 36

Regarding the defense of individual houses, churches, palaces, etc. there is little objective that can be said. Those who steadfastly stick to the rules of engineering textbooks of course will not think very highly of these means. But experience shows by way of many nice examples, that it is possible in such circumstances to make a big name for oneself. Even if those who set up such positions must believe in the ease with which, according to the rules, they can be overrun, so as not to expect too much from them, so too must those who find themselves within these positions believe in the possibility, through determination and sacrifice, to become useful and to distinguish themselves.

§ 37

Examples:

1. The example of Charles XII in Turkey is well known.[29]

---

[29] Charles XII, King of Sweden (1697–1718). During his exile in Turkey, the Swedish colony in Bender was attacked by a mob and Turkish elite infantry soldiers (Janissaries) took the Swedish King prisoner in 1713.

2. The Marshal of Saxony defended himself in the year 1715 with 18 men against 800 Poles in a house for an entire day and broke out by night.[30]

3. In the war between Charles-Gustav, King of Sweden,[31] and Casimir, King of Poland,[32] five months before the battle of Warsaw, a Swedish Lt. Colonel Aschenberg was sent to the town of Radom with 300 horsemen. He encamped for the night in a noble estate named Sakersau. In the morning, when he was ready to depart, 1500 Poles broke into the village and he was compelled to defend himself at the estate. The enemy had no cannons; there were only three entrances, namely two gates, which led into the courtyard and the house door. The courtyard was surrounded by a wall; the entryways were barricaded in haste with beams, through which hand to hand fighting could be avoided. A firefight ensued and after this had lasted a certain time and parts of the buildings were burned down, the Swedes dashed against the Poles and fought their way through. They even took prisoners and captured an enemy standard.

4. Often the enemy does not know how weak the garrison is. King Sobiesky of Poland[33] fired upon a small village Nemiszi, in which no more than 19 riflemen were positioned, for four days.

5. 60 Hanoverian riflemen defended themselves during the 7 Years' War for an entire day in the fortified Palace Friedewald against a large corps under General Stainville.

6. 1. In the year 1759 the allied army of Cassel advanced against Bergen. During this march, the column of the Duke of Holstein came across the mountain castle Ulrichstein, in which 400 men were said to be located.

   2. When, during the campaign of 1794, the Observation Army advanced on St Winox across the mountains, a small location called Esselbeck was attacked by a battalion of grenadiers under Captain Hotze. He conquered the town in which a palace was located. Immediately thereafter, the men dispersed in order to plunder. The French returned and attacked the Germans. A heated battle ensued in the streets. The Germans were driven out again. A corporal with 14 men was left behind in a wine cellar, and when he found the streets full of Frenchmen, he retreated with his men to the palace. He pulled up the bridge and occupied with his 14 men both towers. As soon as the French approached, he gave fire; and as evening was approaching, he remained in his position until the next morning and then was liberated by the allies [see Figure 3].

---

[30] Moritz, Count of Saxony, later Marshall of France (1696–1750), natural son of August the Strong and Aurora of Königsmark.

[31] Charles X, King of Sweden (1622–60).

[32] John II Casimir, King of Poland (1609–72).

[33] John III Sobieski, King of Poland (1624–96).

Figure 3. Defensive Occupation of Palace Towers.

Source: Clausewitz (1810: 101v.) Copyright © Universitäts- und Landesbibliothek Münster, N. Clausewitz 4,001.

7. In 1777, during the American War, General Washington[34] wanted to attack the English army under Lord Howe,[35] which was located two hours from Philadelphia. After forced marches General Washington suddenly approached, fell upon the right flank, dispersed the light infantry, which was positioned a half-hour forward, and would have attacked the army if Lt. Colonel Mousgrave, who had remained behind with three companies as *soutien* near Tews' country house, had not retreated into the house with the firm determination to sacrifice himself. In haste, he blocked the entryways with tables and chairs and defended himself with such persistence that General Washington, who had fastened onto this position, was delayed until the English army arrived, attacked the Americans, and defeated them.

8. Lieutenant Gauvain of the fusilier battalion defended himself with 35 men on the 20th of March 1793 on the Goldfels near Stromberg for a half-day against 700–800 Frenchmen.

(Some remarks about the dangers of such a defense and the nature of attacking such positions. Ewald's rule to never ask for advice.)

§ 38

Whatever the ends or objectives with regard to defending a locality and whatever the means one wishes to apply, the following issues are important:

1. To be informed early about the advance of the enemy.
2. To quickly take position.

---

[34] George Washington (1732–99), Commander-in-Chief of the Continental Army 1775–83 and first President of the United States 1789–97.

[35] Willliam Howe, Fifth Viscount Howe (1729–1814), British General and Commander of the English troops against the Americans 1775–8.

The chief concerns of an officer who mans such positions are thus the following:

1. Security vis-à-vis the enemy, therefore the deployment of forward posts. Here the rule is **never to believe your rear is secure.** (Example of Hoya[36])

2. Barriers to access, mainly blocking of entries to villages. One should never neglect this, even if very few means are available.

3. A certain policing. It provides for order and security from within. One delegates the supervision to one of the most highly regarded inhabitants and makes him responsible.

4. An adequate allocation of quarters. At night one either remains under arms or one stays together in some houses or fully dressed in quarters. Furthermore, in every quarter someone must hold guard.

5. An adequate allocation of duties. An officer is commander of the forward posts; he must be responsible for their vigilance. A second supervises the police; a third the distribution of foodstuffs and the allocation of quarters, etc.

(Reasons why such arrangements are better than giving orders one after another.)

6. Determination of alarm stations. Here the following rules apply:
   6.1 For companies in the precinct.
   6.2 For the entire unit, if one does not want to stay in the locality, if possible outside of the village.
   6.3 No unnecessary distances; that is, if it is not especially necessary, no specific alarm stations for battalions but only for companies and the entire unit.
   6.4 The alarm stations must be chosen with regard to function, namely, the retreat, if this is the main purpose.
   6.5 If one has cannons but does not want to defend the locality, then these are brought to the alarm station to be guarded.
   6.6 Cavalry has to have its alarm station whenever possible outside of the village.
   6.7 If possible, cavalry and infantry should not cross paths on the way to their respective alarm stations.

§ 39

Very often one has erected entrenchments near localities that could not defend themselves, be it in order to provide at least some defense of the position

---

[36] Town in Northern Germany where, according to Scharnhorst, French troops under General Chabot lost a secure position due to false reliance on forward posts in the winter of 1757/8.

through such entrenchments, or just to provide a secure place for assembling the garrison where they can await the return of their forward posts. Such entrenchments are called *place d'armes*.

1. If the point itself is to be defended by the entrenchment, then the locality is secondary, the troops have occupied it merely for their convenience. But this is not the issue here.

2. If, however, the entrenchment is merely meant to be an assembly point for the troops in which they await the return of their forward posts, then it has to be noted that this is a very dangerous measure. If the point at which one wants to assemble and line up is determined by the entrenchment, then the enemy will move against this point. And since the entrenchment manned only with a weak guard rarely offers resistance, the enemy will take it before or while the garrison occupies it. (Example of the entrenchment of Mosbach near Mainz[37]).

§ 40

All partisans[38] also regard the following as important:

1. To make friends amongst the inhabitants of the locality through cordial behavior.

2. To maintain a determined but calm attitude toward them.

3. To draw on them for information. (Ewald[39] himself advises that if informants cannot be found in enemy territory, one should compel them in a sense, and make the principals of the village responsible for it.)

§ 41

Although cavalry is never used to defend a locality, in connection with the infantry it can contribute by chance or purpose to its defense.

Thus it will be deployed outside the locality.

1. To fall upon the enemy as soon as he attacks and to assault his flank and rear.

---

[37] The entrenchment at Mosbach was attacked only days before Mainz capitulated October 21, 1792.

[38] In Clausewitz's time, the term *Parthey* (sometimes written *Partei*) generally referred to a band of armed fighters. The terms *Partheygänger* (sometimes written *Partheigänger*) and *Partisan*, translated here as "partisan" referred to their leader. See Rink (2006: 360). Clausewitz's definition of the terms appears below.

[39] See Ewald (1790: 45).

2. For small unit chases through the streets where people are shooting at each other.

4. Varied But Nonetheless Accessible Terrain

§ 42

Little can be said here about defensive measures as such. They are always very weak. Gardens, trenches, and hedges are obstacles that can be easily circumvented or broken through. The less that can be said in such cases about defensive measures as such, the more we must apply what has been said in the chapters above regarding the planning and conduct of defensive battles. Offensive defense is absolutely essential if the battle is to be anything more than a slow retreat.

§ 43

Such features as accessible mountains, rivers, morasses, villages, trenches, woods, hedges, gardens, etc. etc. do provide some cover against the first assault and allow any number of combinations; advantages which one would have to do without in completely flat lands. One quite correctly favors such areas over flat lands for the deployment of small defensive posts.

SOME ADDITIONAL RULES FOR THE ENTIRE UNIT

§ 44

If one arrives at a position during the night and does not know the area, then one remains at arms, deploys sentinels around oneself, and sends patrols to the villages closest to the enemy to collect information.

§ 45

The measures taken up at defensive posts, of which we have heretofore spoken, differ from one another in part according to the objective of the post. The officer assigned to such posts must therefore first know the objective. If it is not clear from his instructions, he is well advised to ask. In many, if not most, cases the objective of the post is quickly revealed by the location and other circumstances, as long as one examines these without preconceived ideas.

On the Use of the Art of Entrenchment with Regard to Defensive Posts

§ 1

The art of entrenchment is taught separately. It does not belong here. But because it so closely touches upon the former chapter, and since we have availed ourselves of it in the cases just examined, it will nevertheless be an element of our instruction at least to link our analysis to the art of entrenchment as such, and to use the latter for the analysis of our cases.

§ 2

The advantages of entrenchments are:

1. To shield oneself against continuing fire.
2. To defend against the force of the assault (bayonet assault).

Both measures require small posts, especially when facing a superior enemy. There is no doubt that in this way a small troop can gain the capabilities for strong resistance. On this, a few additional remarks.

§ 3

The disadvantages of entrenchments are:

1. One cannot attack the enemy unexpectedly.
2. In most cases one has to forego the idea of retreat.

§ 4

Obstacles to entrenchments are:

1. Insufficient time.
2. The terrain. Rocks. Woods. Morasses.
3. Too few men for defense.
4. Uneven terrain.
5. Too steep a camber.

Elaboration of these points.

6. Ease of circumventing the position of the entrenchment.

§ 5

The most difficult aspect of application is found in weighing the advantages and disadvantages and in choosing the best option.

§ 3 [sic!]

When located behind a causeway that cannot be circumvented, then without a doubt, an entrenchment that provides cover against superior fire conveys great advantage. Here, this advantage is the only objective. Under such conditions one erects open rather than closed structures, because if they by chance are lost, we easily can take them back from the enemy. This, by the way, is almost the only case for which open structures are advisable.

§ 4 [sic!]

If the causeway can be circumvented, the entrenchment must in every case be closed. But then the problem arises that one is often too weak and suffers from the disadvantage that no retreat is possible. Both must be accepted if holding the position is essential and the area does not provide for any further cover. A steep profile can correct for the first disadvantage.

§ 5 [sic!]

In the mountains, entrenchments are essential for the defense of passes, when enemy columns cannot circumvent the point in the road somewhere nearby. If they can, the entrenchment at times becomes ineffective, whereas troops not assembled in entrenchments could have followed enemy movements.

§ 6.

The difficulty of avoiding the problem of too strong a camber (which we discussed earlier) has led to the well-known blockhouse.

Nothing can be said against blockhouses as such; but their construction requires so much time, that using them in the way we are discussing is hardly possible in the midst of a campaign. They can only be used:

1. In fortifications and aforementioned entrenched camps.
2. In defensive *cordons* that were built for the defense of the province long before. However, these *cordons*, having a purely *defensive* objective (and not one of the objectives of which we have spoken), are precisely the most dangerous and objectionable. Therefore, these measures count for little in the field of battle.

§ 7

The rough terrain in mountainous areas often presents an obstacle to erecting entrenchments, if one does not want to place them directly on the road. For on the one hand, one cannot build on a very steep surface with many small canyons and hills. On the other hand, one cannot observe anything properly from such entrenchments.

§ 8

From a different perspective, entrenchments are less necessary in the mountains. The advantage of the terrain protects against the sudden assault, the woods against the effects of enemy fire. When encountered by the artillery, an irregular terrain can diminish the effectiveness of fire, often by a half, sometimes by 2/3.

§ 9

The consequence of all this is that in the mountains one avails oneself of entrenchments only when one has the time and means to clear away any obstacles, when defensive measures have been taken in advance, and when an absolute defense is expected.

There are only a few examples from the 7 Years' War[40] where light troops entrenched themselves in the mountains. They usually occupied existing entrenchments but almost never erected such entrenchments themselves.

§ 10

Entrenchments in woods present problems of their own because of the many roots. Moreover, the woods themselves provide cover against the cavalry and the trees provide some protection against enemy fire. Hence [entrenchments] are not as common [in the woods] as in the plain. However, the difficulties are not insurmountable and strong abatises covered by fire from the entrenchments provide them with greater strength. Because one cannot rest with wagons at many points along a road in the forest, one often finds points where the enemy cannot avoid being attacked from the entrenchment, and where he is unable, at least with artillery, to attack the entrenchment with concentrated artillery fire. These are reasons that very much speak for the erection of entrenchments.

If it is a matter of defending an isolated position in the woods, one will entrench oneself and build abatises and palisades for reinforcement, and choose, wherever possible, a point on the road where the enemy is constrained in the use of his artillery.

§ 11

If villages and other localities are to be defended in war, the art of entrenchment very often is used but more in Large than in Small Wars. But here too there are cases.

---

[40] While the Seven Years' War (1756–63) involved most of the great powers of the time, Clausewitz refers mainly to the Third Silesian War waged between Prussia and Austria over Silesia.

Hereby, the following points are the most essential:

1. One no longer encircles entire villages with entrenchments[41] as was previously done. This is even less the case when speaking of Small Wars.

2. Blocking entrances does little good when everything else is accessible. Only when everything else is inaccessible and one intends to fire upon the enemy at a distance is it advisable to erect *flèches* and redoubts in front of the entrances. Otherwise one can content oneself with bringing guns into position in the streets.

3. Erecting entrenchments for lateral defense in closed villages is only sensible when one seeks to elevate the locality to a fortified position and the time and energy for this is not lacking. Such cases do not arise in Small Wars.

4. Therefore, in most cases in Small War there is probably nothing better to do than to erect the entrenchment apart from the village or behind it.

5. An entrenchment with a steep profile can in general be made better and stronger than an entrenchment erected in an expansive or open location. Thus, if there is time to erect an entrenchment, one will prefer its advantages to those of the village.

   If one views the entrenchment in combination with the village, it may gain by this connection great strength.
   In this case it can be situated behind the village so that the village presents a barrier to access; located in such a fashion that the enemy has to advance under our most effective fire. Or, it can be placed in front of the village, the latter covering to some extent its rear. This will in the main only be the case if one is able to simultaneously occupy the village and the entrenchment.

6. It will not be the case that one prefers the advantages of the entrenchment to those of the village, if the village is to be occupied as a goal in and of itself, which is sometimes the case when one occupies a village because there was no better access barrier. Most common are cases in which one wants to use the locality merely for quarters. In the latter case, one calls the entrenchment a *place d'armes*.

   The most important thing to note in this regard is the difficulty of securing this *place d'armes* from any attack if the garrison is not in the entrenchment but in the village. To have but a guard in the entrenchment is dangerous. The danger here is twofold. First, that the *place d'armes* is lost before we arrive. Second, that the enemy, because he knows our exact assembly area, can prevent us from assembling. In any

---

[41] At this point, Clausewitz uses the French term *retranchment* rather than the German term *Schanze*.

case, such entrenchments have to be situated close to the quarters and heavily protected.

If the entrenchment is the primary issue, then it is safe to quarter in or next to it, and if quartering in the village is the primary issue, to take defensive measures there.

§ 12

Entrenchments in completely open or varied but easily accessible areas are the simplest to build and enjoy great advantages. However, they suffer from the disadvantage that they should be built at a location that the enemy cannot circumvent. Since they are usually erected in such a way that they intersect direct routes, the enemy does not gladly ignore them. Advance detachments can be defeated if they do not retreat via detours: one can steal a march on them along straight paths, etc. For these reasons, one does not leave a manned entrenchment to one's rear lightly. Habit and preconceptions add to this and one can assume with some certainty, that if one fortifies a small post with an entrenchment along the path of the enemy, the enemy will first take it before a further general advance. But this does not prevent the enemy from circumventing the entrenchment at the first opportunity, cutting off the garrison's route of retreat.

From time to time cases also will arise in which the enemy decides to continue his march via small detours before taking the entrenchment.

It is self-evident that those light obstacles of the terrain that are found in the region must be taken by effective fire.

§ 13

With regard to the positioning of the entrenchment, in general, the following applies:

1. The entrenchment should strafe a certain point with its firepower. (In most cases artillery)
2. The entrenchment should hold a certain point, preventing the enemy from establishing himself there.

The first case is more common in Small Wars. Here, the entrenchment has to subordinate its self-defense and try to achieve it through other means. One can strafe the area *a d* quite well from the rampart *a*, thus the entrenchment completely defends the access to its trench. The area *b c* cannot be observed, and because it is so large that point *c* is out of the range of cannon fire, the entrenchment does nothing else than defend itself and point *a* [see Figure 4].

The rampart *d* allows for the strafing of the area *e c*, but not the area *d e* nearby the entrenchment.

This case arises quite often, because in general this is the shape of all mountains, and the summit is rarely so flat that they can be observed from the ramparts.

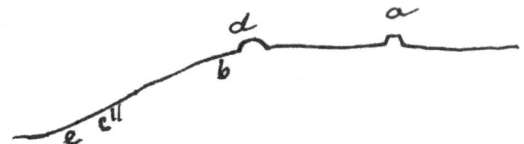

Figure 4. Positioning of an Entrenchment.
Source: Hahlweg (1966–90: 321), own reproduction.

Thus the entrenchment *d* has to help itself by other means, mainly through profiles, palisades, trench defenses, etc.

The purpose of the entrenchment and the circumstances must determine which position is to be chosen.

§ 14

If we take together everything that has emerged from observing individual cases and add the general thereto, the following propositions follow:

1. Individual entrenchments of small defensive posts must be situated in such a way that the enemy cannot pursue his intentions without attacking them. (Consequently they cannot prevent assaults as was the case in Dittersbach.[42])

2. In woods and mountains they are most difficult to erect, but since they are also more easily dispensed with, they are less common, even if here they are most likely to fulfill their purpose.

3. Indeed, entrenchments do not offer more defensive strength than open villages with stone houses, but one takes fewer chances, because one doesn't lose sight of the people.

§ 15

As far as the construction of the structure itself is concerned, the following issues are the most important ones and should be taken into consideration in any case:

1. Never build open structures.

2. Provide steep profiles. Trenches 15–18 feet deep and never less than 9. The main difficulty with deep trenches is the water. Working in water is very difficult. What one cannot achieve in the depth of the trenches must be added to the height of the parapet. 6–8 feet high ramparts.

---

[42] Scharnhorst describes an assault on a Prussian infantry regiment in 1759 by Austrian forces. See Scharnhorst (1980: § 58).

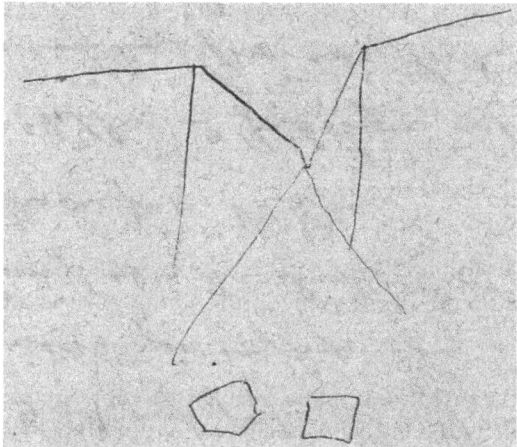

Figure 5. Barriers on the Edge of a Trench
Source: Clausewitz (1810: 113v.) Copyright © Universitäts- und Landesbibliothek Münster, N. Clausewitz 4,001.

3. Other barriers to entry, palisades, and pitfalls[43] on the edge of the trench. Small spikes, etc., through which storming is impeded [see Figure 5].

4. Simple redoubts are preferable to all other forms. The sideward defense of the trenches through small structures with inward-looking angles cannot be maintained anyway and the inward-looking angle unnecessarily narrows the area. Even outward-looking angles are defensible only in the case of a dodecagon (namely if the inward looking angle is square). As regards small star-forts successful defense results from steep assault, on which nobody likes to depend.

5. A unit in the trench.

ON THE EFFECTIVENESS OF THE ARMY FORWARD POSTS, THAT IS, THEIR BEHAVIOR IN GENERAL

§ 1

Having spoken of the establishment of the new forward post system, we went through the behavior of the outposts and their *soutiens*, spoke about small defensive posts, because the actual forward posts can be regarded as such. Now

---

[43] The German term is *"Wolfsgruben,"* and denotes a 0.6–1.6 meter deep, cone-shaped pit with a sharpened spike pointing upward from the bottom, typically placed in front of entrenchments as a physical obstacle.

it is a matter of getting to know how the entire forward post system fulfills its purpose when the enemy advances, how the individual elements relate to one another and to the whole.

This is possible if we clearly think through the behavior when facing an enemy advance:

1. Of the individual brigades,
2. Of the *soutien-corps* and the whole.

Some examples from forward post wars. Forward post battle upon the river Boxtel 1794 and on the river Vechte in the winter of 1794 and 1795.[44]

§ 2

It is very often the case in war that a weak group confronts an enemy three or four times its strength. One should believe the ruin of the first to be the most likely consequence. But this is only the case if the stronger knows exactly the strength and situation of the weaker and support is not close enough to prevent the detachment's entire destruction and dispersion.

In most cases the advancing party does not know enough about the position and strength of the troops he first encounters and the area they occupy, and thus will be compelled to that caution that is considered to be a norm in war and which is only violated in specific cases.

This caution plays an inconspicuous but nonetheless extremely important role in war, presents itself in every development, and only through it are we able to explain phenomena that otherwise appear incomprehensible.

Remark:

One can compare this caution to a very general force of nature, for example gravity, or friction, etc. without whose existence phenomena as we see them would be entirely impossible.

§ 3

It is primarily this caution that provides the endurance for the resistance and effectiveness of the forward posts, which otherwise could not be explained.

An outpost and its *soutien* cannot be pursued hotly and destroyed by the front line of the advancing enemy cavalry because the latter has to fear being lured into an ambush or suddenly being confronted with a superior enemy.

In order to drive out a posted brigade, it is necessary to analyze its position, call on the infantry, develop a plan, form columns, etc. This leads to the loss of time, which the defender gains, whereby this does not include the amount of time won by the resistance itself.

---

[44] Clausewitz refers to battles during the War of the First Coalition in which British, Dutch, and Austrian troops had attempted to invade France through Flanders.

It is equally unlikely that the enemy will be able to pursue rapidly and to destroy retreating brigades with a substantial cavalry, for similar reasons as in the case of outposts and their *soutiens*. Thus, the enemy can pursue only in large mass and therefore less rapidly.

If a substantial corps is located in the area, it will have to await the arrival of its columns. If the area is at least somewhat varied, as is the case in most cultivated regions, the enemy will reconnoiter the area before him only after he has occupied the terrain that was formerly occupied by the forward post brigades, and then he will find it difficult to distinguish between a substantial corps, *c.* 10 battalions and 20–30 squadrons, from the army itself. He will not be certain of this before he has given his columns directions for their efforts against the army itself, and the battle has already begun at some places. Even if this corps does not want to provide any resistance but rather to retreat, by its mere appearance time is won, which in most cases probably is sufficient to fulfill the purposes of the forward posts.

This time, gained through the methodical advance of the enemy and the retreat of the forward posts, constitutes the actual and general effectiveness of the forward posts.

One nonetheless cannot completely avoid actual combat, that is, resistance as such. Because:

1. The resistance of the individual brigades in any case must endure long enough for their guards and *soutiens* etc. to return.
2. They can be attacked during retreat.
3. They must be able to defend themselves against a rapid and carelessly advancing enemy, otherwise the aforementioned would no longer obtain.
4. It is not always the enemy army that forces them back, but often only a relatively small corps, because the enemy is interested in possessing the terrain that they occupy.
5. One should in general only retreat when facing a superior enemy, and even then only if one can assess him accurately, because otherwise one would be retreating before every weak detachment. This also applies to the *soutien-corps* in their relations with their brigades.

§ 5

Thus the battle of the forward posts can be divided into two phases.

The first consists of the resistance of the individual brigades, the other in the uniting of the *soutiens* with several or all of the brigades.

§ 6

Consequently, for a commander of an individual forward post brigade, the rule applies that if there is no hope of conducting a successful raid against the enemy, or if he believes he is not up to the challenge, his resistance should be limited to compelling the enemy to prepare an attack and to adopt precautions, which slow him down. Thereafter he should retreat to the *soutien*. Whatever measures are adopted, this retreat to the *soutien* must never be left out of sight.

§ 7

Besides a strict defensive, for which there is seldom an opportunity, there are various postures, which are suitable for the forward post brigade.

The first is when one defends a single point, the [second] when advancing with a large part of one's forces to attack the enemy.

For the former case, infantry and artillery are best suited, in the latter, cavalry. This assault can only be effective if it is directed toward the flanks and rear of the attacker.

This posture is appropriate only against an enemy that is not too preponderant, for example, an ordinary reconnaissance unit. It thus can only be adopted at that moment when the enemy is close and his strength can be estimated relatively well.

In general, the posture is more appropriate to the wings of the forward post positions than to the center.

§ 8

The second posture is retreat without great resistance upon enemy attack, but immediate return to the attack before the enemy contemplates any defensive measures.

In most cases, it is the unexpected that generates here a large effect. If one is again expelled, a considerable amount of time nevertheless thereby is gained. The enemy will always believe that we had returned with reinforcements and therefore will want to reinforce himself.

Of course this idea can only be executed if the enemy position is not strong and he does not occupy it with a large column.

§ 9

The third posture involves occupying a weak position with cannons and infantry to make the enemy believe he is confronting the true position. With the remaining forces one retreats and takes cover. As soon as the enemy breaks through, he is attacked. This posture is appropriate in those cases where the terrain is not conducive enough for local defense. If the enemy arrives in great numbers, however, the attack can only be directed against the front lines of the columns.

§ 10

All these elaborate postures require precise knowledge of the area and other preparations. If there is not enough time, as is very often the case for the forward posts of armies that march a lot in war, then only one thing remains to be done.

§ 11

Fourth posture. One rather concentrates from the start and favors a concentrated assault against the enemy over a dispersed resistance, which usually cannot be sustained for long in an unsuitable terrain.

§ 12

All these postures of battle, however, can be successfully applied against an enemy which is not vastly superior. If one confronts a main enemy column, the attack will be repelled.

In most cases this can be duly assessed and thus one can avoid taking on more than is advisable; sometimes, however, one believes oneself to be assailing a weak enemy only to discover he is quite strong.

There is no avoiding this in detachment wars, as otherwise one would easily be expelled by every weak enemy, and in any case, it will not lead to ruin.

§ 13

By means of these three types of resistance the retreat to the *soutien* is eased greatly because one has all one's troops close together and does not need to attack the enemy any more than one believes advisable.

§ 14

With respect to all these operations, the chain of outposts and the double or single chain of *soutiens* serve to report on the enemy's arrival and to delay him long enough for the post to take necessary measures.

§ 15

All these measures are at the discretion of the individual brigade commander. There exist other measures, however, which depend on the superior commander. The *soutien*, in which the latter is based, is mainly intended to accommodate the brigades and rarely in a position to support them in their moment of battle:

1. Because it usually arrives too late.

2. Because it is uncertain of what is taking place at other positions, and thus cannot devote itself too much to anyone.

§ 16

In addition to the accommodation of the forward posts, the measures at the disposal of the aforementioned commander for their benefit are:

1. The reinforcement of some posts with cavalry or infantry, which he either attaches to them or places closely to their rear, taking infantry or a part of the cavalry from others. Cannot be withdrawn in the plain.

   A post will rarely be able to do without cavalry completely.

   The infantry which one withdraws must not be divided amongst the other brigades, but deployed behind their brigade or as a *soutien*.

2. The redeployment of the brigade if one is informed of an enemy attack and believes the enemy has gained knowledge of its position.

   In this way one at least maintains the advantage of surprise.

3. Placing the *soutien* closer to the most dangerous spot.

§ 17

With regard to the behavior and effectiveness of the *soutiens* themselves, one might say the same as was said about the forward posts of the brigades.

Nevertheless, the following particularities should not be overlooked:

1. The *soutien* has the main purpose of accommodating the returning brigades and since it is located relatively far away (¼, ½ mile), it will have to set out to meet up with the brigade if it is hard-pressed. This will often prevent it from offensively advancing against elements of the enemy forces.

2. If the *soutien* and its attached brigades want to undertake an action against an enemy that has advanced:

   2.1 Either because they believe themselves able to fight him under favorable conditions, or

   2.2 Because it is essential to stop the enemy,

   then a concentrated assault on an enemy column without much posturing in most cases would appear to promise the best success.

§ 18

The strength of the forward posts is discretionary. Stronger ones allow for greater resistance and provide more security. But because they suffer many losses through continuous combat and exertions, it is not economically wise to strengthen them any more than one believes the conditions require.

If one confronts an enterprising enemy and does not want to risk much, strong forward posts are essential.

In general, this provision depends on the way in which one wages the war and thus cannot be dealt with here.

§ 19

With regard to the relation between the brigades and the *soutien* the following must be mentioned:

1. If too weak, brigades suffer from the disadvantage that they would be unable to offer resistance without support, which would lead to a continuous marching of troops back and forth.

2. A *soutien* that is too weak would not allow for measures appropriate to the circumstances. One would have one's forces distributed equally, but one would no longer be in a position to create more of a barrier for the enemy where it is stronger, because the reinforcement of a brigade through others has several difficulties. Moreover, the retreat of the brigade thereby would be less secure. For only that which directly accommodates the withdrawing troops guarantees the retreat with any reliability. Counting on the flanking effect of other brigades would betray a very limited knowledge of war.

Finally, even with overly strong brigades one would not be able to impress the enemy with considerable corps of the *avant-garde* before he reaches the army, because the brigades will not always be able to unite.

If the *soutien-corps* are equal in strength to forward posts, one has the advantage that they can replace them.

If this feature is absent, then it is good to have more cavalry and mounted artillery in the *soutien*.

§ 20

If a forward post system is to be reinforced under specific circumstances, then this is best accomplished by establishing new *soutiens* and not by reinforcing the brigades themselves, on the very grounds of the frequently reiterated principle that with regard to the defense, one should concentrate more on active than local and passive defenses.

§ 21

What has been said thus far regarding the forward posts applies mainly to middle-sized armies. Very large armies such as those of the last war, of 100 and 150 thousand men, cannot easily be surrounded by a fully integrated forward post system. In such cases, every *corps d'armée* of 20–30 thousand men has its own forward posts. However, most of what has been said above also applies to them.

EXAMPLES OF THE FOUR POSTURES
IN FORWARD POST WAR

1. The battle at the river Dommel in September 1794.

2. The winter posting of the English on the river Vechte in the winter of 1794 to 1795.

3. **Fictitious example from the region of Berlin.**

    3.1 One has occupied the lower Panke from the river Spree to Luisen-brunnen against the enemy advancing from Spandau with two forward post brigades, which consist of 4 battalions and 8 squadrons. The infantry builds 9 defensive posts at the bridge of the Invaliden-haus, at its windmill and at the bridge of the Hamburger Strasse. The cavalry is positioned behind Wedding and Luisenbrunnen. The infantry has the order to offer the utmost resistance, the intention being to cross with the cavalry the river Panke and to attack the advancing enemy on its left flank.

    3.2 A post of 2 battalions is located in Biesdorf and Friedrichsfelde; the enemy approaches from Marzahn.

    The entrances to the villages and the bridges, which cross expanses leading to the enemy, are occupied. The battalions in this way disbanded into several street posts. The commander does not believe that such resistance can be very successful. Therefore, he issues the order to retreat if a strong enemy approaches, and establishes a point in the woods to which the troops should withdraw.

    Once they have united and the support that he perhaps expected from the *soutien* has arrived, or whenever else the moment appears opportune, he returns to assault one of the two villages, attacks it with several columns from various sides, and expels the enemy from it. It is most likely that considerable time lapses before the enemy returns with reinforcements; by then, either support has arrived for our troops or they also withdraw at nightfall.

    3.3 4 battalions and 2 squadrons are to defend the varied terrain between Kaulsdorf and Köpenick. The area around Kaulsdorf is defended by cavalry.

    At Otten's Hill, one chops down the trees and erects some entrenchments on the heights of the Wuhle. Additionally one builds an abatis to the breach; but on the Königswege at the bridge across the Wuhle, again an entrenchment. At each of these different posts one places one or two battalions with some cannons and gives the order to withdraw if circumvented to the area of Kikemahl. One remains here with the two squadrons and the remaining infantry and attacks the first enemy in sight with united force and tries to repel him as quickly and far as possible. Without energy this assault cannot be effective.

If one were to be cautious with one's right flank and therefore attack the enemy from the left in the region of Wulfs Garten and only use part of the troops to protect the flank, then one would be unable to accomplish anything, but instead promptly be compelled to retreat before one had even attempted anything. In addition, this retreat would be very hurried and with great losses. This would be the effect of a half-measure.

But if one hurls oneself with any regard against the enemy's left and decides if necessary to retreat to Friedrichshagen, then one is in a position to defeat completely the enemy attacked, inspiring fear in the others. It is unlikely that the column that is advancing along the Königsweg will continue its march if the other column is completely repelled across the Wuhle.

3.4 If one has just arrived in the area and thus has neither abatises nor rods, such that one is unable to position troops along the Wuhle without exposing them unnecessarily to the danger of being overrun, then one positions only guards at the Wuhle and keeps the troops together in the area of Kikemahl in order to adjust to the circumstances.

DEPLOYMENT OF FORWARD POSTS

Reflections on the Deployment of the Entire Forward Post System

1. The forward posts occupy the access routes to the army at a distance which is conducive to the purpose at hand.

2. One occupies those areas which the enemy could approach in an undetected fashion.

3. One has to be careful not to be drawn into disadvantageous battles by deploying forward posts in certain areas. If the enemy is superior and enterprising at the same time one has to act with great care. This does not mean that one should not venture anything against him; for great objectives one may always risk a great deal. But one has to be careful with regard to minor matters that have no decisive purpose, and among these are forward posts.

4. One surrounds the army's flanks to the degree they are threatened.

5. One occupies main roads and other important points with single brigades. If the brigades are insufficient for this purpose, or they would be positioned so far from one another that they could not observe the area

without difficulty, they are to be divided. This division, however, may not be undertaken unless necessary and not with the intention to maintain a light chain of posts. Practice alone may provide a solid judgment.

6. The first division of the forward posts is usually made according to plan by the general quartermaster or another officer of the general staff. He sends the brigades out to the most important points of access and only there where it is obvious, decides to detach from the brigade, leaving it to the commander of the forward posts to decide what other points should be occupied by detachments.

7. When detaching, one does not divide weapon groups unless necessary. Ideally, one keeps the cannons on the main road.

8. In most cases an intermediate post is useful only:
   8.1 If in connection with the terrain it prevents the rapid advancement of the enemy toward the flanks of the main positions.
   8.2 If it is necessary for guarding the area, since this is the first requirement of all forward posts.

9. The forward post *soutien* maintains its position behind the middle or somewhat closer to the threatened point. Whenever possible it must remain covered, because if one wants to impress through a show of strength, one can reveal it at any moment.

10. In most cases, after they have left their positions all forward post troops unite and create an impressive corps. Camp guards and their pickets serve to accommodate these corps as well as single brigades that returning separately, or even dispersed, otherwise would be prevented from uniting.
    Given the distance of the forward posts one cannot do without them. Therefore, they are doubly useful.

11. The camp guards are located 1000 to 1500 paces in front of the bivouac, camp, etc.

12. To position these in *flèches* given the cannons is not inappropriate. The enemy generally does not come close to the army with great speed; a light cannonade might easily erupt in which case a *flèche* is always useful. Ordinary, closed entrenchments are of no help if the army does not intend to fight here; or if the army does not intend to feign a passive defense before the enemy.

13. The strength of the camp guards depends precisely on the number of necessary sentinels. Their *soutiens* can be located as pickets within the army. These guard chains are deployed by the general of the division or his general staff officer.

14. The essence of this entire forward post organization, to repeat it once again, is to provide the army a certain degree of freedom of action. Woe

to the army that must accept in every situation the enemy's rules, must fight as soon as he appears at its front, or must retreat as soon as it senses his approach and now, pursued and driven, does not find any rest and peace, and is so thrown off-balance, that it misses the best opportunities to regain a solid footing.

In addition to the proper forward posts, every bivouac and cantonment has its own guards, partly for keeping the internal order, partly vis-à-vis the enemy, because in extraordinary cases, one cannot completely rely on the forward posts, which are quite often rather far away. The enemy might sneak through at one point; he might attack the post etc. and thus quickly penetrate our cantonment or camp. Were one to have no guards at all, one would be ambushed.

These guards also serve the purpose of accommodating the forward posts if they retreat.

They are located in cantonments, usually at the entrance to villages, on bridges, etc. With regard to bivouacs and camps, they are best located at a distance of 1000–1500 paces from the enemy on appropriate terrain. Their strength depends only on the number of necessary sentinels.

If they are supported by *soutiens*, then these are pickets, which stand ready in the camp, etc.

Patrols and Reconnaissance

§ 1

We are not talking here about small patrols, which are sent by the outposts in order to visit their own sentinels and to search the surroundings. Their job is quite simple. Wider-ranging patrols can be stronger or weaker. The stronger they are the more they resemble reconnaissance units.

Larger patrols are usually called reconnaissance units, and are used to scrutinize more closely the enemy position, if need be with a certain amount of violence.

On Patrols

§ 2

1. Kinds of patrols.
   1.1 In-depth reconnaissance patrols (*Schleichpatrouillen*).
   1.2 Which are sent toward the enemy.
   1.3 Which are to gather information about the enemy.
   1.4 Which should appraise the enemy position.

2. Strength and composition.
    2.1 Very weak. Infantry often better than cavalry. In-depth reconnaissance patrols.
    2.2 5-man cavalry. The customary.
    2.3 The rather strong 20–30 men; if the area is varied, with infantry.
    2.4 Ditto.

Patrols that are sent out in order to be informed about the approaching enemy are very weak; they consist of a few men. If they are supposed to report on whether a specific point is occupied and this point is not far away, then they also are only a few men strong. If they venture several miles; if they are to search out the enemy, because one has no information about him; if they are to investigate the surroundings, because one wants to determine whether the enemy is present; if they are to investigate the features of the area; if the sentinels return in fear; then they must be made much stronger, because in this case they must divide themselves into as many groups as the situation requires and at times must secure themselves with side patrols.

General Rules for all Patrols

§ 3

(General Scharnhorst suggests the fastest horses and vigorous men.[45])
    On the strength and composition of patrols. Only in very thick forests infantry; otherwise the cavalry and infantry together. In areas that are relatively flat, cavalry alone. If, however, defiles are to be occupied in order to guarantee the retreat, then infantry is very useful. Patrols are sent out not by outposts but by *soutiens* troops and the post itself, indeed sometimes even by the *soutiens-corps*.

§ 4

Routes

If it is possible to march off-road, this is better. The patrol should never return via the same route.

Examples:

If patrolling one path, do not ignore another nearby. If the road parts at the beginning, then better to send two patrols; if it only parts later, a strong patrol

---

[45] Clausewitz refers to Gerhard von Scharnhorst's *Militairisches Taschenbuch zum Gebrauch im Felde*. See Scharnhorst (1980: 3).

that then divides the task. In the 7 Years' War Lt. Colonel Poleretzky of the French army was assaulted when encamped with 300 men in the village of Stokendrebber because the patrol, which was orienting toward Rethen and Alden, chose the road via Hören, ignoring an alternative via Gilten on which the Prussians happened to be advancing. Scharnhorst page 17.

During the campaign of 1758, Hoya was likewise attacked, because the prince took the footpath beyond the main road. Scharnhorst page 13.

§ 5

Intelligence

It is very important to gather information from the inhabitants; otherwise patrols would return with little news. For this reason they choose paths through villages and apply thereby the following precautions.

§ 6

A patrol, which has been sent out in the direction of the enemy, regularly reports back whether or not it has found the enemy. The English army near Breda sent out an engineering officer who made it to Leuven, sending back reports all along the way.[46]

§ 7

Patrols sent to find the enemy should march as clandestinely as possible; they should never return before having first seen the enemy for themselves.

If the enemy is nowhere in the area, they are to return with sworn statements from the mayor or other office holders.

One cannot rely on the information that one gains from the peasants. In the campaign of 1776,[47] General Ewald was ordered to take 10 riflemen and 30 grenadiers from Bordentown to Burlington in order to determine whether the American oar boats still held station at this point along the Delaware. During a vigorous daylong march he passed by the left flank of the enemy corps at a distance of two hours and arrived at Yorkshire Bridge at dawn, a half-hour's distance from Burlington. He found two houses that were occupied to prevent anyone from escaping. A strong snow flurry aided his undertaking. One of the inhabitants attested to the fact that the ships' soldiers had occupied Burlington and that the oar boats were beached there, another claimed the opposite. General Ewald thereupon took four men, positioned his command post in a concealed location, and gave the officer the order that if he were to hear shooting, it would

---

[46] Clausewitz expands on this incident in his *collectanea*. See Hahlweg (1966–90: vol. 1, 553–4).
[47] Clausewitz refers to the New York and New Jersey Campaign during the American Revolutionary War between British forces under General Sir William Howe and the Continental Army under General George Washington in 1776 and 1777.

signal that he had been captured. In this case the officer should retreat through the woods along the Delaware. He then went to the mayor and ordered the four men to follow him, walking one behind the other, and to give fire the moment they heard his pistol shoot and then to rescue themselves. The mayor answered his questions equivocally, whereupon Ewald himself sprang through the town to the harbor, convinced himself of the presence of the oar boat and also saw some men who looked like ship soldiers, and then sprang back.

Ewald's Treatise on Small War, page 108.

§ 8

The March Formation

A front line at a distance of 100 to 1000 paces and even further; then the main group; then at a certain distance, the rearguard. The same on the way back [see Figure 6].

(The further the front line the better. A strong patrol can extend it further than a weak one, because it can have single men between it and the front line. The further forward the front line, the more secure the march, which cannot be completely secured by the side patrols.)

The main body of troops searches the surrounding area for flankers.

(This is necessary because of ambushes.)

§ 9

Side Patrols

If the area is to be searched, they develop by themselves. But also for security reasons, a larger patrol needs smaller side patrols, namely on the nearest paths to the left and right.

§ 10

Rearguard

At defiles and other points prone to circumvention, some men have to remain behind; in the worst-case scenario they will be able to report back and through shooting to inform the patrol that danger is behind it.

(Infantry if the terrain is suitable.)

§ 11

Marching through large forests is dangerous. If the danger is great, one follows guides along back trails. In this case infantry is necessary; it forms the front line. One hides quickly. March through defiles. Never move into a defile without first having scoured it. (Ewald treatise on the service of light troops. Page 88. Example of French officers with a forty-man field guard. (Villages to be searched.)

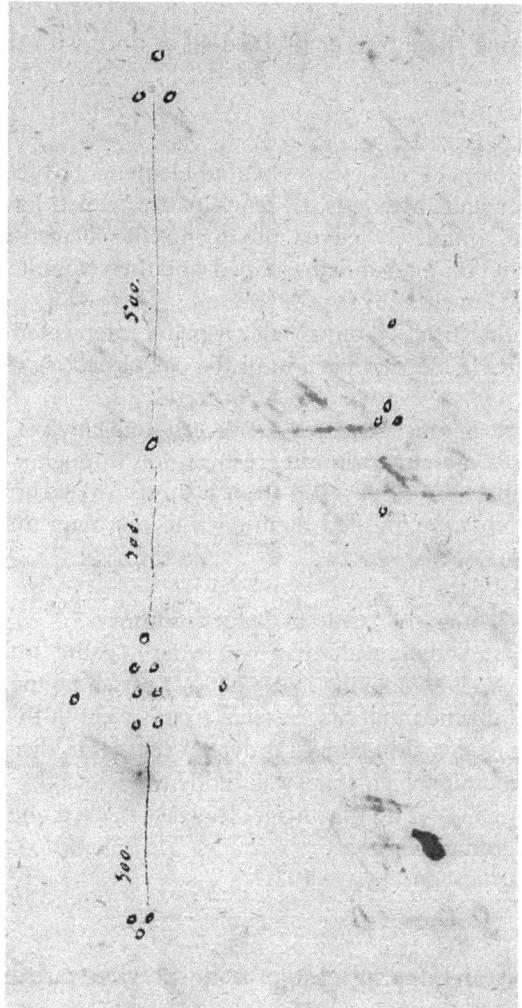

Figure 6. Positioning of Side Patrols and Rearguards along Paths and Defiles.
Source: Clausewitz (1810: 131r.) Copyright © Universitäts- und Landesbibliothek Münster,
N. Clausewitz 4,001.

§ 12

Marching through a Village

As in the case of defiles. If one has information or is suspicious that the enemy
is hidden in the village, then some men have to be sent out to carefully search
the farmsteads and in the meantime to try to secure a concession from the
inhabitants.

(In most cases, they will reveal it.)

Nevertheless, one should never proceed all at once with the entire squad into the village.

(Scharnhost, page 8)

Scharnhorst TB, page 14[48]

Example: Lt. Colonel Freitag leaves behind Lieutenant Thies hiding with 39 horses near Uslar and intercepts a French patrol, which having earlier patrolled the village, completely moved into it, once the villagers gave assurances the enemy was not present. No man escaped, and these volunteers from Alsace were attacked in Hemeln.

In a village not far from Hamm, Major Scheiter intercepted a patrol during the 7 Years' War. He hid in a barn until the patrol had passed and was in a narrow street.

In the year 1760 an officer ordered to proceed to the area of Marburg with a patrol of 20 horses, marched without great caution through a long defile with an *avant-garde* that was 50 paces in front of him. A detachment of Hussars attacked the *avant-garde*, pushed them back to the main unit and took the entire squad as prisoners.

Scharnhorst TB page 14.

In the year '59, after the battle of Bergen, Emmerich[49] was sent into the region of Würzburg with a cavalry patrol in order to gather information about the imperial army. Upon arriving in Nieder Weißbach he inquired about the enemy and was informed that no Austrian troops were in the region. Hence, he entered with his detachment and ordered them all to dismount and feed. An enemy commando of Hussars was hidden in a nearby forest and had observed Emmerich entering the village. He was attacked and taken prisoner with his entire commando.

Emmerich, *Partheygänger* page 102.[50]

§ 13

The men sent to search the village approach with great care during the night; not on the paths, but through gardens, look into windows, etc. If the enemy is in the village, the patrol may have the opportunity to attack it and take prisoners.

§ 14

In wintertime, if it is impossible to march off-road, if one is strong, one has to split up into small units that follow one another at a large distance. In this way, one can prevent being completely cut off.

---

[48] See footnote 45.   [49] See footnote 13.
[50] Clausewitz references Emmerich (1791).

§ 15

Whenever the fear of interception is large, as for example in large forests, one sends out very small patrols of 2–3 men; each patrol following the other at distance of 1000 paces.

It would be advantageous always to send small patrols if not for the fact: that bigger ones can search a large area much quicker; that a large patrol is less easily cut off than a small one; that small patrols are afraid of a stronger enemy. As a rule, use a larger patrol if it should advance boldly.

§§ 16 17 [sic!]

One encounters the enemy. 1. As soon as someone at the front of the patrol comes to a halt, everyone in the field must stop. 2. Some good horsemen must receive orders in advance to immediately ride back and report if one is unexpectedly attacked. 3. One has to keep the men oriented. That is, one has to keep them informed of the enemy location, the location of our own army, and of morning, evening, noon, and midnight. 4. As long as one has not been detected by the enemy, nobody is permitted to fire.

(With these measures, even in the worst situation one cannot be intercepted without the army receiving word of it.)

§ 18

1. If the enemy is under one's control, that is, one has discovered him first and recognizes that he is not much superior, then the opportunity presents itself to strike successfully. But one must first send back one man.

2. If one comes across a strong enemy and is pursued by him, one likewise immediately reports back and retreats with a patrol as with a field guard as long as it is safe to do so, keeping the enemy in sight and under frequent fire.

(A patrol is not for combat, but the officer who withdraws too quickly and loses the enemy from his sight will not be in a position to deliver a proper report.)

3. If in spite of every precaution one is unexpectedly detected by the enemy and cut off, then one falls upon him and fights one's way through.

(Example from the American War. Scharnhorst TB, page 4)

ON RECONNAISSANCE

(Here we are concerned only with the reconnaissance of the enemy; reconnaissance of the territory will be dealt with when we turn to the work of the general staff.)

Composition and Strength

§ 19

They usually comprise all three weapons groups, but the cavalry is commonly the most important and the artillery must be light, or even better, mounted.

The strength of the detachment depends on the strength of the enemy corps that is to be reconnoitered. If the position of the enemy is known, or if one needs to remain in his vicinity longer, then the danger is greater and return more precarious if the detachment is not of sufficient strength.

(Reconnaissance usually involves the attack of enemy posts. Only if these are located entirely on the plain and consist only of cavalry, will cavalry be sufficient. In most cases, infantry is also necessary. If the area is very wooded or varied, then the infantry is indeed the main service arm, otherwise it is the cavalry. For assaulting posts and especially for retreating, artillery is required. With regard to strength it can be said that less time, distance, effort, as well as fewer assaults are needed for the reconnaissance of a division's position than the position of an army. Thus, the enemy has more time to bring up reinforcements and to react against the reconnaissance unit, something for which one must be prepared.)

(The primary intention is to push back the enemy forward posts and to alarm the enemy army, as if an attack were imminent, and thereby induce it to reveal its plan of action.)

§ 20

Before beginning a reconnaissance one asks for instructions (preferable written) regarding its purpose. One familiarizes oneself with the region as much as possible by way of a special map. For this, a writing tablet, telescope, and special maps are indispensable.

§ 21

The reconnaissance is directed at the most important point of the enemy positions, or at several points simultaneously, and develops prior to this a plan for attacking and expelling those troops that stand in the way of our intentions.

One preoccupies other positions with mock assaults. Not to prevent the enemy from coming to the aid of the position under reconnaissance, but in an effort to prevent the enemy from guessing that a reconnaissance is underway.

§ 22

One selects several officers to observe the enemy's position and strength, and provides them with small units for their personal security so they can use the time to detect as much as possible without having to concerning themselves with the actual course of battle. The commanding officer would be well advised to take the task upon himself and to transfer command of the battle to another officer.

§ 23

If one is relatively strong, one can proceed with the attack methodically. If one is too weak, however, one has to try to conduct one's march as clandestinely as possible so as to gain momentary advantages through a surprise assault.

(The enemy cannot differentiate between large columns of 20, 30, or more squadrons and the army. Thus he cannot undertake countermeasures until our intentions become apparent. In this time span one has the opportunity to achieve one's purposes. The enemy would easily recognize small detachments of 5 squadrons and a few battalions for what they are, and adopt quite early such measures that they would not only fail to achieve their purpose but would be in danger of not returning.)

§ 24

What cannot be observed must be established through reports, and therefore it is important to:

1. Try to capture prisoners, who can be interrogated by officers.
2. Ask the inhabitants of the area about the enemy's position.

§ 25

The prisoners are mainly questioned about: 1. the regiment in which they serve; 2. high-ranking generals they have seen in the corps; 3. the strength of the company in which they serve; 4. the strength of the corps; 5. about the foodstuffs they receive; 6. the strength of their quarters, the location of individual divisions, whether there are entrenchments, etc. (One can ask other questions that a common solder usually will not be able to answer; the answers therefore will be very unreliable.)

The inhabitants of the area are questioned about the strength of the quartering in the villages and about any of the areas where the enemy is located and finally about the character of the region.

(A peasant rarely knows whether one or two divisions are in village *A*, the soldier knows this better. But the common soldier does not know whether there are any troops at all stationed in town *B*, this the peasant knows better.)

(The best information comes from educated inhabitants, such as preachers and office holders, especially if they are well disposed, which then can be compared to what one observes oneself. Since time usually is precious and short, it would be good to assign these tasks to several officers. If an officer identifies a highly valuable man, he shall bring him to the commanding officer.

In any case, some conclusions can be reached by the corresponding elements of various statements.)

§ 26

If the enemy's march is to be reconnoitered, one inquires as to his direction in every village the enemy has passed through. If one is next to him and has approached him to a certain degree, one leaves his detachment in a concealed location and proceeds for observation with a smaller team as close as is possible without being detected.

§ 27

Retreat

Usually the enemy takes revenge, if he could not prevent the reconnaissance, by trying to defeat the detachment on its retreat. Therefore, strong *soutiens* must rush forward from the camp to meet the detachment. Mounted artillery provides an invaluable service during retreat.

Examples:

1. A weak detachment has occupied Charlottenburg. But the enemy has moved into Berlin in large numbers.
   A spy patrol is sent out in order to see whether the enemy has occupied the Tiergarten and what measures he has taken to secure the city.
   1.1 If the bridges are occupied, nothing else but the trench is left for reconnaissance.
   1.2 If the bridges are not occupied, the patrol proceeds alongside the road as concealed and cautious as possible. For this, infantry would be better suited than cavalry. Here no side patrols, but not together. 3 men, no more than 5.
2. The detachment from Charlottenburg has to retreat via Schmargendorf and Dahlem and discovers that the enemy has already occupied these localities.
   A spy patrol to Wilmersdorf and from there to Dahlem. It reports back from Wilmersdorf and thus has to be somewhat stronger, about 5 men. Already has a man on every side.
3. The enemy is not in the region surrounding Wilmersdorf. The detachment has withdrawn to Steglitz and sends at the break of dawn a strong patrol to establish the strength of the enemy in Berlin and whether or not he is also in Schöneberg and Wilmersdorf.
   It would be advantageous to make this patrol 20 to 30 men strong. First, it has to detach to Wilmersdorf; secondly, to send a unit to

Schöneberg; thirdly, to Tempelhof; and fourthly, it would be good if they could take some prisoners.

As regards the occupation of Berlin, the patrol would not be able to secure any information other than that provided by the peasants and prisoners. Moreover, they could draw some inferences from enemy behavior.

4. The enemy approaches from Niederlausitz. A strong patrol is sent out from Spandau to establish whether he has already arrived at Groß Ziethen etc.; whether he has already occupied Köpenick. One is not familiar with the area. It is daylight.

    4.1 20 man infantry and 30 man cavalry.

    4.2 In two units, one in the plain, the other in the varied terrain.

    4.3 Instructions for the first unit.

        4.3.1 Attack if you come across the enemy.

        4.3.2 Send reports from Tempelhof to Rixdorf, von Rudow to Köpenick.

    4.4 The main detachment in two parts. One from Rixdorf to Johannis Thal. The other straight to Köpenick.

    The infantry either remains in Rixdorf if one has not heard anything on the enemy, otherwise 10 men are to be taken along to form the front line.

    4.5 The patrol in the plain

        1. Finds the enemy

        2. It does not find him and returns via Marienfelde and Teltow

        The other unit

        1. Comes across a field guard, does not withdraw immediately

        2. By day approaches two guards from Rixdorf, but by night, if necessary, just one

        3. Field guard in front of Köpenick does not move in

5. A Hussar field post with 30 horses is located near Reinikendorf, whereby its post is located in Panko[w]. Another stands in front of Niederschön-hausen. During the night, the latter sends from time to time three patrols, one comprising two men to Dahldorf, another of two men to Rosendal, another comprising four men to Tegel.

    So that one man can go right, one man left, and two men can remain on the road, this patrol returns via the Chausée House.

    The post at Pankow sends from time to time a patrol of five men in order to learn earlier of the enemy's approach and at the same time to revive the guards' vigilance. They have the order to take the following route.

    Field guard from Niederschönhausen, Rosenthal, Dahldorf, through Tegel Forest, toward the Chausée House bridge. Here they split up: one to Reinikendorf, the other to the sheep farm.

6. A patrol is sent by night from Spandau to Charlottenburg and Berlin.
   6.1 [sic!] It may not be too weak.
      1. At the edge of the Grunewald Forest some infantry and one cavalryman remain.
      2. The same in Charlottenburg.
      3. Those on the way to Berlin send a side patrol toward Hofjäger.
      4. They can return via Wilmersdorf.
7. The enemy has an encampment of 1000–1200 men near Rosenthal. We have occupied the river Spree; he the Jungfernheide. We want to reconnoiter his camp.

   A column near Charlottenburg, with the other near Berlin.

   The first weak and with infantry. It is only intended to alarm the enemy.

   The other ten squadrons and four battalions, ½ mounted battery strong, advance toward Königin Plantation and Niederschönhausen. 10 squadrons advance to Wedding with one battery of mounted artillery.

   5 squadrons remain near Pankow towards Blankenburg.

On Small Observation Detachments, Which Are Sent Some Miles in Front of the Army toward the Enemy

§ 1

Such detachments do not belong to the forward post system because they are positioned far ahead of it and are not permanent. They are needed if one is far away from the enemy thus not able to observe him from one's forward posts. And one can only separate them for a short time from the army lest one expose them to very unfortunate battles.

§ 2

In the plain they can consist only of cavalry, but if the terrain is varied, they can consist of both weapons groups. In very rough terrain, like woods, very few cavalry are to be found. Sometimes one provides them with light cannon, be it to delay at suitable points the pursuing enemy, or just to make noise with them.

They comprise select troops and are commanded by officers well suited for this duty.

§ 3

They are deployed on roads or in their vicinity; in front of the enemy's position or at his flanks. They are intended to observe points of access and the position of the enemy corps.

§ 4

Their strength varies greatly: from twenty to thirty horses, to several battalions and squadrons, depending on whether secondary objectives are also present.

We will consider only the actions of the weaker, namely up to a few hundred men, because those with more battalions and squadrons are in a different situation. They can provide for their own security more or less through the usual means of forward posts and must act more or less as any other corps.

§ 5

The smaller ones of which we are speaking have some particularities that we want to investigate further.

Detachments of this type are not at all designed for resistance. They won't allow themselves to be pushed back by a weaker enemy. This is demanded by military honor. They will resist a somewhat superior enemy with cunning and courage and this explains the reputation of light troops and partisans. In both cases, there does not emerge great danger for them. In the face of a considerably superior enemy, however, they retreat without any resistance, since it is enough to have detected him. They do not need to impede his advance, which is not necessary at this distance, and for which they are not appropriate. Nonetheless, they should not lose sight of the enemy while retreating, a rule which was already recommended with regard to other situations.

They never allow themselves to be drawn into battle with a superior enemy, unless to battle their way through.

§ 6

As a connecting chain of posts they will not be able to occupy the area they have been instructed to observe because they are too weak. If they were to accomplish this by dissolving the chain, they could not support the individual positions and the enemy could seize one or the other daily. Thus, they must adopt other means both to accomplish their task and to secure themselves against too great a danger.

§ 7

For this purpose they position individual weak posts far to the fore, either in the field or in villages.

In this way, these weak posts will be able to observe the area just as well as a forward post *cordon*, however this is not necessary:

1. Because the enemy at such a distance from our army would hardly act with that caution and effort that he would employ to circumvent our forward posts and to approach the army covertly.

2. Because it is not important to detect the enemy in the first half-hour, which would be very important for the forward posts. However, while the enemy marches several miles, it will not be very difficult to learn something about him.

3. The enemy will not send out weak detachments at this distance, or at least they will not be of great importance; but large columns are easier to detect. By contrast, the forward posts must be able to detect even a weak detachment in a timely fashion.
   Finally,

4. These detachments are often in a region where the enemy is not. They are to provide reports of his arrival. This is possible without difficulty in a hundred ways.

§ 8

The individual posts do not need to be very strong and they must not be. Because of the abovementioned reasons they do not need many sentinels and *vedettes*. In most cases, one will be sufficient. If they are weak, they are in less danger of being intercepted, because the enemy will not bother himself too much about a few men. The commander thus keeps his detachment together and does not run the danger of losing a part through the ineptitude of others. Where necessary he can assemble strong patrols and reconnaissance.

Only in specific cases, when the enemy juxtaposes a relatively strong detachment to ours, might one feel compelled to provide ours with a similar strength, so that it is not in too much danger.

§ 9

Small observation detachments have to be deployed as far forward as possible, because the enemy can only be observed with success in close proximity. Moreover, because of the provisional nature of this observation system, one must have the ability to calculate the time it will take for the enemy to advance to the main detachment from our outermost posts.

The main detachment may not be deployed so close to the enemy that its strength would provoke him to take immediate measures.

The danger to which small posts are exposed owing to their great distance has to be considered inevitable. Because they usually are comprised primarily of cavalry they are not easily completely destroyed. A few men can escape more easily than many, and hence the loss is not too great if such a post is taken.

For all these reasons, if one does not want to put them into villages, it is necessary to position the posts next to them. But if they are located in villages, and the enemy is in the region, they have to come out at night and change their position.

§ 11 [sic!]

For such detachments, positioned beyond the forward post chain, it is neither necessary nor feasible to constantly patrol the area in which they are located. It is essential to observe the enemy in his positions, because every activity precedes or follows a change in his location. Hence, it is necessary to reassure oneself daily that the enemy guards and forward posts are still in the same position. By night, this is accomplished most easily by very weak or spy patrols through the observation of enemy campfires; by day, through reconnaissance with stronger troops, ideally at dawn.

The officer conducts, wherever possible, such patrols himself, because he is principally responsible for observing the enemy, and one sees more with one's own eyes than through others.

§ 12

Another method for gaining information about the enemy is through detachments of 15 to 20 horses with very able and enterprising officers, which are sent by the commander of the entire detachment into the flanks and rear of the enemy army to sneak around and report on what is going on behind the army. This, however, cannot be undertaken under all circumstances.

§ 13

Such detachments gather most of their information from the inhabitants. Of course it is not always true, but the sheer quantity allows one to compare and to draw in the end the most certain conclusion. Thus, it is very important for the commander to make acquaintances in the region and to endear himself to the population.

The reports that one receives from actual spies also belong here.

The means of providing information for the army are thus:

1. Proper spies.
2. The inhabitants.
3. The observations made by the small posts themselves.
4. Patrols and reconnaissance.
5. Everything the detachment has come across.

§ 14

What we have said thus far concerned primarily the way in which the detachment fulfills the purposes for which it has been established. Now we must say a few things about its own safety. For even if one were to think that a detachment had been dispersed and to a large extent destroyed by the enemy columns, yet nevertheless thereby achieved its purpose of informing the army of the enemy's arrival, one will still try to avoid such mishaps as much as possible. Indeed, a partisan will have the ambition of losing as few men as possible.

None of the means we have discussed thus far for detecting the enemy's arrival are sufficient for preventing the detachment from being completely destroyed, being ambushed, etc. Hence, it must deploy the necessary field guards near its position in order to detect the enemy at some distance. This will not be difficult during daylight and only a few guards will be necessary. Since such detachments are often so small that after the redeployment of the distant posts there are insufficient men left for a proper field guard, they have to be content with mere sentinels, which during daytime are usually sufficient, especially if one deploys two in opposing directions.

But it is different by night. On the one hand, a small detachment cannot deploy enough sentinels to prevent the enemy from stealing in. On the other hand, a closely linked chain of sentinels often is insufficient for the security of a strong detachment because the enemy advances simultaneously and the detachment, even if it were alert, would have insufficient time to mount its horses.

In such cases there is no better response than to change position. Such a detachment marches out during the night and often assumes another position or, when the season is quite raw, remains together in some remote barns.

CONDUCT OF A DETACHMENT DURING MARCHES AND CANTONMENTS

§ 1

If a detachment undertakes a long march, it must conduct itself in a different manner than a patrol, which remains close to the army. While underway, it must assume and secure its camp and quarters. This subject shall be dealt with here. The purposes for which the detachment is sent out at a greater distance are quite diverse. The following are the most common.

1. To occupy outlying locations.
2. To reinforce distant corps.
3. To search for the enemy and deliver intelligence about him.
4. To pursue his march.
5. To conduct small offensive actions against bridges, depots, convoys, etc.
6. To neutralize individual posts, detachments, couriers, etc. in the rear of the enemy army (clandestine marches).
7. To collect foodstuffs, contributions, weapons, clothing, etc.

Where appropriate, we will discuss the conduct of these individual tasks to the degree to which special mention is warranted. But here we limit our discussion to the conduct during marches and cantonments that is common to all these detachments.

§ 2

A. Marches. 1. Ordinary

We have already discussed in connection with the field guards what an officer has to observe before decampment; what he has to take along.

On the *avant-*, *arrière-garde*, and the side patrols.

§ 3

In completely open terrain, the *avant-garde* consists exclusively of cavalry. In varied terrain and in woods, of cavalry and infantry. The more varied the terrain, the more infantry, yet always some cavalry for communication.

§ 4

Likewise, the side patrols ideally consist of cavalry unless defiles are expected, in which one would leave infantry positioned, or the terrain is altogether too difficult for cavalry.

These are of two types. Very close to the detachment some men search secluded areas in order to prevent a lateral attack. This is only necessary when the enemy is in the vicinity. At a greater distance, stronger patrols march along the nearest routes left and right, in order to gather information on whether the enemy is located in the area.

(Example from the area of Berlin.)

§ 5

In retreat, the *arrière-garde* consists ideally of both infantry and cavalry and if possible of one or a few mounted artillery. When advancing, infantry is sufficient for the *arrière-garde*, yet some cavalry should be present.

§ 6

Never march without any *avant-garde*. It is extremely dangerous to proceed along a single street if one has to retreat and was so careless as not to have an *arrière-garde* while advancing.

§ 7

The strength of the *avant-garde* depends on the strength of the detachment. ⅙ for strong, ⅓ for very weak provide rough ratios.

§ 8

When retreating, the *arrière-garde* is at least as strong as is the *avant-garde* when advancing. The latter [when retreating] is a bit weaker.

When retreating, the *arrière-garde* is central.

§ 9

The strength of the side patrols depends on the size of the area they have to search. If no less than six men, they are more reliable.

(In some cases, 6 men can be the side patrol for 1500 men and can cover them as effectively as could 50 men. If, however, the area that the side patrol is intended to search is vast, then it is better to strengthen it. For a detachment of 1500 men, for example, it could comprise 20 men without any difficulty, which would not be the case if the detachment were only 30 men strong. Moreover, sideward deployments from weak detachments do not create such difficulties because they do not serve the same purpose; hence the detachments are not afraid of dividing their strength.)

§ 10

The distance of the *avant-garde* depends on the area and the position of the detachment. An *avant-garde* deployed far ahead has the following advantages.

1. It is easy to come into battle formation. This is not so important here.
2. One can choose a good position. This is very important.
3. One can retreat from a dangerous area.
4. One can create a hideaway.
5. One can retreat in a timely fashion.
6. One can more easily secure supplies.

These advantages depend on very timely information.
The disadvantages of an *avant-garde* deployed too far ahead are:

1. One loses sight of them.
2. One attracts the enemy.

From these observations follows the rule that:
The *avant-garde* should never be so close that an attack is possible; never so distant as to lose sight of it. If a detachment is not at all supposed to engage with the enemy, then an *avant-garde* deployed far ahead is good. If, however, its purpose is in some sort of attack, then the *avant-garde* should not be deployed any further to the fore than security demands. This is precisely the case when the detachment intends to slip through enemy lines. At night, weak detachments must have their *avant-garde* very close in front of them, stronger detachments can push them further forward as circumstances allow.

§ 11

The distance of the side patrols is even more difficult to determine in the abstract. If the detachment is supposed to return, as is the case for all detachments that are sent out for information, for collection of contributions and requisitions, then it has to cover its considerably extended flanks. If it is supposed to reinforce a remote position, then the side patrols proceed only as far as the security of the detachment requires. If the detachment is supposed to undertake an offensive action against enemy posts, then a part of the army often moves forward to guarantee its retreat. Then there is no need for it to weaken itself through side detachments. If the detachment proceeds at a larger distance and does not return right away, as is the case for all who operate to the enemy's rear, it should send out its side patrols only so far as is necessary to inform the detachment about the enemy's presence in a timely fashion in order not to be attacked. By the way, such detachments march clandestinely. We will return to clandestine marches below.

In spite of these differences in purpose, one nevertheless can assume the usual distance of side patrols to coincide with the nearest roads and villages. Villages are particularly important, since their inhabitants can provide additional intelligence.

A detachment that was sent from Gross Ziethen to the area of Tegel in order to provide information on the enemy, certainly will visit and perhaps even occupy Charlottenburg with a side patrol. The same detachment sent to reinforce the corps at Tegel will not dispatch to Charlottenburg unless necessary, so as not to attract the enemy, and it will not march via Britz and Rixdorf without having a side patrol on the road from Köpenick to Berlin. A detachment sent after the enemy from Ziethen across the Spree to Rosenthal will not only patrol the nearby villages because some ambushes might have been positioned there, but will also occupy the crossings as soon as it has passed the river and send side patrols to Jungfernheide along the Hamburger Straße in order to find out whether the enemy has not marched to Tegel as well. The same detachment, sent out to requisition in the villages of Niederschönhausen, Panko[w], and Reinikendorf, will have to secure itself in a similar fashion through side patrols, which occupy Jungfernheide, Weissensee, and Heinersdorf. The same detachment sent out on the road to Oranienburg in order to attack convoys to the rear of the enemy army will cross the river Spree during the night close to Charlottenburg and position some men on the other side in order to observe Charlottenburg quietly. It is self-evident that the strength of the side patrol influences its route and distance from the detachment.

§ 12

Conduct of the *Avant-Garde* and the Side Patrols

The *avant-garde* and the side patrols form a front line and side troops. Once the front line comes upon the enemy without being discovered by him, it stops right away and if one man stops, everyone stops.

By day, the commander of the *avant-garde* interrogates the population of the area as to the enemy. By night he has to rely on his ear. Ewald recommends that the officer place himself at the front and often hides along the way in order to destroy enemy patrols. One night he captured in this manner 7 American officers, among them one major, all of whom were sent by the commanding general with written orders to arm the country folk. This service was extremely important.

Diligent and appropriate reporting is one of the most important obligations of the *avant-garde*.

Detached units must not lose sight of the main unit. (What this means)

An *avant-garde* under pursuit never retreats directly toward its detachment.

(The conduct with regard to defiles, villages, woods, etc. was dealt with in the discussion of patrols above.)

§ 13

If an *avant-garde* repels enemy *vedettes* and field guards, it is necessary to take great care while pursuing, and only if the field guard finds itself in a decidedly inferior position is rapid advance appropriate.

§ 14

Arrière Guards

(*Arrière* guards usually remain closer to the detachment than *avant-gardes*. This lies in the nature of things.)

1. They may not be located further than the time necessary to bring the detachment into battle formation, should the enemy advance.

2. They must always be divided into two components that withdraw alternatingly.

3. They never pause unless necessary.

4. They must not lose sight of the enemy as long as he is in the vicinity.

5. The commander is present.

§ 15

In heavy fog one marches as in the night, that is, one draws all the detached troops closer to oneself. (The fog is more dangerous than the night: firstly, because it deceives the eyes; secondly, because one does not hear well.)

§ 16

Routes, Guides

The officers who command the *avant-garde* and side patrols must know the route along which one is supposed to march to the extent possible, and to ask for a list of the villages that one wishes to pass. They have to take along guides from village to village (preferably woodsmen and shepherds), who guide them and try to orient themselves with a map.

§ 17

If there is a danger of encountering the enemy, it is safer to march on back roads. Small detachments often can do so without great discomfort.

§ 18

Even with small detachments, the order of the march is not of the same importance as with armies. Yet, in most cases, it will be most appropriate to march with the infantry to the fore, the cavalry to the rear and the artillery in between.

§ 19

One keeps the detachment as close together as official regulations suggest and does not allow anybody who is not ill to fall out or to remain behind. In return, one takes 3, 4, or 5 short breaks during every daylong march.

§ 20

Should the *avant-gardes* and side patrols encounter the enemy, one hastens to deploy his detachment concealed; (to hide it;) if there is no other possibility right in the middle of a village, pushed close together. Previously one started marching. This closed and concealed deployment allows all combinations, eases retreat, etc. The rest is here out of place.

§ 21

While the detachment is pursuing its objective, from time to time (at least once a day) it sends information back to the army, if this can be accomplished without danger, in part to give notice of its own fate, in part to share the information that has been gathered on the enemy.

§ 22

Absent any obstacles on the path of the enterprise for which we are under-taking the march that could cause us to turn around at the outset, we cannot allow ourselves to be deterred easily by difficulties that concern only the march. If the direct route is blocked, one often can get through by back roads. It is often said that the road is closed when the enemy either is not there or only weak. Often one can attack unexpectedly a sizeable detachment and open the path. Through strenuous marches one often can take an indirect route and happily get through. All these are alternatives that one has to think of before turning around too soon only then to be admonished and ridiculed.

Examples:

1. [sic!] One enemy corps stands in the vicinity of Rosenthal, another on this side in the vicinity of Tegel. Two battalions, three cannons, and three squad-rons are to march from Spandau to Küstrin. The enemy patrols up to the area of Berlin and Köpenick.

> 1. **Marching route**
>   It goes via Charlottenburg, the Hallesches Tor, Rixdorf, Köpenick, Mahlsdorf, etc. The detachment spends the night in Köpenick, as it set out only after noon.
>
> 2. **Situation in general**
>   One fears the enemy has been informed of the detachment's march, has crossed the river Spree, and has concealed itself in order to attack and destroy it. One has little to fear from the right side; yet one has to remain vigilant.
>   The *avant-garde* has been equipped with one squadron and one company of fusiliers in order to send out side patrols when necessary. Because it is not the objective of the detachment to search the area, it does not split up further but rather contents itself with small troops left and right to guard against assault.
>   Because one will not arrive in Rixdorf long before the onset of evening, one has to march the last mile to Köpenick with great caution: partly because of the night, partly because of the terrain.
>
> 3. **Instructions of the Commanding Officer to the Officer of the *Avant-Garde***
>   You begin to march a short half-hour before the detachment.
>   It is your responsibility to survey the area all the way to Rixdorf, in order to prevent the detachment from falling into a trap; or to encounter the enemy unexpectedly. You advance only to Rixdorf and await there the detachment. You occupy the Spree river crossings with some caval-rymen until the side troops of the detachment arrive. From time to time

you report back and inform me even if one has not learned anything about the enemy. As soon as you arrive in Rixdorf, you send out small patrols towards Köpenick.

4. **Conduct of this Officer according to the General Instructions**
Under the command of an officer, he sends out 10 infantrymen and a number of Hussars from Spandau to Grunewald and from there to the Fasanerie and the Hallesches Tor.

1 non-commissioned Officer and 6 cavalrymen to Charlottenburg with the order not only to patrol the village but also to search for the enemy beyond the bridge. As soon as he arrives with the *avant-garde* in Charlottenburg, he sends one officer with ten infantrymen and twelve cavalrymen to Berlin, in order to patrol the Tiergarten and to occupy the Berlin Bridge. This is achieved by a few cavalrymen who stay until the main detachment occupies the bridge with a side troop. The rest of the side patrol moves through the city via Bergmüle and Treptow toward Rixdorf.

The officer sends a patrol of 6 or 8 infantrymen and a few cavalry from the Hallisches Tor to the Hasenheide, which stretches from there to Rixdorf.

As soon as the officer of the *avant-garde* arrives at Rixdorf, he inquires about the road to Köpenick. He discovers that two roads exist: one via Johannisthal, the other along the Spree.

At the same time he learns that an enemy infantry detachment had arrived in Köpenick at noon, but that one does not know whether it has stayed there and how strong it is. The officer at once dispenses sentinels around Rixdorf and informs the commander of the detachment. Then he sends out two small patrols toward Köpenick, which are only three or four men strong and have been ordered to inquire about the enemy at the next houses they come across, and to return as soon as they have some certainty of the enemy's presence in Köpenick.

1. The entire detachment is assembled in Rixdorf, the patrols report that only one enemy infantry patrol had been in Köpenick but immediately had left the village.

   Hereupon, the commander of the detachment decides to march toward Köpenick as soon as possible. Having heard that the route via Johannisthal is not difficult, he chooses it. He sends ahead one officer with one infantry company and 20 cavalrymen on the main road with the order to occupy immediately the bridges and to deploy forward posts towards Mahlsdorf and Friedrichsfelde. This officer simultaneously serves as side patrol. Another patrol proceeds via Johannisthal. Smaller patrols follow the larger at a distance of 600–800 paces. The *avant-garde* now remains at a distance of 300–400 paces from the detachment and only individual flankers

ride through the shrubbery right and left along the way. One marches
with the greatest silence and order. If an ambush has been planned
against the detachment, it will presumably be triggered by the *avant-
garde* along the main road, leaving the detachment enough time to
retreat.

As soon as the detachment arrives in Köpenick, patrols are sent out
in the same night to Mahlsdorf, Kaulsdorf, and Biesdorf, which bring
the necessary information for the next day.

2. Information is received that Köpenick is heavily occupied by infantry,
   while the patrols have covered the area to the gates of the town
   without having encountered the enemy.

If he could be certain of the Fürstenwalde passage, the officer would
rather decide to go via this route than attack Köpenick. Nonetheless,
he would like to know whether the enemy is indeed in Köpenick and
whether he perhaps is not so weak that he would leave the town upon
our approach.

Therefore, he marches with the detachment to Johannisthal and
sends from there 100 infantry volunteers and 20 horses to Köpenick
with the order to advance across the bridge into the town, unless they
find it impossible. If the attack fails, the officer of the *avant-garde* has
the order to retreat to Britz, in order to mislead to enemy while he
himself marches via Fürstenwalde.

If, however, Fürstenwalde, is occupied by an enemy corps and thus
there is no hope of crossing the Spree at that point, an attempt should
be made on Köpenick.

Thereupon, the commander of the detachment is to approach the town
as clandestinely as possible and to attack the garrison if possible.

He inquires whether it is possible to cross the Wendische Spree with
cavalry. His intention in this case is to march to Rudow, allow his cavalry
to cross the ford, then, however, continue to march with the infantry
along the Spree via Schöneweide and suddenly attack the town.

But having heard that the Wendische Spree cannot be crossed, he
keeps the detachment together and marches with caution up to a
location 600–800 paces in front of Köpenick. There he holds up in the
woods and forms an *avant-garde* that suddenly assaults. If the attack
fails, the detachment retreats via Adlershof and Britz.

He informs the commanding general in Spandau of this decision.

3. Information is received that the enemy has been seen with cavalry
   and infantry on the road from Köpenick to Berlin; that a quarter of an
   hour from Köpenick a number of *vedettes* were present and that some
   of the houses have been found to be deserted. The commander of the
   detachment no longer risks advancing by night instead deciding not
   to move through the varied terrain of Köpenick before daybreak.

He takes his security measures in Rixdorf and sends patrols of 10–12 infantry and 5–6 cavalry along every road at the break of dawn.

He does not march before he is certain that the enemy is not in Köpenick and the adjacent area. If this not the case, he awaits orders from Spandau.

2. Clandestine Marches

Notion of Such Marches

§ 23

If one is supposed to attack, assault, or reconnoiter a position, it is only natural to conduct one's march as clandestinely as possible. This is usually not very difficult. Usually, such marches take place at night. One has to pass the enemy's chain of posts, the position of which is vaguely known, and to avoid the enemy patrols, whereby, of course, much depends on chance. But there is another kind of march that has to be conducted in particular secrecy and is more difficult. It involves marching through areas that are under the complete control of the enemy and lasts for several days. Such marches often occur:

1. As measures against enemy convoys.
2. Against bridges, depots, etc.
3. For the elimination of individuals.
4. For the gathering of intelligence.
5. In the retreat of detected detachments.

(In civil wars, the arming of the nation, etc. such circumstances are more frequent than otherwise was the case with armies. If they now seem to be less, or not at all, common to armies, we nonetheless should not believe that they have lost their importance. On the contrary, they have gained in importance.)

In addition to the organization of the marches, some additional rules apply.

§ 24

On the Organization of the March If One Intends to Conduct It as Secretly as Possible

The *avant-garde*, side patrols, and the *arrière-garde* are very close to the detachment and only at a distance that can be secured against an actual attack. Hence, one marches with greatest discipline and stops as often as one senses a danger.

(What is lost in terms of security must be replaced by exertion. It is not possible to sustain this exertion and vigilance during a march. Therefore, one keeps one's detachment, wherever possible, far ahead of oneself and to the side. Where circumstances do not allow this, one has, of course, to accept the momentary exertion.)

§ 25

Time, Route, and Further Conditions

1.1 One marches, wherever possible, during the night and rests by day in the woods.

1.2 One takes the most concealed routes.

1.3 One arranges for the delivery of supplies from the nearest villages or individual houses to a location where one does not intend to remain and does not reveal the entire detachment; this ideally occurs in the evening.

1.4 Also, one takes the guides by night, wherever possible from separate houses, and does not release them until they no longer can do any damage.

1.5 The information one hopes to secure must be extracted from the country folk.

1.6 If, by chance, one is discovered by inhabitants, one detains them until they no longer can cause any damage. Since one is dependent on them to such a great extent, a friendly treatment, money as much as one can give, and ultimately even threats that one could take revenge through murder and setting fire, are necessary means for reaching one's objective.

(If one is unable to pay for foodstuffs, one must at least issue generous receipts, and the guides must never be released without having been rewarded.)

1.7 If the season is so unpleasant as to render the open air unbearable, then one has to establish quarters in a nearby barn.

1.8 One often and suddenly changes the direction of one's march and positions oneself vis-à-vis the inhabitants as if one had quite different intentions than truly is the case.

(If one does not do so, despite all caution, one will be eliminated, because the enemy receives information in any case and the main issue is therefore that he does not know where to find us.)

1.9 Ewald recommends discretion and to inform only a few individuals of the march's aim.

Example:

An army has advanced from Magdeburg via Plauen and Brandenburg to Berlin and encamps from the river Havel to Wusterhausen. In Plauen, large amounts of foodstuffs and ammunition are stored in order to be loaded onto ships. An average sized corps (6000–8000 men) has proceeded on the right bank of the Havel toward Spandau in order to cover these supplies. It has the order to retreat to Brandenburg and Plauen if the opposing army advances with superior force. This opposing army stands between Berlin and Spandau. Its general has been informed by a trusted spy that Plauen is occupied only by a weak battalion, further weakened by detachments that have been deployed as forward posts against Ferchesar, etc. It is late fall. A partisan of this army receives permission to take action against Plauen. He intends at some distance to circumvent the right flank of the enemy army with 50 cavalrymen and 100 infantrymen and to attack Plauen from a side where no enemy is expected.

Preparation

1. Men and horses are selected.
2. Every man takes along ten Congreve Rockets.[51]
3. Bread and feed for three days.
4. The officer receives a good special map and 100 *Louis d'or*.
5. He receives written instructions on his mission in which only the purpose is specified, whereas the means are left to his discretion.

March that Could Be Undertaken by this Officer

The Frankfurt Road to Fürstenwalde. In the evening, the officer crosses the Spree here or at an earlier point and marches during the first night on the other side of Lake Scharmützel to Neuen Mühl, where he arrives at daybreak. He sends one man into the town who presents himself as a deserter and inquires as to the enemy. He returns with the information that the next quarters are in Storkow. Since the officer still has foodstuffs and is very close to the enemy army, he remains in the woods during the day without disclosing himself. He decides to break camp in the evening and to advance to Teupitz. In the second night he arrives at the Hermsdorf forest station. There he learns from the forest ranger that Teupitz is occupied by a detachment that has issued requisition regulations for the area. He declares his intention to destroy this detachment, but marches during the same night through the Teupitz Forest and arrives by morning near Halbe. He keeps the guide who led him there close by for the entire following day and talks with him about routes to Lübben. If he has sufficient foodstuffs, water etc., he remains undetected in the woods and breaks camp around evening and in this third night marches 5 miles to the vicinity of Luckenwalde.

---

[51] The Congreve Rocket was originally a British military rocket designed by Sir William Congreve in 1804, inspired by the armies of Tipu Sultan and his father, who was of the Kingdom of Misore in India.

This location is not occupied by the enemy. The partisan hears that the next quarters are located in Belitz and Trebin. He assumes position near the Lindenberger Mühle, and sends someone in the night there to bring back enough grain for 2 or 3 days. He also takes as much bread as possible and pays the miller for both. He keeps the miller with him for the entire day and threatens to shoot his family if he is betrayed. The miller serves as a guide during the next night and he rewards him when he releases him.

He intends to march during the fourth night to the vicinity of Brück and Belzig but learns that a considerable corps had arrived at Belzig and Brück in order to proceed on the next day to Potsdam. Thereupon he decides to go only to Treuenbrietzen and to stay there in the woods until the march has passed by, and then to approach within one mile of Plauen by means of a forced march of 7 miles. He intends to hide here until he has gathered information through a number of disguised men about the position of the posts and especially about the means to cross the canal, in order to attack then according to circumstances by day or night so as to disperse him and to set the depot in flames. He decides to inflict as much damage as possible on the enemy while retreating along the right bank of the Havel and then to return to the army on the other side of the Havelland Lowland through the district of Ruppin.

B. Cantonments, Camps, and Bivouacs

§ 26

The issue here is conduct in cantonments, quarters, camps, etc., but only to the extent that these are intended to provide rest for the troops. Such rest can be enjoyed only if it does not impede the very tactical and strategic purposes. The issue is above all security and a few other things. In this regard, those rules must be observed that are meant to secure the foremost goal. Otherwise, however, the true tactical or strategic purpose of the cantonment, quarter, camp, etc.—for example the defense of the location, taking up of forward posts, etc.—should not be mentioned here any further, as it was dealt with above under small defensive posts.

§ 27

Cantonments

Cantonments assume a higher degree of security than bivouacs and camps. If an entire detachment can be accommodated at a single location, the difference is not that great. If one is forced to divide up, the difference is considerable. The enemy's proximity and danger alone, however, do not determine whether or not to establish bivouacs. If the detachment is very exhausted, its maintenance not easy, aggravated perhaps by very harsh seasonal conditions, then one might be compelled to settle in cantonments under great danger, or at least to separate so as to establish bivouacs in small villages.

Of importance here are the conditions to which the commander of a detachment, which has established cantonments in one or several locations, should direct his attention.

§ 28

A. The Individual Quarters

BEFORE ONE MARCHES INTO THE QUARTERS

1. One sends in advance the quartermaster sergeant (*furier*) and his men as early as possible, if possible with three officers. The first secures the quarters, the second the foodstuffs, and the third surveys the area in order to position the forward posts. If the quartermaster and his men arrive at the same time as the *avant-garde* then the latter officer also serves as commander of the *avant-garde*.
   (These three officers retain this duty for a length of time.)

2. When the detachment arrives, it comes to a **halt, either as a whole or in parts. The guards are brought forward. The orders are distributed.** These must include:
   2.1 How the troops are to behave in the quarters at night.
   2.2 The time of decampment in case the march is to continue.
   2.3 The place of assembly.
   2.4 The point to which one will retreat if attacked.

§ 29

SECURITY MEASURES

1. The forward posts and patrols usually only close, the next bridges and nearby defiles. Patrols, field guards.

2. The entries into the village are blocked, with the exception of two entries opposite one another. If place and time require doing the same with distant entries, security is greatly increased, provided that the barrier is kept under observation by a guard.
   (Means for blockade: Wagons, rocks, haystacks, trees, abatises, etc. etc.)

3. **Assembly places.** Already have been mentioned. Cannons and equipment are brought up behind the villages to the side not directed at the enemy.

§ 29 [sic!]

ADDITIONAL MEASURES

1. **Division of duties among the officers.**
   Already has been mentioned.

2. **Reports and guides**. One has to compare several statements with one another. Several guides for the next day. Reasonable men.

§ 30

CONDUCT UNDER ENEMY ATTACK When a detachment is not intended for defending the location it must have another purpose assigned to it that it must try to fulfill as soon as possible if the enemy approaches the quarter, engaging the enemy only to the extent that it is unavoidable. The following principles thereby always are important.

1. The disposition is simple to the highest degree.
2. It is based less on defense than attack.
3. One tries to secure a concealed position.
4. The route of retreat in every case is precisely predetermined.
5. One marks the paths one would have to march with *Strohwische*.[52]

§ 31

REGARDING THE VARIOUS SERVICE ARMS Cavalry needs more time to assemble than infantry, and artillery more than cavalry. Therefore, the infantry must be assigned the most dangerous quarters if different troops are in the same cantonment. However, one tries to avoid this because of the disorder that easily can develop.

§ 32

If one cannot accommodate all of the troops, usually the cavalry is ordered to assume bivouacs, partly for reasons of security, partly because infantry marches are more arduous.

B. Rules to Be Observed When Taking Up Several Quarters

§ 33

If one cannot be accommodated in a single village and if one has to take up cantonments, the following issues are important.

CHOICE OF QUARTERS

1. One tries to reach a town in which one can stay together.
2. One tries to reach a piece of terrain behind which the quarters enjoy some security if one mans the entryways.

[52] A *Strohwisch* is a bundle of hay attached to a post of roughly one meter length used by farmers to demarcate territory.

None of this is possible if it leads to detours. For as regards marches, advance is the chief objective.

3. Wherever possible, one chooses a quarter close to the road and thus rather positions the troops behind instead of next to one another.

§ 34

ORGANIZATION OF THE CANTONMENT

1. The quarters next to the enemy are assigned to the cavalry, the furthest to the artillery. (If the terrain suggests a well-founded reason for deviating, that would be different.) The reason for observing here a rule that runs contrary to those in Large War is that a small detachment is only capable of providing resistance if all service arms are kept together. It is much easier for the cavalry to retreat without serious losses toward the infantry than would be the case vice versa. (Moreover, this does not contradict § 20.)

2. If bivouacs are taken up at several points, one can leave the cavalry and infantry together, if the infantry is not weakened too much by this partition.

3. The commanding officer remains in a quarter close to the enemy.

§ 35

1. One remains together until immediately prior to quartering and designates for the following day, when the march is to continue, the rearmost or the foremost quarter for *Rendezvous* depending on whether one is moving forward or backward.

2. If possible, the villages are chosen during the morning *Rendezvous* and quartermasters sent there in advance. These are best taken from the cavalry.

3. A unified *arrière-garde* or *avant-garde* commanded by a select officer constitutes the forward post vis-à-vis the enemy. If there are impediments to access then infantry is introduced. Otherwise it consists solely of cavalry; but where possible, one or two mounted artillery. Besides these unified forward posts, every quarter deploys its own guards and the commander of the same is responsible for security.

4. Orders are given prior to the dispersion of the troops. The orders include the following:

    4.1 The *Rendezvous* for the following day and if one is advancing an additional one in case of enemy attack; the rearmost or middle quarter being best suited.

    4.2 The hour of decampment.

4.3 The general terms of the following day's march. In case the commander has reason to keep it secret, then he will advise only the individual quarter commanders or in an emergency remain silent.

5. Upon encampment, every quarter dispatches to headquarters a young courier (*Ordonanz*), who remains there.

6. If there is no reason to conceal one's march, patrols are dispatched toward the quarters that one intends to assume.

§ 36

1. If the enemy attacks a quarter during the night, then it retreats as well as possible to the *Rendezvous* but at once informs the nearest quarters and headquarters.

2. One agrees on signals that, in event of emergency, will allow one to communicate one's location by night. Three shots, two in rapid sequence, the third somewhat later.

§ 37

Camps

Although camps provide more security than cantonments when an entire detachment is in the same locality, cantonments are nevertheless to be preferred in this case because one can provide for security through vigilance and the troops prefer a bad cantonment to the best camp. Troops are ordered to set up camp only if it is essential to maintain them in a specific location that is devoid of houses.

§ 39 [sic!]

Setting up a camp for 24 hours is hardly advisable since it requires material and time. If one remains at a location for a longer time, material for building huts needs to be secured. Straw and wood. (Thus, camps are more commonly used by great armies than in Small Wars.)

§ 40

Bivouacs

They provide the highest degree of security. Since the men are not supposed to undress here, and are not protected against the weather, one should avoid allowing the troops to bivouac too often and for too many nights in a row, which one commonly feels compelled to do in Small Wars due to the enemy's proximity.

§ 41

1. Bivouacs and camps near villages are quite commodious for small detachments, but the proximity of the woods is even more important.

2. One should not camp or bivouac on a meadow without good cause, as Vegetius maintained.[53]

3. Next to the proximity of wood, the proximity of water is of utmost essence; in summer it is key; at most ¼ mile.

§ 42

When choosing a bivouac in most cases tactical considerations are determined first by its purpose, although most of the time a concealed deployment will fulfill all of them.

ATTACKS AND ASSAULTS ON SMALL POSTS

A. Purpose of Such Undertakings

§ 1

We will deal here only with such measures as are undertaken for the sake of the post itself; that is, with appropriate but also superior numbers of troops. Attacks on small posts, which occur during the general advance of entire columns, do not require much preparation. Nevertheless, the following particularities can be specified:

1. One enjoys a disproportionate superiority.

2. One seeks to remove the barrier constituted by the enemy post as fast as possible.

3. To inflict as much damage on the enemy detachment as possible is only a secondary purpose.

From this follows the subsequent guideline:

If the front of a column encounters an enemy forward post, then the chief objective is to clear it out of the way quickly, to overwhelm him more through vigorous advance than through maneuvering, and to inflict losses more

---

[53] Flavius Vegetius Renatus was a Roman military writer of the fourth century.

through hot pursuit than through circumvention and annihilation. Cases in which a single guard post can be annihilated, and our advancement thereby concealed from the enemy, do not belong here. But it is hard to annihilate entire detachments without word getting out.

§ 2

If, however, the attack of a small post is not the consequence of the general advance, then there must be another reason for the undertaking.

Usually, such undertakings have the following purposes:

1. If the enemy post poses a burden, which is often the case with forward posts.

2. If the position is particularly threatening and crucial to the conduct of the undertaking it invites attack.

3. If one intends to take revenge on the enemy for similar losses suffered.

4. If the enemy post is intended to defend important objectives that could be taken thereby, such as bridges, warehouses, depots, generals and other important persons.

5. If it occupies a location important for the operations.

§ 3

In general, we can say the following about the purpose of such undertakings:

1. The loss of troops, which one thereby inflicts on the enemy, is never decisive and can become significant only through repeated raids of this sort.

2. If the campaign is very quick, undertakings of this sort may be rare or completely absent. If defending, one does not have the opportunity since one's hands are full with the necessary general measures. If attacking, one does not have the time necessary for such undertakings since more important measures can be adopted.

    Only when roughness of terrain, shortage of men and foodstuffs, sieges, fear of the enemy, etc. compel or necessitate the attacker to proceed less adventurously, more carefully, and hence more slowly, is there enough time remaining in both cases for such small undertakings.

3. The intention to instill courage in one's troops and to provide combat experience without the danger of great losses through small undertakings of this kind, over which one always maintains control, causes one to think of such undertakings, which go beyond the cases addressed in § 2, more than would otherwise be the case.

Almost all authors have regarded this game of Small War as excellent training for the troops, as one has the opportunity to ruin the enemy's troops through frequent alarms and to instill the spirit of terror in them through individual successful raids.

One should not forget, however, that this already implies superiority over the enemy, for otherwise he would not allow this to happen. Rather, he would try to take revenge immediately following the first undertaking through similar measures.

4. In cases of national mobilization (*Nationalbewaffnung*) and defense, as Spain is currently mounting and Tyrol has mounted, in cases of civil war such as the *Vendée*, nearly all battles are attacks against small posts or at least these are the most common. The *Landsturm* are unable to do much else, which provides them with the greatest security. The countless posts, which he who seeks to hold a hostile and rebellious nation must maintain, provide ample opportunity.

B. Rules for all Cases. Superiority

§ 4

Such undertakings are usually carried out with great superiority of force in order to secure success. The gain that can be achieved thereby is not substantial enough to warrant exposing oneself to the danger of great losses.

It is carried out with equal or weaker forces only if one has no more at one's disposal or if the detachment that is supposed to undertake the attack is not near the army. Partisans, who undertake operations of this type, are often compelled to attack many with few troops.

It is most opportune to do so when the detachment, which is supposed to be attacked, has not yet arrived and one has the chance to locate a concealment behind the position it intends to take up.

In any case, the weaker the attacking detachment, the greater must be the speed of execution and cunning of the plan.

§ 5

If such an attack is to be carried out, one usually is not content with a force two, three, or four times as strong, but also designates a substantial unit of the army's troops that moves forward in order to be able to absorb one's attacking detachment in the event the undertaking fails, and to provide means for any unforeseen eventualities. The enemy, by accident or purpose, could have placed his troops between our detachment and the army, etc. etc.

§ 6

In most cases, nothing can be done without a number of reliable persons with precise knowledge of the area. One cannot rely on even the best specialized maps, the more so as one is considering an attack.

The individuals of which one avails oneself have to be relatively intelligent human beings; otherwise they will not be able to understand the idea. It is much better if the commanding or other officer knows the region. Nevertheless, one cannot do without the people from the region entirely, since the execution of the entire plan often depends on great detail. It is good to have more than one such person. One should mind them well, promise them a gift if they are not too noble, treat them well, etc.

Besides knowledge of the locale, knowledge of enemy measures is required. Usually, such undertakings are based on reports that one receives about the enemy's negligence, and usually these are the best.

Depending on whether the operation is smaller or larger, more or less an attack, it is more or less important to have specific knowledge of enemy positions. Regarding attacks on smaller quarters, outposts, etc., which can evade attack with the slightest notification, approaching undetected depends on knowing the position of the outpost, *vedettes*, etc. Reliable spies from the lower classes have to secure here the necessary information and when possible they should accompany the operation. It is easily said that one needs spies, but they often are difficult to secure. In addition to the information provided by proper spies, one also receives information:

1. From disguised men sent out to proceed and await us at a certain point.
2. From people from the region where the enemy is located; or who have lived there; or were born there. Such people almost always are found in the countryside within a few miles of the posts.
3. From deserters.
4. From envoys.

§ 7

Secrecy is of the utmost importance for such undertakings. Whoever wishes to carry them out must conceal them until the very last moment; otherwise they will be disclosed to the enemy despite the best of odds. Since no additional measures are required, in most cases it is not necessary for the one with the idea to share it with others; and it is nothing more than common human loquacity when such secrecy is not observed. If it is a principle of such undertakings not to inform anyone of anything prior to the moment of execution, or none other than those persons who absolutely have to know, because they have to provide information, etc., then it is the duty of every officer assigned to a superior officer to guard closely the secret that has been entrusted to him. Nothing is as unmanly as loquacity.

The troops that are needed for the operation should receive their orders either while decamping or even better during the march.

Regarding other means of concealment, the following is to be observed:

1. That the march itself is carried out clandestinely. (See clandestine marches.)

2. That one tries to conceal the decampment of the troops since this most certainly informs the enemy spies that something is going on. For this reason, if one cannot march by night, many have advised beginning the march after exercising.

C. On Proper Assaults

§ 8

Almost all attacks in Small Wars are carried out by means of assault because they are operations of small components of the army against other small army components. If the enemy were to learn about the operation before its execution it would be sufficient for preventing it. Even if he were to learn about it during execution, one would have to fear in many cases that he will have set traps for our returning troops.

The real assault differs from assault-like attacks, insofar as one does not want to take the position but rather to benefit from the confusion in order to take prisoners and loot, to destroy something, etc. and then quickly remove.

It is even more necessary to assault the enemy one intends to attack if one is oneself so weak that success can only be found in the enemy's confusion. Remarks on the effects of assaults on morale—enemy troops are fatigued; terror is easily spread amongst them.

§ 9

The best time for assaulting is:

1. At night; more precisely, in the middle of the night, not in the early morning, as is the case with substantial and large operations, for which one only uses the night to approach undetected.

2. If it is supposed to occur by day, midday would be best, as people are cooking and usually least likely to be thinking about the enemy. Sometimes the enemy's security is enhanced by falsely alarming him during the previous night and thereby only exhausting one's own troops.

§ 10

The difficulties that one has to overcome in the conduct of assaults tire the common soldier. Other conditions serve to facilitate the assault.[54]

1. Stormy weather, snow flurries, rain, severe cold.

2. Through continuous alarms, one can lull the enemy.

3. If one discovers in advance that the enemy intends to take up a position and can place oneself in a concealment behind it.

4. If one comes across a post that has just arrived and neglected to deploy sentinels.

5. If one slowly retreats and quickly reappears from another side.

6. If one can approach the enemy unexpectedly through vigorous marches. This is where the operations of partisans belong.

§ 11

Weapons That Are to Be Used

Cavalry and infantry are almost always combined.

1. The infantry marches less noticeably; thus, at the moment one reaches the enemy one can approach him herewith undetected.

2. By shooting, the infantry can, under certain circumstances, inspire terror. It can intrude into houses, tents, and huts more easily.

3. The cavalry is necessary for taking prisoners; it can easily disperse assemblies; its speed increases chaos and terror.

Artillery is not employed in very small operations. It would offer little assistance and only run the risk of being lost. If such a detachment nevertheless comprises artillery, then it is best employed to provide rear cover or in that section that moves against enemy support.

Artillery is only necessary for positions one intends to maintain.

Also if one has to pass through and occupy defiles on the way back.

Finally, in all larger operations which could not be decided by night battle.

Infantry can always be used alone. However, in open areas one cannot proceed too far, either because they cannot march fast enough or because one

---

[54] The original text is here opaque. The alphabetical numeration in the original text is confusing. The translators have tried to reconstruct Clausewitz's thinking from the principal text and relevant marginalia in his own hand.

has to worry a great deal about the retreat. Except in very mountainous areas, cavalry can be employed alone. One uses then whatever arms one has at hand, combines both when both are present, and provides light cannon only in special cases.

§ 12

Order of March

1. The *avant-garde* consists of infantry, is very weak, and very close to the detachment. Only if the detachment is very big should a part of the cavalry be close to the *avant-garde* in order to achieve something through quick intervention in the event it is detected too early.
2. At the front of the *avant-garde* the most trustworthy men, whether officer, non-commissioned officer, or private.
3. Envoys, under the watch of two men, with the *avant-garde.*
4. The infantry to the fore, the cavalry to the rear.

§ 13

Defiles that have to be passed must be occupied with some troops, even only a few. In the worst case, if the enemy disperses them in our rear, they will be able to inform us, through gunfire or otherwise, of what is transpiring and we can retreat via another path.

At the same time a unit is sent to thwart anyone who might come to the aid of the enemy.

It occupies those defiles through which the enemy could advance, or makes them impassable. Without these precautions one could be assaulted while assaulting.

Neither precaution is to be neglected unless:

1. The assault is decided in the very first moment.
2. The enemy cannot immediately move forward to the *Souccours.*

§ 14

1. One assaults the enemy from several sides and tries to cut off his retreat.
2. One first has to separate into several units only if one has already come close to the enemy. In cases of small operations that are only calculated for immediate terror and are quickly decided, it is hardly possible to act jointly and with the highest degree of precision if the columns are

divided from the start and follow different routes. Thus, one circumvents the enemy position together and separates into multiple units when one comes near to the enemy position.

3. The *avant-garde* remove their shot because a careless gunshot can easily spoil everything. Whether one should allow the remaining troops to shoot or not is disputed. What is certain is that one should shoot as late as possible and only deliver a general salvo at a very close distance. The fire causes terror and distress. If one is detected, then one pursues the enemy with great speed and in many cases arrives together with the guards or patrols and assaults.

4. One divides one's troops into many units, for which one appoints exceptional commanding officers, who coordinate with one another or rather must cohere.

5. One designates, if one is not too weak, a unit to receive the prisoners.

6. One agrees to a signal by which one can be identified.

7. One designates a place of assembly or two, to which one retreats after the attack.

8. One designates a signal with drums, horns, etc. for retreat.

D. On Assaulting under Particular Circumstances

§ 15

1. Assaulting an outpost

For this, cavalry is most appropriate. Infantry will rarely take many prisoners, which is the purpose. In highly varied terrain and against infantry, one surely can make use of infantrymen, but several cavalrymen will be very helpful in such cases.

  1.1 One does not divide oneself into too many units.

  1.2 One races with greatest speed toward the enemy.

  1.3 One detaches against enemy *Souccours* only under special circumstances, simultaneously establishing a rearguard. It is best to be absorbed by other troops advancing from the rear.

  1.4 One beats retreat as soon as possible and withdraws along different paths and wherever possible through woods.

§ 16

2. **Assaulting an open quarter**
   2.1 The detachment is divided into as many units as there are exits and in addition, one unit is designated to proceed against the *Souccours* and another for the prisoners and for later assembly.

   2.2 One provides the commanders of the individual units as much as possible with a sense of the position and character of the locality.

   2.3 If the cavalry and infantry are united, then every unit is composed of both service arms.

   2.4 A unit is never entirely disbanded. About one third is designated to storm the houses if the enemy is still in them. This is infantry; weak cavalry units of three or four men chase through the streets to take individuals prisoner. The remainder of each unit stays together at the entrance or other suitable point so that the enemy cannot readily escape and takes charge of the prisoners who are immediately delivered to reserve units. If the enemy has already assembled at a given location, then the remaining combined component of the unit advances toward him with bayonets.

   2.5 One of the units is sent toward the market, the main guard station, or wherever else the enemy's place of assembly might be.

   2.6 A number of designated men are immediately sent out toward the commander's quarters.

   2.7 If the enemy has erected entrenchments near his quarters, then the main rule is to observe these with a part of one's forces to prevent anyone from retreating to them. To remove them would cause unnecessarily delay, although in most cases it would not be that difficult.

   2.8 In this case gunfire should be avoided as much as possible, even if is impossible to prevent it entirely.

   2.9 Every infantry unit carries with it some axes in order to remove obstacles.

§ 17

3. **Assaults on fortified locations with *Escalade*.**[55]
   3.1 They are usually only successful if one had the opportunity to hide in near proximity to the location.

---

[55] An *escalade* is a storm ladder.

3.2 Other useful means, such as disguises, wagons, ships, etc. are well known. One cannot come up with an exhaustive list but anyone who is capable of conducting such an operation will easily find the means demanded by the circumstances of the particular case.

3.3 Here it is dangerous to concentrate one's entire detachment in the town and to focus exclusively on the markets and squares. The example of Cremona demonstrates that nothing is won if the garrison assembles on the wall and remains its master.[56] Because of the concentric and eccentric effects, the point is rather obvious. Thus, regarding fortified locations, one is well advised to leave a gate occupied once one has taken it; to allow the cavalry to chase through the streets; also to send some weak infantry detachments through the streets in order to shoot and to search for the superior officers in the houses; to advance against the wall with the remaining troops immediately and from here to direct one's assault on the enemy.

3.4 Since nailing up the cannons[57] is essential, some of the troops, preferably from the artillery, must be specifically designated for the task.

3.5 The remaining issues should be dealt with in the same fashion as open locations.

§ 18

4. **Assault on a position covered by a wide river.**

4.1 The security that such a post believes itself to enjoy provides the best opportunity to assault it and to do so with even fewer men, which in any case is necessary, because otherwise one could not approach it undetected.

4.2 In addition, the proximity of the magazines, bridges, depots, etc. provides good reason to attempt such assaults; for if one wants to undertake measures against such targets one often has to overcome difficulties such as crossing a wide river or covering a great distance without being noticed, etc.

4.3 The means of crossing a wide river once the enemy has seized the ships for himself, as is always the case:

4.3.1 Fords; often the widest rivers have them.

4.3.2 Row boats of fishermen; those the enemy overlooked.

4.3.3 Row boats that are brought over land from nearby rivers.

4.3.4 Flotation devices.

4.3.5 Swimming.

---

[56] Clausewitz refers to the battle of Cremona where French and Spanish troops defeated Austrian troops under Count Eugen of Savoy in 1702.

[57] That is accomplished by hammering a thick jagged iron nail into the vent.

One of these means is almost always available.

5. **The assault of several quarters.**
   We can deal here only with those that are carried out by small detachments, namely partisans. Here the following issues are essential.
   5.1 Quick and concealed marches.
   5.2 Assault in the rear; when possible the rearmost quarters first.
   5.3 Disruption of guard posts and patrols.
   5.4 If one was successful with a bold attack on a second one, better not one of the next nearest.
   5.5 To intimidate those not yet under attack.

CONCERNING ATTACKS WITHOUT ASSAULT, OR, WHEN THESE ARE MERELY INCIDENTAL

§ 19

The actual assault is associated with the intention to use the initial terror, the chaos, and the gloom to inflict heavy losses on the enemy, to take prisoners, to seize cannons and other loot.

If the intention is to take and hold the position from which the enemy is expelled, then we are talking about attacking a stronger detachment, and in order to expel it or to inflict heavy losses, we ourselves have to use a considerable detachment. In this case, the mere effect of an assault is not enough. Even if it is very advantageous or necessary to start an operation with an assault, as has been previously discussed, one has to adopt those measures that are necessary to continue the battle by day and to assume the presence of a more or less well-prepared enemy.

It is very difficult to approach an enemy with a strong detachment without detection and in most cases he will be prepared to receive us or even will have achieved full readiness.

§ 20

Therefore, such an assault has to be conducted according to the rules of Large War. What distinguishes one from the other is the following:

1. The great superiority with which one can arrive, and which one tends to exploit, enables one more or less to cut off the enemy posts' retreat.

2. In most cases this is the purpose of such assaults as otherwise they would not be worth the effort.

3. As it is impossible in Large War, either in the offense or defense, to dispense with any of the service arms, so it is here as well; but one usually employs more cavalry
   3.1 because it is essential to destroy the enemy detachment upon his retreat;
   3.2 because speed in the execution is essential and because one can move forward and retreat more quickly with cavalry than with infantry. Finally, one takes along less artillery, because one cannot be delayed with a large number of gunners.

4. The entire skirmish must be decided more quickly and thus conducted in a more rapid and bold spirit than is the case in battles and larger engagements.

5. If one is not strong enough to approach the enemy from all sides, then one attacks his rear with the entire detachment, for a detachment is not as easily truncated as is an army.

§ 21

Examples

1. From Hoya, page 174, Scharnhorst's pocketbook.[58]
2. Attack and ambush of the French *corps* under General Glaubitz near Emsdorf in Hesse. With Captain Rozière's map.[59]

ON AMBUSHES AND CONCEALMENTS

§ 22

Ambushes can be used for many purposes. They also can be effective as a kind of offensive defense. In most cases, however, they are attacks on small enemy detachments and thus they take their place next to assaults.

§ 23

Because troops that are positioned in a concealment are usually quite exposed, these can be used successfully only under specific circumstances and can be dangerous if they fail.

Under the following conditions, the ambush is better suited than other types of assault:

---

[58] Scharnhorst (1980: ch. 2).
[59] Hahlweg (1966–90: vol. 1, 409, fn. 21) indicates that Clausewitz refers to survey maps of Hesse from the year 1760.

1. If one intends to attack a small detachment on the march.
2. If one intends to attack a detachment that is assuming position.

Convoys and foraging almost always fall under 1 and 2.

3. If one intends to destroy small detachments completely, which include patrols.
4. If one intends to halt a pursuing enemy.
5. If one intends to punish an enemy that harasses our forward posts.
6. If one intends to eliminate single persons in the rear of the enemy army.

These goals are unlikely to be achieved by means other than an ambush. As a condition, we have to add, however, that the terrain needs to be suitable.

§ 24

It is no longer as common as it used to be for detachments to march without due precaution; in this regard one has become much more prudent. Consequently one will have fewer opportunities to achieve something through ambushes. Nevertheless, the following issues are to be considered:

1. If one can position oneself with superior strength in a concealment, then even if the enemy detachment were to be careful and detected us, one would be able to conduct an advantageous battle, to take prisoners, etc.; and since on the other hand, the danger to oneself of suffering losses is not great, it is worth such an attempt.
2. Many environs have to be searched with extreme diligence, such as woods, mountains, etc. If one places an ambush here, one can indeed be detected if the enemy sends out side patrols. Detection need not be inevitable, rather is more by chance, and hence in such regions there is still a chance of success even against a careful enemy. In such areas the retreat also is not too much at risk.
3. As a rule, convoys and foragers should be attacked from ambushes; if one is detected, one still enjoys every advantage of a direct attack.

    The recurrence of such circumstances is the reason for the continuing use of ambushes, insofar as armies wage Small War at all.
4. They are almost always successful when the enemy is in hot pursuit.
5. They are necessary when the enemy harasses our forward posts. There is almost no other effective means of punishing him.
6. For this it is advisable to place a lure, for example, a field guard, a patrol, etc. that entices him to follow.

§ 25

The danger that is associated with an ambush is great:

1. If the enemy is quite superior and we are detected.
2. If the ambush has been disclosed and the enemy has the opportunity to encircle it with superior force from all sides. Therefore, ambushes in enemy territory are less advisable than in one's own.

§ 26a

Combined cavalry and infantry are best for ambushes; although each of them can be used separately as well. United they provide the advantage:

1. That the enemy can be thrown instantaneously into chaos with very close and unexpected fire, which cannot be accomplished through cavalry attack. Cases in which one can place the concealment so close to the road, however, are today seldom.
2. That one accomplishes more by shooting at the cavalry than by the attack itself.
3. That infantry is easier to conceal than cavalry; that they more easily take up arms, etc.
4. That one takes prisoners with the cavalry and the enemy's initial retreat is turned into stampede.
5. That in retreating the service arms protect each other according to whichever is favored by the terrain.

§ 26b

The most important rules that have to be observed in the conduct of ambushes are the following:

1. Secrecy of the forward march.
2. Supply of bread, water and fodder.
3. No neighing horses.
4. Trustworthy men.
5. If one intends to destroy the enemy completely, two or three units are left in the concealment. If one is very strong, one divides into units. If one fears one might be detected at several nearby locations, then one places one unit significantly to the rear. If it is not intended to completely encircle [the enemy], it is at first not a matter of sheer numbers and the

approaching *soutien* certainly will have a strong effect, because the enemy will be convinced that we are strong in the vicinity.

6. One must not strike out too soon and the men must be strictly instructed.

7. One conceals some smart men as sentinels who send out an agreed-upon signal upon enemy contact.

8. One agrees upon a signal for the assault; another one for retreat. One determines a location for the retreat.

9. One detains anybody one suspects of having taken note of us.

10. The moment one is detected, one thrusts oneself, without any further planning, upon the enemy.

11. If one is detected too early by enemy patrols without previously having been revealed, one often will have enough time to escape, and because the enemy is uncertain about our strength and the distance of our other troops, he will not engage with us in the first moment. In this case, the infantry is sent forward and the cavalry tries to cover the retreat as well as possible.

12. If it is too late and the enemy is encircling us, one attacks the unit that blocks our path. Thus, at least some individuals will escape. Losing the unit is no worse for the supply chief and the army's esprit than capitulation.

ON RETREAT

§1

The retreat in Small War quite appropriately deserves its own chapter:

1. Because it often occurs.
2. Because often it must be carried out under difficult circumstances.
3. Because it provides the best opportunity to distinguish oneself.

§ 2

The first and perhaps most important question is **when** one should retreat.

Retreating too early from an important position is very dangerous for the commanding officer's reputation, even if the army suffers no further damage as a result. But the cause of premature retreat is not always a lack of good will and eagerness, but quite often a false appraisal of the situation and timidity.

It is very difficult if not impossible to determine through abstract rules whether in the individual case the time is right to retreat, but some caveats nevertheless might be possible and appropriate here.

§ 3

1. A detachment that is supposed to observe the enemy whenever possible must not retreat without having seen the enemy.

2. Absent evident danger of being cut off, such a detachment must not retreat so far as to lose sight of the enemy.

3. The fear of being cut off is the most common ground for retreat. Very few detachments are intended to defend themselves to the utmost. Thus, this fear is well founded and reasonable. But the problem in such cases is that one judges the danger to be much larger in advance than it later turns out to have been and that having given in to the fears of the moment, one later must admit that one was too timid. Such timidity is hardly advisable and in many cases one incurs the greatest blame through early retreat. The only rule that applies here appears to be the following:

   Never retreat from a position on the basis of rumor, or rely on the statements of country folk, refugees, etc., but rather confirm the danger with a patrol. If one is convinced that a short delay would lead one to be cut off completely, and if one has not been ordered to defend the post at all cost, then one can call the retreat in good conscience. The retreat easily can be justified.

4. One must be aware, as always in war, but especially in this situation, that the enemy will do everything he can. This assumption inspires incredible fear. But first, one should remember that the enemy cannot do everything he is capable of at once; further, that he does not know our position and all of its disadvantages, as we do; and finally, that in most cases he will not do what he could and should, because in war, more than is otherwise the case, the execution falls short of the theory. Thus, through the theoretical prediction of what the enemy will do, one acquires an inflated estimation of one's own danger. Consequently, the rule is:

   Always base one's behavior on those things one knows rather than those one believes it necessary to assume.

5. One should not ask subordinates for advice since they undermine the best resolutions with their own ideas.

6. If a post is to be defended to the utmost, one must surrender any idea of retreat.

7. Much as an early retreat is not very honorable, likewise it is not laudable to give up the idea of retreat entirely if this is linked to danger. I will not allow myself to completely rule out capitulation, but I regard the following remark to be necessary:

    If ever one finds oneself in the sad situation of having to think about capitulation, then one should consider what would happen if one were to charge the enemy or to allow one's men a disorderly retreat.

So much for reasons for retreat.

Principles for all Cases of Retreat

§ 4

1. The main objective is to escape. If one can march, one should not be delayed by foolish rules of parading.
2. One must not, on the other hand, run away from every enemy Hussar out of fear if one has just paused to allow the men to rest.
3. One has to inspire, as far as possible, respect in the enemy, so that he does not advance recklessly.

On the Various Cases of Retreat

§ 5

The diversity of these cases originates primarily in the distance of the retreat, the service arms that are retreating, and the terrain.

1. A retreat within sight of our army does not present great challenges; although it provides an opportunity to distinguish oneself. A courageous resistance of short duration is demanded.

    1.1 **Cavalry alone.** We assume a great superiority of the enemy cavalry. The enemy will try either to cut us off before the army can come to our support, or to chase us so that we arrive entirely disbanded and confused. The only way to prevent this is to break up into two or three units and in case of emergency to hurl oneself blindly against the enemy, thus perhaps preventing a too rapid pursuit or at least allowing an honorable defeat.

    1.2 **Infantry alone.** In woods, between hedges, etc. the infantry will rarely come into great danger. In the plain, mass is the only means of rescue. In case of close support, the danger for such masses is not too great. Here everything depends on the quality of the troops.

1.3 **Both arms united.** Insofar as we are discussing small detachments and the proximity of support, the cavalry may never abandon the infantry, even if the terrain is not entirely suitable for it. One dismisses redundant cavalry only if one has more than can be accommodated by the terrain. One would do the same if the enemy cavalry were far superior to our own and could annihilate it easily in full view of the infantry.

§ 6

2. **The retreat of an isolated detachment if it is several hours away from any support.**

Such a retreat within sight of a superior enemy is undoubtedly the most difficult task in the entire art of war; and therefore, only a few rules apply:

Alone in the plain, **infantry** masses or if there is more than one battalion instead creates several groups. They surround themselves with sharpshooters and try to gain terrain to the rear as well as possible. One stands still only if the enemy is so close that any movement would create the expectation of chaos, and first scares him away with rifle fire.

If one were pursued only by infantry, the danger would not be that great. But the appropriate order always would be to mass. If, however, one is pursued by cavalry, everything depends on the quality and fortuitous steadfastness of the troops. History provides a number of examples of infantry withstanding cavalry. In such moments, this should inspire courage in the infantry and since there is no other choice, nothing else can be done but to think about the possibility, proven by experience, of a successful resistance. Perhaps it also can be demonstrated historically that there is even the possibility of fortuitous success for the infantry if the cavalry lacks artillery.

Mounted artillery is the chief means of providing access to the battalion's masses. An easy success is quite natural under such circumstances. Nevertheless, one should not believe that everything is now lost. Artistry certainly won't do. But this much is certain: if the masses are dispersed into an unorderly crowd by artillery fire, this crowd nevertheless will be able to resist the cavalry by holding close ranks. For the orderliness of the formation in any case is not decisive.

This observation is intended only to help those who find themselves in such an unlucky situation and to remind them that everything is not yet lost and that such cases have occurred in the past.

Infantry in varied terrain. The most advantageous terrain is undoubtedly the forest. The denser the better. A defile, if it cannot be circumvented, would end the pursuit. But if this is not the case, defiles are of little value, unless one is so strong that a small unit can be sacrificed to save the rest. Mountains, woods, and meadows. If the infantry is able to reach such terrain, it is usually safe.

If one has artillery at one's disposal, then one enjoys a great advantage because one can keep the cavalry at a much more respectful distance from oneself.

VERBAL OBSERVATIONS ON THE SUPERIORITY OF INFANTRY VIS-À-VIS CAVALRY

1. From the sheer probability[60] that the infantry can withstand the cavalry the general superiority of the former does not follow. The cavalry enjoys the same advantage if we turn the argument around.

2. If the infantry were in general a superior branch of the army, the cavalry would not need to feel embarrassed, since it is superior in some particular cases.

3. The fact that the infantry under normal circumstances is as likely to succeed in its resistance cannot intimidate the cavalry. For on the one hand, it has the prospect of completely destroying the infantry if things go well, whereas it can never be destroyed completely, even by the very best infantry. On the other hand, war provides hundreds of thousands of cases in which one had to act against all odds of success, namely, when nothing better could be done. **Very very** [sic!] much could be said about this.

Although it has been argued that experience, demonstrating that the infantry can withstand the cavalry with a certain probability of success, should be withheld from the cavalry, and that one must demonstrate to them the opposite so that they do not become intimidated, the argument is one-sided and utterly baseless.

Position of Several Massed Units

a and *b* are two units that defend one another; the riflemen and cannons can be placed at *c*.* [See Figure 7.]

(Regarding the positioning of guns in the units and the mutual defense of massed units.)

---

[60] Hahlweg notes that the following remarks, up to *, were added later by Clausewitz to the margin of the main body of his lecture notes.

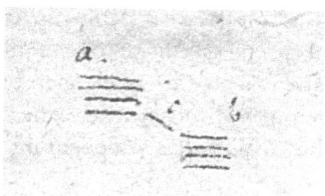

Figure 7. Positioning of Massed Units.

Source: Clausewitz (1810: 165v.) Copyright © Universitäts- und Landesbibliothek Münster, N. Clausewitz 4,001.

1. **Cavalry alone.** If it is pursued by a superior cavalry and does not wish to be destroyed or cut off, then it will always find it necessary to hurl itself repeatedly with the greatest determination against the nearest part of the enemy cavalry. There are few rules governing the use of the terrain. However, it is certain that troops concealed by a narrow point along the way can achieve great effects.
   Mounted artillery renders great service here.
2. **Both service arms united**
   2.1 **In the plain**
       One assumes that a superior cavalry is pursuing, as otherwise there would be no great danger. Two cases are to be distinguished.
       2.1.1 If there are very few infantry but much cavalry. Then one has to send back the cavalry, as General Lukner once did, in order to save it.
            (Remarks on the ignoble spirit of such measures. It is still regarded as acceptable for a general, but never for the cavalry regiment itself.)
       2.1.2 Few cavalry but substantial infantry. Then the above rule applies again, because then the few cavalry, if they are not placed directly under the protection of the infantry, will be lost immediately. If one can place them amidst the infantry so that they cannot be attacked by the enemy cavalry without also attacking the infantry, then they will contribute to the infantry's protection. This requirement is not easy to meet, yet there are cases and arrangements that have a fair chance of success. For example, if four battalions are positioned as indicated in the figure [see Figure 8], so that a space of 400 paces remains in the middle, one certainly could accommodate some squadrons. (Considerations concerning this.)
            If, however, this arrangement is also deemed too dangerous and one sends the cavalry away, it may not go too far, leaving the infantry utterly alone. It retreats until the enemy cavalry ceases to menace it with great superiority and then it stops again. If they are pursued only by a small part of the enemy

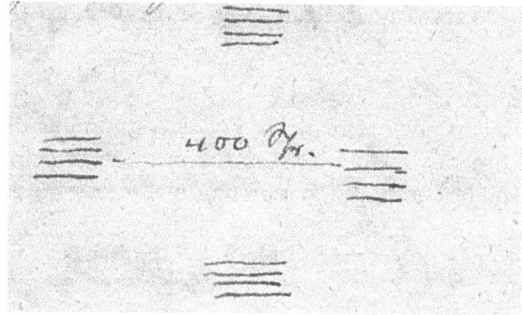

Figure 8. Positioning of the Cavalry amidst the Infantry

Source: Clausewitz (1810: 166r.) Copyright © Universitäts- und Landesbibliothek Münster, N. Clausewitz 4,001.

cavalry that is not too strong, then they attack it. In this way the cavalry will be useful to the infantry, even at a distance.

2.2 In varied terrain

Here, in most cases, it will not be necessary to abandon one service arm for the other.

Although when the enemy is not pushing too hard one is well advised to send the infantry forward in order to gain terrain, one nevertheless has to place the cavalry behind the infantry the moment one could come to blows with the enemy.

§ 7

On the Advantages of Mounted Artillery during Such Retreats

1. The artillery is an extremely effective service arm in every retreat because it keeps enemy fire at a distance, owing more to perceptions than actual effects. On the other hand, it has the disadvantage that it provokes the enemy to take risks, because a captured enemy cannon is always a shining coup.

2. If the artillery is mounted, the danger of losing it is slight since it is as agile as any other unit and in addition has the great advantage that man and horse work alternatingly and thus one is rested if the other is tired.

3. If one wants to exploit every advantage of mounted artillery upon retreating, then one has to employ it with the *Prolonge*.[61] (Verbal elaborations.)

---

[61] According to Hahlweg, a *prolonge* is a rope fitted with a hook and used for towing a gun carriage.

Marching Retreat over Several Days

§ 8

For small detachments such retreats are not as common as they are in Large War. Yet a detachment can find itself in the position of being pursued by a superior enemy and be compelled to march retreat for several days to the army or to a fortress.

Here one has to pay due regard to the following issues:

§ 9

One marches by night if one:

1. Intends to sneak through completely undetected, or
2. Otherwise has the intention to march secretly to gain a head start on the enemy, to take an unexpected path, etc. In short, to get out of his sight.
3. Needs to avoid the heat.

Under normal circumstances, however, one is better advised to march by day.

1. Because marching by day is less tiring and can be conducted more orderly and thus more quickly.
2. Because during the night there is less danger of having one's rest disturbed by the enemy.
3. Because during the night one may venture a skirmish with the enemy with less danger.

§ 10

If severe cold does not prevent it, one bivouacs. In every case, one positions the bivouac near a village, or even better, close to a town, to facilitate rapid delivery of supplies.

If one is too numerous to be sustained by a single village, one divides into two or three units and positions them in the vicinity of the next three villages.

One does not march into the bivouac before complete darkness and one leaves it after daybreak or once the men have had enough rest.

Four to five hours are enough for a rest. If the men are well fed and if one pauses for an hour several times during the march itself, then one always will be able to cover seven to eight miles and perhaps more, every 24 hours.

§ 11

One takes along as many wagons as one can procure.

1. To carry away the exhausted, so that the drifters do not all fall into the hands of the enemy.

2. To carry stocks of foodstuffs, mainly meat.

The wagons are changed in every quarter, if possible, but the used ones are not abandoned unless one has replacements.

§ 12

Securing foodstuffs is essential.

Thus one dispatches an officer with some soldiers to requisition the necessary number of rations. One requisitions double the amount one needs, to be certain one hasn't received too little.

The rations can consist of beer and wine, brandy, of bread, cooked and smoked meat, and cooked vegetables.

One should only take raw food in case of emergency.

In addition to those rations that are delivered to every nighttime quarter, raw foodstuffs are delivered so they can be carried along and be available in case of hardship.

§ 13

If possible, the wood is delivered in advance so that the men are not fatigued by the need to fetch it.

The fodder for the horses is collected in one, two, or three barns, where it is distributed. The number of the barns follows the number of the squadrons, batteries, etc.

§ 14

Since one is only bivouacking, one does not need many forward posts.

1. One leaves some Hussars a half-mile behind the bivouac, who signal upon enemy approach, avoiding detection by him. This is the simplest forward post arrangement and is completely sufficient here. (why?)[62] If one can leave stronger detachments behind to serve as forward posts and *arrière-garde* all the better.

2. One places infantry sentinels at a distance of 1000 paces around the bivouac.

3. One sends patrols toward the enemy and the region to which one intends to set out the next morning.

---

[62] The "why?" appears in the original lecture notes. Presumably this was a cue to remind Clausewitz to elaborate on the reasons why this arrangement of the forward posts is sufficient.

§ 15

1. One retreats along the shortest route and refrains from taking a detour on the basis of every rumor. Should one in this way come rather close to the enemy, it will nevertheless be possible to evade him through a strong unexpected march to the side.

2. If one unexpectedly encounters an enemy detachment, it is better to throw oneself at him resolutely than to lose time with a detour.

   Ewald says if you don't run they won't chase you and tells a story from the American War, when he was in the rearguard foraging. Riflemen were hot on his heels such that he could not move on. He at once frantically charged against them, struck some of them down, and had his peace.

3. If the enemy with the front of his *avant-garde* is so hot on our heels that we are delayed thereby, then one hides in ambush with the entire cavalry in the next best defile and assaults the front line upon its arrival.
   Ambushes always play a large role in retreats. They are the only means to earn the enemy's respect.

   As the army of Prince Heinrich retreated toward Dresden in the campaign of 1758,[63] the *arrière-garde* was harassed in the area of Kesselsdorf by Austrians, Croats, and Hussars to such an extent that they could not move on. Lt. Colonel Belling[64] hid with his Hussars in an ambush in a village located to the side. While Meineke's dragoons and an available battalion from Wunsch engaged them head-on and lured them out, Lt. Colonel Belling assaulted them from behind and took 2000 prisoners. That helped.

4. If one is very weak, escape is easiest if one frequently changes the direction of one's march.

§ 16

1. The infantry always at the front and the cavalry and mounted artillery remain behind.

   A retreat of several days requires a certain head start. Hence, it is very unlikely that the entire detachment becomes engaged. Rather, it will be only the front of the enemy column and our *arrière-garde* that always deal with each other. If the cavalry is delayed in this way, it nevertheless easily can catch up. This is the reason it stays behind.

---

[63] Clausewitz refers to an episode of the Seven Years' War.
[64] Wilhelm Sebastian v. Belling (1719–79), Prussian Hussar general under Frederick the Great.

2. One has to familiarize oneself as well as possible with the region through which one is going to pass:
   2.1 With maps.
   2.2 Through interrogation.
   2.3 Through scouts.

3. If one fears that the enemy could reach a pass prior to us, then one has to resort to extraordinary measures and load part of the infantry onto wagons, even if only a hundred men, sending them ahead, and to hold the commander responsible for the success.

   In many, indeed most, cases, the enemy will believe nothing more can be done, since we have preempted him.

4. Good envoys must be cared for on the evening of the march; they have to remain in the bivouac at night.

§ 17

ON BREAKING THROUGH

This is one of the most glorious acts of war; it is the best way to a great reputation.

One breaks through if one attacks an enemy detachment, which has placed itself on the path of our retreat, and either completely defeats it, or at least throws it into such chaos that one finds the opportunity to pass it.

Naturally, this can only be accomplished by assault; and usually, this will only be possible by night.

One always chooses to break through at night; not only because the enemy is assaulted more easily at night, but also because he who wishes to escape can do so better by night than by day.

If one considers that there are only a few cases in which a detachment is encircled in such a way that it encounters enemy defenses on all sides, as this requires a quality of terrain that is rare; if one considers that chaos is inevitable in every battle during the night, but in most cases is more advantageous to those breaking through than to those who seek to prevent it; and finally, if one considers the advantages of a completely unexpected attack—then it becomes understandable how an undertaking, which at first sight appeared to be the boldest in the entire realm of warfare, nevertheless is so often successful, as history shows us.

§ 18

The following rules are to be observed:

1. Divide the ensemble into several columns and divisions in which all service arms are present and place a clever commander at the top.

If one directs the columns to different positions one probably has the chance to break through with one or more. But one should not suspect a collective effect of such columns. Strength alone is of little value in such cases; it is easier to break through with a small division than with a large one.

2. The arrangement of the columns should be such that the infantry is at the front, the cavalry follows, and the artillery brings up the rear. If there is freight and the like, this follows at the very end. This and the artillery are not of primary importance.

3. Under no circumstances should the infantry unreel, and when fighting, it must fight in closed ranks.

4. The commander of these columns should become familiarized, as much as possible, with the location of the villages and the route of retreat.

5. All men should be informed of two points of retreat, to which they should proceed if they are cut off.

6. If a column is repelled in battle with the enemy, it may not retreat to its point of departure.

7. Perhaps remove the ammunition.

Examples:

1. In the year 1760, six hundred French infantrymen and one detachment of cavalry were attacked at Nordheim by Major Bulow of Freitag's infantry corps with a half-brigade of riflemen (*Jäger*) and two hundred and fifty cavalrymen. The cavalry galloped away, the infantry assembled in a churchyard and started to retreat through a gate, in front of which eighty cavalrymen had already taken position. The infantry had formed a *quarrée*[65] and the eighty men had not the courage to attack. The *quarrée* retreated into the mountains without loss.

2. Just how much the determination of a few men can achieve is demonstrated by an example from the Seven Years' War.
   In 1758, while retreating from Moravia through Bohemia, the Cuirassier Regiment Bredow from the Retzow's column, which constituted the *arrière-garde*, was attacked in a defile by 1100 cavalrymen under the command of General St. Ignon. At this point, Lieutenant Korzhagen from the Zieten's regiment arrived with fifty Hussars. He was sent from the king to Field Marshal Keith with correspondence. He seized the opportunity and while pursuing, resolutely attacked the Austrians'

---

[65] A *quarrée* is a rectangular formation.

flank. Bredow's regiment caught its breath, reorganized, joined the attack, and took three hundred prisoners.

3. In the year 1758, after the battle of Zorndorf, General Wedel marched against the Swedes and learned that a detachment had advanced via Fehr-bellin in order to forage. Hereupon he advanced with Möhring's Hussars and Plettenberg's dragoons and encountered 100 cavalrymen and 200 infantry at the village Tarnow, half a mile from Fehrbellin. The hundred horses bravely charged against the Prussians, but were immediately scat-tered. The infantry, however, had time to form a *quarrée*. Herewith they were able to retreat happily to Fehrbellin, which was located at the end of a long causeway, and the attacks of the Prussian cavalry were to no avail.

4. Example of Menin.[66]

In the year 1794, the fortress Menin, originally a strong structure built by Vauban but later ruined and now in a very run-down condition, was occupied by two thousand Hanovarians under the command of General Hammerstein when General Pichegru arrived in Flanders.

The position was rather more a bad retrenchment than a fortress, and a defense of a few days was possible only through great effort and exertion, because almost everywhere the enemy could enter the town over the walls without hindrance and thus could only be deterred with a defense *à force de bras*.

On April 26, the locality was surrounded by a column of twenty thou-sand men under the command of Generals Moureau and Vandamme. General Hammerstein resisted until the 29th by keeping the garrison almost always on the walls. Two demands [for surrender] were refused.

The English army stood at Courtray. That of Clairfait at Mouscron.

On the 26th, Courtray was taken by the French. The defense of Menin depended on whether or not General Clairfait, who stood at Mouscron, would be defeated by the French.

The garrison in Menin was stretched to the limit. The enemy ad-vanced closer to the wall every day with his snipers and columns. The garrison's ammunition was running short and the danger of being taken by storm increased day by day.

The garrison consisted of:

the first Hanoverian Grenadier Battalion	354 Men
two Battalions of the 14th Hanoverian light infantry regiments	1148
one Battalion of loyal immigrants[67]	400
	1902

---

[66] The siege of Menin in 1794 was an early French victory during the campaign in Flanders.
[67] Abbreviation of note from Hahlweg: A unit of French immigrant mercenaries paid by England.

General Hammerstein decided to hesitate no longer and to break through in the night of the 29th–30th.

Observations

1. The cannons caused the first and greatest disruption of order. Since in such cases they are not central to the operation, one is well advised to leave them in the rear.

2. If the two Battalions of the 14th Infantry Regiment had been in columns and remained that way, then the enemy would not have been able to scatter them, even if he had surrounded them.

3. If one had had the chance to divide into two columns, the outcome would not have been so bad. The first column would have marched along the path taken by the immigrants, the second along the street. Then only the second would have encountered misfortune, the first would have escaped without difficulty. No doubt chance played a major role, however chance is always in play, and if one has two columns, as a rule one makes it through better than the other.

ON PURSUIT OF THE ENEMY WHEN HE RETREATS

§ 1

We are not dealing here with the way in which those circumstances, which induced the enemy to retreat, can be exploited to compel him to accelerate his retreat to the utmost. This is usually the task of the army or larger corps and not a matter of Small War, but rather of strategy. By pursuit of the enemy, we mean the harassment and hindrance of his march that makes his retreat more arduous and leads to larger losses.

§ 2

Either the army's *avant-garde* or a specific detachment is ordered to follow the enemy so closely that it can detect and exploit every mistake of the enemy, capitalizing on the disadvantages that are related to the retreat, in order to inflict heavy losses on him. If the terrain is completely flat, one employs cavalry and mounted artillery, but since this is seldom the case when a march lasts for several days, the infantry is only rarely completely dispensable. The infantry becomes more important the more the terrain is varied and in real mountains, it is the main weapon and is only supported by the cavalry.

§ 3

The great disadvantages, to which the retreating side is subjected, comprise:

1. The troops are dispirited. Ewald argues that much can be achieved with soldiers during pursuit and nothing during retreat. He was never short of volunteers in an emergency, regardless how tired the men, but while retreating received from even the bravest of men no more than that to which they were obliged.

2. As retreats are usually strenuous marches, there are always many stragglers. The pursuer doesn't have any fewer, but he doesn't lose them as is generally the case with the retreater. The result is a large number of captured.

3. Although the retreater has more opportunity and means to arrange for his provisions, his men are nevertheless less well fed than those of the pursuer. For if it is relatively crowded and dangerous, then the retreater rarely has the time to provide for the supply and preparation of essentials. Usually he is overrun by the attacker who consumes that which was intended for him. Additionally, the peasants always tend to conceal their resources more from the retreating than from the pursuing forces; the sense of the victor's superiority comes over them as over the troops themselves. Furthermore, they believe that the retreating forces cannot further delay and if one can only hide the provisions for a few more hours, they will be salvaged. They have not the same opinion of the pursuing forces, although they usually have as little time to halt as do the retreating forces. They fear revenge from them for which the retreating forces in their sorry state haven't the time.

4. The pursuer can afford his troops a certain amount of time for rest. During this time they can enjoy their rest to a certain extent without worry. The pursued will be startled by every footstep and unnecessarily withdraws from many a bivouac.

§ 4

If one intends to maximize the disadvantages for the retreating forces and at the same time intends to reap the resulting advantages, then the following items are important:

1. One spares no effort to achieve one's goal. The private is animated by the prospect of plunder. One has to march with the very same exertion that would be required to rescue oneself. For otherwise the enemy would soon gain an edge.

2. Whenever the enemy halts, one tries to reach him with the front line of the *avant-garde*. If the enemy commander does not conduct himself accordingly, its appearance usually will be enough to deny him rest and foodstuffs, as he will immediately continue to march.

3. One tries to cut off the enemy. If this cannot be accomplished successfully because one would bring oneself into a dangerous situation, then one would try to pretend to cut him off by allowing very weak detachments to move ahead of the enemy, by spreading false rumors, etc. It is hard to believe what sometimes can be achieved if the enemy commanders are not resolute or men of much experienced in war.

4. One tries to compel the enemy to march by night. Night marches are always slower than daytime marches and exhaust the troops infinitely more. Every sort of confusion occurs and a spirit of terror readily overcomes the troops.

   However, it is easy to coerce the enemy to march by night, if one attacks or tries to circumvent him during the very night he tries to afford his troops rest in a bivouac or in villages. He will then most likely decamp and not stop again throughout that night. He will reach his next position during daytime and rest there. While the enemy marches, we take rest and begin marching around noon so that we approach him again in the evening in case he intended to stay the night.

5. If the area through which the enemy retreats is favorable to the infantry, then it can be of great use for impeding his retreat. One approaches the enemy with a detachment of riflemen or snipers to a distance from which one can fire into his formation with bow shots. If this measure can be applied in defiles and similar situations that are given to disarray, it will often result in outright flight.

   For this purpose one should always have infantry near the forefront.

6. If the enemy intends to decamp in the morning, units of riflemen are deployed during the night, approach his position as much as possible, and greet him with unexpected light rifle fire. Ewald argues that this fire, as ridiculous as it may seem, has a great effect on the retreating soldier's heart, insofar as it foreshadows how dangerous and arduous the coming day will be for him. It is certainly all too easy for a spirit of terror and anxiety to take over retreating troops and to lead to great results for the victor.

7. If the retreat is through mountains, one attempts to reach defiles at the same time as the enemy. One proceeds with the infantry to the right and left as far as possible, accompanying the enemy columns and exchanging fire the entire day with the enemy's forward, rear, and side units, thus delaying the enemy's march.

Ewald argues: "One tries to gain the heights in mountainous areas and the deepest forests with riflemen and sharpshooters who constantly harass the enemy with gunfire. Exhausted, he loses many men and his march is held up. During the American War, I quite often witnessed how a handful of riflemen often delayed our marches and constantly harassed us and how little could be done against these people, who with great courage attacked our columns, our vanguard and rearguard. I saw few of them killed, while we were constantly losing many men. And if they were pushed back, they quickly returned" etc.[68]

All of these measures, which are the result of principles and great exertion on the part of the victor, only *seem* to be the result of his sheer audacity, only appear to be the simple expression of his natural superiority, therefore leaving such a devastating impression.

§ 5

These are the means at one's disposal for causing as much damage as possible to the enemy during his retreat and bringing the enemy troops ever closer to a state of dissolution, which can be regarded as the goal of all these measures.

These rules do not lead always to the desired success and the small measures that are undertaken in this spirit do not work out always. As disadvantageous as the enemy's situation during retreat may be, it will never be desperate if the commanders are able and the troops courageous. And even if they are not in the position to prevent every last loss, they will nevertheless find in their conduct means against disproportionate disadvantages. If the retreating troops do not lose sight of the necessary precautions, if they remain courageous and firm, if they know how to punish a brash pursuer, then the pursuer will not only have expended his effort partly in vain, but rather could come into danger himself.

§ 6

One should not be annoyed by the futile endeavor; but the danger in which one finds oneself must be a topic of our attention.

We know from the previous chapter that if the pursuing forces too often push forward, the retreating forces will set up ambushes and by these means attempt to deliver a strong blow. The pursuer needs to guard diligently against this.

§ 7

What one can or cannot undertake against one's enemy, how much, how little, cannot be determined by rules, but depends on a certain tact that one

---

[68] Clausewitz quotes Ewald (1798).

possesses, and on the exercise of that judgment, which one obtains through war. As with every art and performance of human life, these elements are the spirit of action. One can undertake three times as much against a terrorized enemy as against an enemy who upon retreat inspires respect, whose troops are courageous, steadfast, and experienced in war.

Nevertheless, one should not allow them to pass quietly or build them golden bridges. Rather, one should at least try to do what one can against them, and in any case, to inflict that damage that can be caused without endangering oneself, by measures initiated with prudence, caution, and great exertion.

No one doubts that Frederick II would have suffered heavy losses on his retreat through Bohemia after ending the siege of Olmütz,[69] if the Austrians had taken full advantage of the possibilities offered by their many light troops. The transport of wagons, which accompanied the 33-battalion-strong army of Marshall Keith, consisted of 4000 horse and cart. And although the Austrians' main army held back completely, taken together, the generals Zischkowitz, Laudon, Janus, and Buko were certainly much stronger. Laudon indeed ventured a number of bold assaults for which he was punished through skillful countermeasures. Thus, it was quite appropriate that he became more careful. But this need not have prevented the Austrian light troops from harassing and delaying on a daily basis Field Marshall Keith's army and compelling it to take up battle under very disadvantageous circumstances. Obviously, this was a mistake of the Austrian generals, notwithstanding the respect the Prussian troops deserve.

ON THE PARTICULAR PURPOSES A PARTISAN OR SIMILAR DETACHMENT CAN SERVE

§ 1

By partisans, I mean chiefly a detachment of select officers (especially the leader), men, and horses. If such a detachment is permanently organized for the entire campaign or war, then it will be better trained for its type of missions and more reliable in their execution. These are partisans properly so called. It is not always the case that armies have them, but it appears to be certain that although mere partisan attacks are not valued in the new war, such detachments nevertheless are quite useful, because they receive

---

[69] Clausewitz refers to the unsuccessful siege of Olmütz by Prussia in 1758.

hundreds of assignments for which they are better suited than an ordinarily commanded unit.

I specifically deal with partisans here because those matters pertaining to light units, which I still have to address, are well-suited for these detachments; although they also can be employed for previously mentioned tasks, namely for reconnaissance of an area, and on occasion the bearing of all detachments at march, even clandestine marches, to which they are uniquely suited.

§ 2

A detachment with no defensive or reconnaissance objective must have an offensive purpose.

We have already dealt with proper assaults on enemy detachments or posts.

Furthermore, there are additional purposes that can be achieved through smaller detachments and that are commonly the tasks of partisans or similar units. At least we should like to mention these purposes. Moreover, it will suffice for us to offer just a few rules and remarks, because the means of success so often are a matter of pure common sense that rules take on the appearance of pedantry.

The usual such purposes are the following:

1. To collect information.
2. To intercept couriers.
3. To capture generals and other important persons.
4. To collect supplies and other materials.
5. To destroy bridges.
6. To destroy magazines.
7. To block paths.

§ 3

The first and most important element of the accomplishment of such tasks is most often the successful and unnoticed execution of the march. No further rules are necessary here, since in all cases the march remains the same. Stealth is usually decisive and always advantageous. Thus, the chapter on clandestine marches applies.

§ 4

Collecting Information

If a partisan is sent out for this purpose, then the case is different from common patrols or reconnaissance insofar as the former go to where the other no longer can, namely in between and behind the enemy. For such missions, a select officer is needed with chosen men and horses. Training is also required, which differentiates the partisan from an ordinary patrol.

Such deployments are rarely directed at merely reporting on whether the enemy is here. Rather, a specific task is usually the primary objective. Hence, the following remarks seem to me to be important:

1. When one receives one's instructions, one attempts to ascertain a clear understanding of the **primary subject** on which one is supposed to report. An officer who really does not know what he is to do, is unable to take appropriate measures.

2. One ascertains with as much certainty as possible the status of the main subject. One does not rely on mere hearsay, that is, on reports of the population, but one tries to push one's detachment forward in order to investigate the subject oneself or with one's own men. For example, when, while marching with 40 infantrymen during the campaign of 1776, Ewald[70] was sent around the American army to Burlington in order to gather information on whether the American row-boats were still stationed in the Delaware at Burlington, he could not and would not rely on the information supplied by two inhabitants at the Yorkshire Bridge, but instead took his chances and proceeded to the precise location. This was obligatory, and since he had taken the necessary precautions for an eventual mishap, it was understood by his post if not by his detachment.

3. In most cases one will try to get close to the main subject by means of a clandestine march, and remaining concealed will try to secure the necessary information with sneak patrols by night. Sneak patrols are here the means of choice.

4. Often it will be necessary to disguise some men, who are sent toward the enemy to gather information.

5. Never forget the rule to send back information on a regular basis whenever possible.

§ 5

Intercepting Couriers and Patrols

1. One hides along the road where couriers and patrols are supposed to march and deploys some lookouts.

---

[70] See Ewald (1790: 190ff).

2. One doesn't stop anyone by whom one has not been detected and who is not the target of the ambush.

3. One absolutely forbids shooting and even instructs the removal of the shot.

4. One promises the men the prisoners' money and watches as well as the captured horses.

Emmerich provides a remarkable example of how long one can remain undetected by these means.[71]

§ 6

Capture of Generals and Other Important Persons in Quarters

Ewald[72] reports that such things often happened in the American War because the American riflemen exhibited here, and in Small War more generally, great skill and much initiative. With respect to our armies, it was always uncommon and nowadays perhaps even less so. But such things very often occur in civil wars and when the nation is armed.

Instead of listing every rule, we allow ourselves the simple observation that under such circumstances, namely in civil and national wars, it is not unimportant to direct one's actions directly against the personal security of generals and leaders. In this way it may be possible to inspire unrest and trepidation.

§ 7

Collecting Supplies and Other Materials

1. Foremost, in this case, a written instruction is indispensable: both for one's own authentication and because it makes it easier to meet one's goal amongst the people. They are more willing to pay a contribution to the commanding general because they hope that it will redound to their advantage, whereas what the partisan acting on his own extorts from them they regard as thrown out the window. Regardless of how much power one might have, it is undeniable that a great recalcitrance on the part of the people can impede the collection of contributions to a certain degree.

2. One detains some of the most important persons of the locality, intending to take these hostage in case the demands are not met.

    One has to inspire fear and terror in this way in order to achieve one's goals.

---

[71] Clausewitz refers to Emmerich (1791: ch. IX, 56–7).
[72] Clausewitz refers to Ewald (1798: ch. 3).

3. If it is not money, but cloth, grain, or other provisions, one seizes these in case of emergency by force in the supply magazines of private persons.

4. One secures a bill documenting what one has received.

Requisitions of this type usually occur in enemy countries. Thus, it is unlikely that we will resort to them. We can expect that the provinces in which we are waging war will happily yield what they have.

§ 8

Destroying Bridges

1. Wooden
1.1 One burns them down. A heap of straw and dry wood set on fire in the middle of the bridge serves the purpose. However, one has to remain there because someone might extinguish the fire or it might burn out too soon.
1.2 A bridge that is to be defended can be torn down, this might suffice. However, a bridge that is to be destroyed so that the enemy cannot use it once we have left must be completely burned down, and yet the enemy often uses the wooden posts of such bridges in order to quickly rebuild them.

2. Stone
These are detonated. One places two small hallows with 20 to 30 pounds of powder in two adjacent posts in the middle. For the ignition, one uses a proper slow match and the usual fuse made of loose powder.

If there is not enough time for these measures, one affixes a powder keg under the bridge between two posts with ropes, attaches a long fuse, and lights it as one leaves.

If a powder keg is nowhere to be found, then a 25 lb grenade will do the job instead. However 25 lb grenades are rarer than powder kegs.

3. Floating bridges, like wooden, are to be burned down. Every other measure can easily be counteracted by the enemy. We will not deal here with the detonation and burning of floating bridges through specially designed machines, which are sent down the river. This is in the purview of the engineers.

§ 9

Destroying Magazines

Of course one can set a magazine afire by shooting incendiary or firebombs or if necessary also with grenades. But an ordinary grenadier has only a few of the former and the latter only seldom ignite a fire. Since a small detachment will not easily have enough howitzers to fire sufficient numbers of incendiary and firebombs into the location that one intends to burn down, or to set it ablaze through a complete bombardment with howitzers, the burning of a magazine from a distance will always be very difficult. At most, villages can be set afire in this way; hardly towns. But magazines are usually located in towns.

Thus, if a detachment wants to achieve this goal, it would be wrong to lose time with a barrage of cannon fire, insofar as something else can be done. It attacks the enemy, tries to force its way into the locale and if it cannot remain therein, uses the first success and chaos to set a number of houses on fire as close as possible to the supplies. Several units with determined leaders must have this special assignment and follow the first troops equipped with incendiary rockets, pitch wheels, or torches.

§ 9 [sic!]

Blocking and Mining Roads

This is only possible in deep defiles. For it would be easy for the enemy to circumvent every other road that is too troublesome for him to clear. But usually clearing an abatis is not that difficult. Even if a small detachment should face a situation in which it appears necessary to build an abatis on a common forest trail for its own security, this is not a job for a detachment sent out especially for the purpose; it is something so easy as to require no further discussion.

Here we are talking about a situation in which a partisan or other detachment is sent out to block and ruin roads and trails through the mountains in order to force a significant delay upon the enemy. A delay of one or several days.

A trail is rendered useless:

1. If all bridges and crossings are destroyed.
2. If it is blocked with trees.
3. If stones are rolled into it. If these are heavy, they are better than every tree.
4. By digging through the trail, that is, one digs a ditch as wide and deep as possible and spreads the soil in the surrounding area.

Common sense spurred on by hatred of the enemy will inspire thousands of inventions that are impossible to list exhaustively.

The repairing of roads, which is a more technical issue, will be dealt with elsewhere.

CONCLUDING REMARKS ON SMALL WAR

1. Herewith, gentlemen, I am concluding my [lectures on] Small War in the hope that you will find the principles, opinions and rules that I have presented to you worthy of your continued contemplation. For only through personal reflection and coming to terms oneself, not through memorizing rules, is knowledge of the subject matter and the ability to behave accordingly achieved. Above all, I wish that from time to time in the course of your studies you will come back to these sentences and subject them to the test of your more mature powers of judgment. It goes without saying that I am speaking here only to those among you who have not dealt much with these issues and are less familiar with the history of war, that is, to those for whom the topic of these lectures was partly new.

2. At the start of these lectures I could not promise you much and I must now confess that these hours could have been much more useful for you if I could have conveyed to you, through a very elaborate description of personal experiences in the fabric of particular circumstances, a sense of the whole that is the rule, instead of presenting it to you in a dry manner substantiated with a few meager examples. For the rule is only intelligible and useful to those who remember specific incidences or at least have a vague notion of how war is waged. This is also why I hope you will come back to this after you have dealt for a time with the history of war.

3. I took it upon myself to tell you nothing of which I am not convinced. One is easily misled into repeating others in matters of the art of war. The sheer number of books, which up to the present provide so many examples thereof, prove the point. One can say that many authors have written many things that they did not understand, mainly for the reason that most were mere compilers.

I believe I am innocent of this charge. Whatever I did not understand or clearly grasp I left out, such as the many meandering, abstract, vacuous elaborations, which most authors use to substantiate their principles.

My greatest aspiration is that you might find my rules natural, that is, as close as possible to the subject matter and not in contradiction to the process of war. Although my experience in war is limited, it is nevertheless sufficient to afford me the right understanding of the emergence of most of the incidents in war, of the manifold happenstances with which everything is interwoven, and the various difficulties that impede the precise execution of those systematic plans theory tends to produce. One could call this the friction of the entire machinery, which as every other friction, can only be recognized through experience, and which so many authors completely forget.

Thus, I hope this limited personal experience guards against the danger of pedantry.

4. There are many more authors writing about Small War than Large War. Most cover the same material and in a similar fashion. It is hardly worth the effort to read more than one or two.

Of those books I know, the following stand out through more or less originality:

1. The booklet by General von Scharnhorst. No other book is so rich in historical examples and written in such classic brevity and precision. One could say there is not a superfluous word in it.[73]

2. General Ewald's analyses of the services of light troops distinguish themselves through a number of examples taken from personal experience, which the author places next to his rules thereby making them very practical and instructive.[74]

   In any case this author stands out in that he tries to teach with many examples, which is certainly appropriate. In this regard, he has collected:
   2.1 Examples of great heroes. 1 volume.
   2.2 Instruction in Small War. 2 volumes.
      But they are inferior to his analyses, because the examples are not taken from personal experience and in addition most examples are very poorly detailed.

3. Valentini's treatment of Small War[75] presents most issues rather adequately and accessibly, and has the advantage over the other books of providing maps to accompany the examples. However, it is short on good historical examples.

4. Regarding the forward post service, there is a very wordy but well-written book by a German cavalry officer Süßmilch[76] that has the benefit of shedding light on the new forward post system and in addition grasps the issue in a very spirited fashion.

5. Emmerich's *Partheygänger*[77] is a very small booklet in which Lt. Colonel Emmerich recounts in a very simple and pleasant way the incidents he experienced as a partisan, and provides in the process some rules.

   The opinions of these authors about Large and Small War are very different and thus they are of varying utility. I leave it to you to judge which of them is to be preferred.

---

[73] Clausewitz again refers to Scharnhorst, *Militairisches Taschenbuch, zum Gebrauch im Felde*, Hannover 1794. See Scharnhorst (1980).

[74] Clausewitz refers to Ewald (1790).

[75] Clausewitz refers to Valentini (1802). Hahlweg points out that Valentini's work had just been reprinted when Clausewitz wrote his Lectures.

[76] Clausewitz refers to [Süßmilch] (1805).

[77] Clausewitz refers to Emmerich (1789) and the German translation (1791).

6. Examples as well as individual analyses on Small War can be found in
the military journals. The best are:

6.1 *Bellona*, a military journal Dresden. (In the early '80s of the last
century). (18 volumes).

6.2 *Neue Bellona*, by Porbeck. 9 volumes. (In the first years of this
century, up to the war).

6.3 *Neues Militärisches Journal* (von Scharnhorst) (13 volumes, 1789
until shortly before the war. The last volumes have the special title
Militärische Denkwürdigkeiten).

6.4 Collection of unpublished reports, such as the history of the Prussian
Campaign, 1740–79. *Dresden* in the early 1780s. 4 volumes.

6.5 *Militärische Monatsschrift* by Massenbach. (1785–87. 5 volumes).

6.6 *Magazin der Merkwürdigsten Kriegsbegebenheiten.* 7 volumes (Leip-
ziger and Knesebeck) (93–96).

6.7 *Kriegsbibliothek in 8 Versuchen* (56–69) (contains nothing about
Small War but rather translations of analyses and historical essays
in foreign languages. Beslau.)

6.8 *Militärische Bibliothek* 4 numbers. 82. (von Scharnhorst)

6.9 *Neue Militärische Bibliothek.* 4 numbers. 85. (A continuation of the
proceeding) (both contain no war events but rather notes on the
armies and military literature.)

6.10 Hoyer's *Militärisches Magazin* (The first years of this century. 3
volumes quarterly) (Leipzig).

6.11 Thielke's *Beiträge zur Kriegskunst und Geschichte der Kriege.* (in
the 1770s. 6 volumes).

6.12 Böhm's *Magazin für Ingenieur und Artilleristen.* (in the 1770s).

5. For the time being, I would not advise you to read much about the theory of
Small War but rather to invest the time you intend to spend reading in the
history of warfare. Only subsequently, if you again feel the need to return to a
theoretical orientation and to round out your thinking, will you benefit from
consulting the authors I have suggested to you and from asking yourself: If
I leave all prejudices aside, and if I do not commit myself to any traditional
rule, what if that said by the author still remains true?

Then I hope that you might remember these hours from time to time in
order to reflect on them further.

3

Testimonial

Bekenntnisdenkschrift

February 1812
Motto
Certainly I know the value of repose, the comforts of company, the joy of life; I too would like to be as happy as anyone. As much as I covet these commodities, however, so little do I wish to acquire them through perfidy and dishonesty. The philosopher teaches us to perform our duty, to serve our Fatherland faithfully with our blood, and to sacrifice our repose, or even our entire existence.

Frederick II,[1] from his posthumously published papers

This short text[2] is designed to justify before the eyes of the world, the political opinion of those who regarded necessary the resistance against France, who had to give way to conventional opinion and were denounced as quixotic fools, or dangerous revolutionaries, or frivolous cacklers, or self-serving schemers.

Who can hold it against them that in the moment they departed the scene and abandoned their fortune and all that is dear to them—because they were unable to serve with diligence and honor the enemy whom they abhor from the bottom of their hearts—that in this moment they wished to show themselves to be men of calm deliberation, of mature and cool judgment? Out of acquiescence to the government, their opinion could not be stated openly [and] through foreign tyranny was withheld completely from the public; it is attempted hereby to place it on an equal footing with the other opinions.

---

[1] Frederick the Great (1712–86), King of Prussia 1740–86.

[2] This handwritten memorandum was sent by Clausewitz to Gneisenau in February 1812 and circulated among Prussian military reformers of that time. In it Clausewitz defends his view that only a Small War, i.e. a revolutionary uprising of the people and what he terms "active defense" has the potential to stand up against the overwhelming Napoleonic forces. The translation is based on the printed version in Hahlweg (1966–90: vol. 1, 682–750) and incorporates corrections, addenda, and emphases (in bold) made by Clausewitz but not those of others who also revised the manuscript.

Certainly a king will not begrudge this satisfaction to those of whose unselfish service he is certain; in **whose** hearts his cause has found warmest favor; and who were not amongst the least capable of his officials.

Once Prussia has thrown itself into the arms of France, once the men, whose confession is recorded here, no longer outwardly belong to this state (although forever in their hearts), then this text can be published without compromising the government. Perhaps under these circumstances it will be able to ignite a flame in the hearts and minds of those subjects, who at some point might prove to be the government's salvation.

FIRST CONFESSION

The moment of a new war in the North is approaching. Perhaps the outbreak will be delayed for some months. That the storm will completely dissipate, as some deceive themselves, is impossible.

Anyone abroad who commiserates with the Prussian state (and without doubt there are many) anxiously awaits the fate that shall befall her in the new catastrophe.

Not only the fate of this state, but also its behavior, is the subject of great and general interest. All will hope that Prussia at least will have fought with honor and suffered a glorious downfall.

This short text is directed to those sympathetic friends as a confession of a private opinion, which few, though some, of my fellow citizens share. Furthermore, it is directed to all other citizens as a formal protest against any kind of participation in that which is to be decided, which may transpire, and which at some point will be heavily penalized and regretted.

Perhaps these lines will inspire a sense of duty and honor in the hearts of some; perhaps they will enlighten some minds, purging the phantom monster of fear, showing clearly the danger that truly exists, and distinguishing it from that which does not.

Since 1794[3] Prussia has withstood a single struggle, which by far did not last long enough, and which was conducted with much too little effort and strength of will to justify complete despair.

Rather, the whole of Europe must expect that this state will at last rise against a complete subjugation and annihilation, and in a struggle of life and death, dignify the name of Frederick.

---

[3] In 1794 Prussia had to contend with a military insurrection in Poland, parts of which had been divided between Russia and Prussia and annexed the previous year (Second Partition of Poland). The defeat of the Polish insurrection would lead to the Third Partition in 1795. 1794 also marked the adoption of the Prussian General State Laws (*Allgemeines Landrecht*), a civil code that was in effect until the Stein-Hardenberg Reforms initiated after the defeat by Napoleon at Jena-Auerstedt in 1806.

This name, Frederick the Second, which is on the lips of every Prussian, rightly leads the entire world to expect that we can find an honorable ethos: a feeling for duty, virtue, and honor, that far from being blunted and weakened through the force of time, has instead increased in resilience and filled us with noble ire. Indeed, to speak of honor and glory when both have been acquired and secured is mere vanity; and we could have spared the world the many phrases with which we often have annoyed it. How contemptuous and unworthy this swagger must appear, when one sees that we cower in front of the danger without regard for honor and shame.

It is unbelievable, that of all people, those who were witnesses to Frederick's deeds, and others, who constantly invoke his name, only approve of that which **he** did, and ridicule with contempt that which is not of his manner; that these, through a brazen cowardliness, which they openly display, are completely unworthy to be the heirs of this heroic dynasty, which earned the Prussian name respect and sympathy throughout the world.

It is not my intention to present a complete picture of public opinion and sentiment in Prussia. I lack the necessary experience and mainly know the capital city and the courtly estates. In order to officially break with that public opinion that surrounds me, however, I am obliged to outline its main currents.

The argument that one could resist France has disappeared amongst us almost completely. One believes in the necessity of an unconditional alliance, a submission to benevolence and malice, a final renunciation of the merit of our own dynastic house. One shrugs away these gradations of evil—and at most blushes, by merely looking toward the ground.

This is the general **mood**. Some distinguish themselves through the impertinence with which they insist on safety and the docile indulgence of bourgeois affluence; on the necessity of sacrificing everything thereto, even the rights of the king, even the honor of the king, even the security and freedom of the king!

This is public **opinion** with few exceptions. The various estates, and individuals within the estates, distinguish themselves in the ways in which they express and emulate it. The aristocracy is depraved; the Court and the civil servants are the most depraved.

Not only do they wish for tranquility and safety as others do. Nor have they only forgotten to fulfill their duty when confronted with danger. Rather, they hound with unforgiving hate, those who do not despair.

For what else other than despair, if the current condition and a much worse, which is to follow, is preferred to resistance?

Therefore, whoever does not despair believes in the preservation of the state through duty and honor. Whoever does not believe that duty compels us to the most unconditional disgraceful submission and that there is no need for honor, is a traitor. He can be sure that he will be hated and hounded by

those civil servants who have forgotten their sense of duty; denounced before
the public; accused before the king; and betrayed to the French envoy.

The true patriots, who alone are candid and faithful to the king, are placed
in the scorn of public opinion, and by virtue of the folly and spite of self-
serving weaklings and unworthy gluttons, are accused of being members of a
league directed against the state and king.

Who hasn't heard of the ridiculous pursuit of the *Tugendbund*?[4] Those who
have been accused of being the head of this league and of being its most active
members barely know whether and how this society exists. The most frivolous
lies are needed to evoke this phantom, like a sorcerer's ghost conjured from
smoke, with which one continuously seeks to frighten the Court and citizens
of Berlin. But if it is a matter of scaring a fearful public, such an illusion is
sufficient.

This system of belief easily gives rise to personal hate, envy, and an
addiction to persecution, and they, who shamelessly enough openly avow
this system of cowardice and daily preach its rotten maxims, are not ashamed
to impugn the personal merit, the heart and the character of those whose
political principles they merely question.

Let us, however, turn our attention away from these sorry signs of national
depravity, which, like ulcers, are outward signs of an inner illness that can
enfeeble, poison, and destroy the whole.

Those who through the depravity of their heart and principles have not
succumbed to fear and despondence, as is all too common, are not forever lost,
but could and would elevate themselves to a better state, if offered a helping
hand thereto.

All loyalty to the government notwithstanding, one cannot deny that the
source of general despondence reflects first and foremost a lack of confidence
therein. Equally weak is the government's confidence in its subjects, indeed in
itself. This total absence of confidence in itself and others is the general cause
of our public opinion. The continuous influence of weaklings, reprobates, and
the dutiless on this opinion is the cause of public sentiment.

From this opinion and sentiment, which here is born as if it sprang from
some pristine concern for the welfare of all or were identical thereto,
I solemnly disassociate myself.

I disassociate myself from the frivolous hope of rescue by happenstance;

from the inane anticipation of the future, which a dulled sense will not
recognize;

---

[4] The *Tugendbund* was a club established in 1808 in Königsberg to cultivate Prussian
patriotism and restore popular morale in the wake of Napoleonic victories. On the insistence
of Napoleon, the King of Prussia decreed its dissolution as of December 31, 1809.

from the childish hope that the tyrant's ire can be appeased through voluntary disarmament, his confidence won through base subservience and flattery;

from the misplaced resignation of restrained intelligence;

from the imprudent mistrust of our Godgiven faculties;

from the sinful carelessness of duties toward the common good;

from the shameless sacrifice of the honor of state and people, of personal and human dignity.

I believe and confess, that there is nothing more worthy of a people's respect than the dignity and freedom of its existence;

that these must be defended to the last drop of blood;

that there is no duty more holy to fulfill and no higher law to obey;

that the blot of a cowardly subservience can never be cleansed;

that this poison in the blood of a people is inherited by their offspring, and the strength of later generations is paralyzed and eroded;

that the honor of the king and the government is one with the honor of the people and the only palladium of its welfare;

that a people is insurmountable in the noble fight for its freedom;

that the very defeat of this freedom through a bloody and honorable battle guarantees the reincarnation of the people; it is the seed of life from which a new tree strikes firm roots.

I declare and affirm before the world and posterity:

that I hold the false cunning, with which the small-minded wish to defy danger, to be the greatest bane that dread and fear can instill;

that I would regard the wildest desperation as wiser, if we were prevented from meeting the danger with a manly courage, that is, with a calm but steady determination and clear awareness;

that in the delirium of today's anxiety I will not forget the foreboding developments of the past and present, the wise lessons of entire centuries, the noble examples of renowned peoples, and abandon world history for the page of a tabloid;

that I regard myself free from any self-interest, that I may lay bare all my thoughts and feelings before my fellow citizens, that nothing would please me more than to go down in glory in the noble struggle for the freedom and dignity of the fatherland.

Is my conviction and that of the like-minded deserving of the contempt and scorn of our fellow citizens?

May posterity decide!

I place these pages on the holy altar of history, in the firm belief that once the tempest has passed, a reverend priest of this temple will preserve them carefully and file them in the chronicles of a turbulent human history.

Then posterity shall judge and spare from the damning verdict those who courageously swam against the current of depravity and remained as faithful in heart to the sense of responsibility as to a god.

SECOND CONFESSION

If in the first section of this small text I allowed myself to speak from the heart and to express in the language of emotions what is and should be a matter of emotion. I shall endeavor in this second, to speak in the language of calm deliberation, as it is my desire herein to provide a clear depiction of our situation and thereby demonstrate that emotional people are not incapable of calm deliberation just because the heart they carry in their chest does not retract, as if it were a polyp, whenever touched.

1.

A nine-month-long war conducted with little sacrifice and even less exertion of strength, fought with sparing loss of blood,*[5] would appear to have completely ruined the Prussian state's inner makeup, to have left the nation in poverty, one could say deep misery. But it only appears to be so; for where is the necessary relationship between cause and effect if one is to accept this opinion as true?

It has only arisen from a lack of insight and from the fear of a new war, which some thereby wish to depict as impossible.

The presence of the French throughout the land, imposed by the Peace of Tilsit[6] and the Treaty of Paris,[7] as well as scarcely affordable contributions, which direct the cash reserves abroad; a feigned state administration that is focused only on outward appearance and has subverted welfare; the excessive price of grain; the exorbitant interest rate; the speculation craze of property owners, which has led to changes in land ownership; these are additional arguments brought to bear by landlords quartering troops, the financier and the conscientious civil servant.

We do not wish to measure their value and their weight precisely, but they are overstated if one considers that embargoed world trade is regarded by most to be the least important cause of our misery, is not mentioned by many, and is completely denied by a few paradoxical minds.

---

* **Note**: The Battle of Eylau, where the Prussian state stood at the tip of the *épée*, cost the Prussian troops no more than . . . dead and wounded. It was nevertheless the bloodiest engagement of the Prussian Campaign in which our troops participated.

[5] In the Battle of Eylau on February 8, 1817, 75,000 French troops fought against 67,000 Russian and 9,000 Prussian troops. There were heavy losses on both sides, between 10,000 and 25,000 wounded or dead on the French, 15,000 on the Russian and the Prussian side.

[6] Treatise of Tilsit between France on the one hand and Russia and Prussia on the other signed in the town of Tilsit in July 1807.

[7] Treaty of Paris signed on September 8, 1808 by France and Prussia.

Nevertheless, it appears clearer with regard to human affairs, that nothing is more obvious than the overwhelming importance and effectiveness of this cause.

Trade and commerce flow through every branch of civil society with an energetic spirit. How could this trade, through the refinement of navigation and the development of geography, grow to such magnitude, universality, reliability, and vitality, without to a certain extent having enveloped every element of human society, infiltrating every relationship, and step by step over the course of centuries becoming the very foundation of all these relationships?

It was truly so. Millions of occurrences vouch for it. But it was also strictly necessary and no human authority other than that of a commander victorious from the Ebro[8] to the Niemen[9] could have been in a position to stop, steer, or extinguish this development.

If then this most general principle of our social constitution is forcibly subdued, what else could follow but a sudden breakdown of all affairs and, to be precise, a true **national bankruptcy**, namely, a thousandfold bankruptcy of one against the other, that without a doubt cannot be compared to an ordinary state bankruptcy.

This development has occurred because the equilibrium amongst the states of the continent has been lost.

The Emperor of France blockades trade and the entire continent suffers in misery.

Besides this great general adversity there appears a second enemy of all welfare, all domestic order, and consequently all revival. This is uncertainty.

It disrupts the entire financial system and ruins the welfare of hundreds of thousands of families. It paralyzes the activities of all inhabitants and renders part of the national wealth fallow and a substantial portion of that production, which it should generate, and with it a large portion of the national product, lost.

Lethargy, discontent, and moral depravity must be the consequences of these ills. It is impossible for a state with such poison flowing through its veins to recover its strength.

But how can this uncertainty be overcome?

As long as the relationship of France to the other states continues, the insecurity of all property and all civil existence will continue. Therefore, the only true remedy is the fight for independence.

Would not, however, an alliance with France considerably lessen the ill? Yes! At first glance, as the report spreads through the money exchangers and speculators, but hardly for long. Alliance with France provides no security; of

---

[8] River in northeast Spain.
[9] River in eastern Europe draining into the Curonian Lagoon.

that Spain, Holland, Italy, and North Germany provide evidence. Of all those countries that have dared to enter into alliance with France and the revolution—Northern and Central Italy, Spain, Portugal, Holland, Switzerland, Southern Germany, and several North German Princes—only little Switzerland and divided Southern Germany have remained formally independent. Perhaps 5/6 of the entire territory should be considered the property of France. What an admirable security has been provided by this alliance! Everyone would say it, and hardly anyone would forget what happened with Holland's state debts. The subjects of states allied with France will have as little confidence in public order, law, and justice, as the subjects of any other.

I wish to leave aside whether through a forceful preparation for resistance, through adherence to the existence and honor of the state, through the courageous determination to sacrifice everything for it, more confidence and security could have been provided. The probability of this beneficial effect speaks for itself.

The internal constitution of our state and people is hence unlikely to be restored under such conditions of external pressure. It is truly the same great folly to have hoped on the one hand that this could be achieved through the internal administration, and on the other hand to have demanded it from the administration. It would have been more appropriate if the exertions made in this regard had been used for preparations to fight. Ever since the Peace of Tislit, whoever wished to support the state of Prussia should have thought of nothing else but the preparation for the new fight, and only of that. Thereby, he soon again would have felt himself to be formidable, external affairs would have changed subtly, and the body would have recovered little by little through its own strength.

If the internal recovery of the state and its regeneration are not to be expected through an alignment with France, the question then is whether or not the state can preserve its external independence through the temporary abandonment of all honor and security until the dangerous period of political turbulences has passed.

One hopes that an alliance with France will be a means thereto.

This leads us to a consideration of our external affairs and that which we can hope to achieve through our diplomacy.

2.

If France genuinely had been reconciled with Prussia through the Peace of Tilsit, then an alliance with the same immediately should have followed this peace. Through such an alliance France would have been able to entangle Prussia to such a degree, to so strongly shackle her, as thus far has happened with Bavaria, Württemberg, and Saxony.

From that moment on the Emperor Napoleon could have relied on Prussia. Neither the king nor the nation would have had the bold wish to break free again. Forced to take this step, everything gradually would have become accustomed to the new shackles, and if, as in Saxony, Bavaria, and elsewhere, the mood were against France, it would be as inconsequential here as it was there. If on account of Prussia's size and location one could not be certain of this, there would exist hundreds of means of political tyranny through which the strength of this state could be paralyzed. For example, if half of the Prussian troops were to be sent to Spain, if strong and brave men were to be dismissed from public office, if even more Prussian fortresses were to be occupied, and so on.

Napoleon is too experienced to be at a loss for means, even for a moment, which he could employ against Prussia. The alliance presented itself to him as a ready and natural means, and its consequences surely could not have been unimportant to him.

Whether Prussia would have entered into this alliance is no longer a question. Having heretofore never shown the courage to resist France, it is hard to imagine this could have been the case at the moment of the Peace of Tilsit. Moreover, those men who negotiated the peace on the Prussian side were the primary advisors to the king. And because France discovered in the Peace of Tilsit to what extent they out of fear conceded to French interests, it could have counted on complete submission. Prussia itself has made proposals for such an alliance that were rejected coldly out of hand; and apart from the few months of the Austrian War, there was certainly no moment at which very firm words from France would not have led Prussia to give in.

Instead of turning this state into a tool for use against Spain, against Austria, against Russia, the Emperor Napoleon allows it to remain neutral.

This generosity was an obvious trap. For where else had France provided similar examples of restraint? And how is restraint possible at all for a state that aims with extraordinary means to achieve extraordinary ends, for which every breath is an assault? **In this case restraint would be as unreasonable as is pliance elsewhere.**

France allows Prussia's continuing existence, but leaves it in complete uncertainty regarding its future fate.

It appears neither to recognize what is taking place within this state, nor to concern itself therewith, apart from demonstrating from time to time its harshness, its pride, its enmity and its disdain. The vacillations of the Cabinet, party conflicts, the impatience of the population regarding the uncertain and burdensome condition, appear to leave France indifferent. As the moment of the Austrian War approaches, Prussia, thrown back and forth in indecisiveness, comes perhaps to the point of declaring itself for Austria. France obtains thereby an additional non-negligible enemy, whose influence can create circumstances in Northern Germany, the importance of which should not be underestimated. All these considerations, which at the Peace of Tilsit were completely evident to France, prevent the Emperor from making Prussia his ally and drafting it into his service.

Are these observations at all exaggerated? Certainly not! And what must we conclude? That the Emperor Napoleon had determined to destroy Prussia at the very moment he conceded to the Peace of Tilsit. The remaining strength of this state should be broken once again; above all, however, the dynasty toward which he had directed his hate should be expelled.

The execution of this plan should be accelerated by Prussia's own conduct and mistakes; yes, it should shoulder the appearance of all blame. This is why the Emperor Napoleon put the Prussian state in such a dangerous spot, where it was impossible for any ordinary government to stand fast, and where any misstep could instantly lead to ruin. If the plan can be executed only now, as the year 1812 approaches, then this is due to a number of intervening circumstances, which the Emperor Napoleon could not have foreseen.

The hate that the Emperor Napoleon has directed toward the House of Hohenzollern[10] cannot be made clear to everybody, nor can its origin be explained. For many, it would suffice to hear that at the time of the Tilsit negotiations the behavior of the Emperor Napoleon toward Fredrick William III[11] and his family was characterized by an unmistakable disdainful chill, even a restrained hatred; and that the behavior of the royal family toward him (thanks to a human dignity that could not be suppressed by politics!) betrayed a serene and dignified demeanor, which naturally could further infuriate a vain and impulsive person. There are certain facts over which there can be no doubt. The basis of the enmity lies predominantly in the liberality that characterizes the Prussian government, through which it has become an object of general interest in the whole of Germany. Prussia, especially the royal house, more than any state enjoys public support, of which the Emperor Napoleon is a suspicious enemy. The princes of Southern Germany may be tired of French domination, but they have never enjoyed independence, fear the revenge of others, and are without pride and self-esteem, each half-admirer, half-flatterer of the French Emperor. It is not so with Frederick William III. This king, as everyone knows, is above all a righteous man, incapable of hypocrisy. The hate of the French Emperor comes naturally, and since he is sensitive and easily irritated, the feeling of being upset by the Emperor's constant mistreatment has never abated. If, for political reasons, he has refrained from any mention thereof (as countenance comes naturally to him), and in this regard admirably sacrificed both his dignity and his people, he nonetheless could never mislead the French Emperor and nothing is more

---

[10] House of Hohenzollern is the dynasty of Prussian princes and kings.
[11] Frederick William III (1770–1840) was King of Prussia from 1797 to 1840.

natural than that the Emperor has seen more deeply into the heart of the king than the king has seen into his.

Considering the condition of the Prussian state, it is remarkable that the government did not decide earlier to free itself to some degree from this uncertainty and decide to observe certain standards of behavior; thereafter to create a framework to which they would remain unswervingly true. There appeared to be two ways of achieving this, as was then said. One was utter unconditional subservience, the most devoted annexation to France. In this case, one would have to accommodate France in every way, to a certain extent force oneself upon it in an effort to engender its trust.

Whether this would have led to the objective (the alliance with France) is by no means certain, even unlikely, if one considers that the French Emperor could not be interested in what he himself never wanted, and that he is not the kind of man who is led by the interests of others. Whether the alliance with France would have met the objective of external independence is even less certain. Be that as it may, it has not come to pass. Prussia, always ready to receive commands from France, has still not done enough to place itself in the master's good graces, and thus enhance its security to the furthest extent.

The other way would be the organization of a military state that the French Emperor would fear; the introduction of the general military draft, so that burden more easily could be shouldered by all; the reorganization of the army in a new spirit; the removal of the old weak bad generals and staff officers; the procurement of an abundance of weapons and munitions; the supply of every fortress with sufficient provisions; the establishment of secure depots in entrenched camps, the establishment of a general militia; the strict punishment of committed mistakes and unpatriotic attitudes amongst the military and civilians; the continuous renewal of the army after 2 to 3 years of service, by which one would today, after 4 years, have had an army of at least 150 thousand trained men, and military service thereby would be less burdensome to the population. Of these measures, some were not in violation of the treaty, some were not easily detectable, and France was not capable at all times, as was the case immediately after the Peace of Tilsit, of enforcing Prussian obedience through swift and instant punishment. In this regard, if the negotiations with France had been conducted in a lawful and public manner, if the king had decided, as far as France and Prussia are concerned, to inform the newspapers, he would have had public opinion behind him and would have become doubly dangerous to France.

It might thus have been possible to have turned unexpectedly the tempting but false neutrality that had been conceded to Prussia true and robust; neutrality that for a hundred reasons would have been stronger than that which Prussia observed prior to 1806. But these are matters of the past and we consider them only because the past leads us to the present.

Likewise, this second option was not chosen by Prussia because it lacked the necessary courage and determination as well as political insight. Without **courage and determination** in great matters, nothing can be accomplished, since danger exists everywhere and **politics** is not always a cowardly deceit as many believe it to be.—The king would not have been incapable of such a decision had he not been surrounded by two parties, one of which out of fear of catastrophe advised submission to France with great sacrifice, lack of noble pride of heart, and insufficient historical cultivation. This party chained itself to the best decisions of the king like a lead weight, thus destroying or weakening all those measures that the king, through a courageous resolve, adopted against his own misgivings.

Turning to the present, the question emerges: 1. Is the present moment different from that of the Peace of Tilsit?

Absolutely. At that time, Russia, fresh from the battlefield, was deeply entwined in France's interests, and Austria not to be feared; Prussia itself lay disarmed, sick, feeble. Now Russia, again enraged by France, is rearmed. Prussia, although it has not done everything for its military organization, nevertheless has not neglected the essentials and is by no means without the ability to resist. Spain and England hold down half of the entire enormous power of France.

2. Is an alliance with France now possible?

Absolutely. But only because Prussia has done something for itself, has outdone itself, one last time shown a spark of energy. Thanks to these reasons, France has conceded to an alliance.

3. Is the salvation of the state, or at least its external independence, to be expected from this alliance?

Less than ever. As much as conditions have changed to Prussia's advantage as regards the first two questions, on this point they have changed to its disadvantage.

Had Prussia, as Bavaria,[12] annexed itself to France, Emperor Napoleon might have countenanced its existence, but also might not have—much as the unrestrained will of a successful general defies calculation. But now that a disquieted Napoleon has survived the dangers of a lateral attack from Prussia, now that he has realized that Prussia cannot be suppressed immediately and could become a danger, that in 4 years more animosity than devotedness toward France has been nurtured, that the mistreatments to which it has been subjected have been deeply felt and painfully suppressed, now the impassionate tyrant will not have abandoned the decision to destroy this state, and the alliance he is offering is only the means thereto. Things have turned out differently than he expected. He realizes that he made a mistake allowing

---

[12] Bavaria had subdued itself to the will of Napoleon in a secret treaty in 1805.

Prussia to remain independent; that at this moment he cannot overthrow it, he even needs it. But he is committed not to make the same mistake twice.— Although for 4 years he could not use Prussia's strength, he does not want to have sacrificed in vain. At the next possible opportunity he wants to grab the spoils that he for so long has reserved for himself.

Many will miss the clarity of strict necessity in this reasoning and say: it indeed could be so, but also it could be otherwise. They have to stick to the truly objective facts.

If then, one disregards the intentions of the Emperor Napoleon, his opinion of us and his hate, and strictly sticks to the matter, the question is: which advantages and securities could flow from an alliance with France, and which disadvantages are to be expected?

Advantages of the Alliance with France

1. Guarantee of existence. Roughly half as much as Spain, Italy, Holland, and Northern Germany.

2. Removal of war from our country: certainly does not happen.

3. Delay of the war. Equally unlikely, because the outbreak of war depends on the rupture with Russia. Even an alliance with Russia, which is not necessary, or at least need not be made known, would not accelerate the war for a moment. For the principal offense has already occurred: Prussia has achieved the level of defensive capability that makes it impossible to be treated like Hesse. Further increases would not provide the French Emperor a definite basis for an earlier break with Russia. Russia is continuously increasing its strength and the Emperor does not break. Therefore other grounds are necessary.

4. An alleviation in the prosecution of the war will not occur, for it is not a particular burden of warfare to fight with 20 instead of a hundred thousand men, if one has to maintain 400,000 in either case. In any case Prussia will be the theater of war between Russia and France and experience shows that French allies are no better than French enemies. It may be different with the Russians.

Disadvantages of the Alliance with France

1. One debases oneself and the nation by fighting out of timidity for a government that is our worst enemy, deprives us of our greatness, and that has mistreated us to the extreme. The people must become corrupt, if they are to be compelled to spill their blood for a cause that they abhor.

A government that thus coerces the people compels it to vice and depravity.

2. One delivers oneself, hands tied, to the will of the French Emperor. Every alliance with him will utterly destroy the power to resist. He places one component of the army under his command and the other is so placed that it cannot offer resistance. He incorporates some of the fortresses (most importantly the sea ports), the others are so poorly staffed and supplied, that they cease to be of importance. Those steadfast people who are not acquiescent to France are released. The king surrounded with French authorities and troops, in a state of constant concern for freedom and honor, loses all ability to oppose the impending ruin. Assuming this characterization were exaggerated, and it were indeed possible to conclude an alliance with France on moderate terms, that is, terms under which one's own continued independence would be secured, the question arises, is the latter truly the case? Could that be the case? Are we settling for mere appearances, to deceive ourselves in order to justify our choosing the path of least resistance?

The question is easily answered once one considers that every alliance will necessarily absorb some of our energies, that we already doubt these energies are sufficient for defying the demands of France, and that we doubt even more our trussed, our paralyzed energies. Moreover, having once invested in a cause, nothing is more human than to make additional sacrifices in hopes of recovering the initial investment. It all depends on answering **candidly and honestly** the following questions:

Will the Prussian government, having once taken the first large step toward concluding the alliance with France, even assuming the conditions were this moderate and honorable, ever refuse a new demand, regardless of how oppressive and drastic?

Will one of those, who now advise the king to ally with France and claim only to have the well-being of the king and the nation at heart, then advise resistance?

Will we not then follow with inescapable certainty, one step after another, the road to ruin and end as Charles IV and his son?[13]

Oh those reckless advisors who now credit themselves with wise prudence, because they propose to the king the easy path, and denounce as lunatic those who demand resolve and a worthy sacrifice!

How will they show their embarrassed faces to the king, if overwhelmed with violence and disgrace, abandoned by his people, and forsaken by public

---

[13] In 1808 Napoleon forced Charles IV of Spain and his son Ferdinand VII to abdicate after they had changed sides several times and installed his brother, Joseph Bonaparte, as King Joseph I of Spain.

opinion, he is left standing alone like a sorry captive? How will they face their own consciences?

Hence the situation for the king, but what about the people?

Woe to those who would divide king and people in order to continuously set the interests of one against the other. Such malicious sophistry has only become fashionable so that they, by means of specious arguments, can evade the courageous decision that is demanded of us.

The honor of the prince had to give way to the interest of the nation; and the interest of the nation had to give way to the preservation of the princely house. Thus one was constantly turning in circles and playing with words. The king is the representative of his nation. The nation takes part involuntarily, even undeservedly, in everything he does, in whatever is admired about him, both today and in posterity. The king, who disgracefully decays, brings shame onto the nation and is responsible for her misfortune. The king, who gloriously perishes, exalts the nation and his exalted name is balsam for their wounds.

The people, whose king has lost honor and freedom, have with him lost them both. They will be in a state of internal dissolution and external oppression. They will feel their misery and have no hope of escaping therefrom, because they sense that they are themselves to blame; that too early they carelessly have given up everything. They will despise themselves, daily subjugate themselves ever deeper, elevate their enemy higher and thus with every passing day sink ever deeper into cowardly fear and subservience.

Thus will be the fate of a prince and a people, who surrender themselves—voluntarily and shackled—to their natural, their irreconcilable, their hereditary enemy, at the very moment they could have offered the final and brave resistance; when this was the primary duty that they owed themselves and others.

What would be the fate of this king and his people if, in the noble struggle, which they fought for one another, they emerged unlucky; the king expelled, the people enslaved?

Both would retain their honor, both their mutual affection and esteem!— Would this be nothing in such misfortune? Especially then, when everything is lost, would this noble sentiment be worth nothing? Should not the seed of a future rebirth there lie? Let everyone answer these questions with his own heart and mind!

If there is no external security in the alliance with France, if there is no other remedy for the internal malady than this resistance against France, then this resistance should be regarded as the last and only salvation.

This idea of resistance should be on everyone's mind, even if the heart does not abhor the present condition of subjugation.

From there should arise a clear determination to throw off the yoke.

This determination within the government and the people should lead to a preparation for the great moment of combat, through which alone this combat is made possible.

Thus prepared one should await calmly the appropriate moment.[†]

If this is the only truly political behavior that a people in our situation can observe, then we are so far away from it that we will have to go through a number of steps before we reach this point.

One surely wants to be freed of France's tyranny. One recognizes the benefits of this liberation but not the **necessity** thereof, which is a big difference.

One wishes to wait until chance does something for this great cause—by which one means the violent death of the Emperor Napoleon. Should this never come to pass, then one is prepared to wait for his natural death. Judging by the strength of his body, however, the Emperor could live another 30 years. Who, having carried that yoke for 30 years without murmur, would contest his heir the inheritance of his thus acquired and affirmed rights? Would not the same reservations set in? Is one certain that it will be a weak regent that follows him on the throne, and if he were weak, is there not the example of Rome, which survived its great dynasties by 400 years?

But the question remains whether this situation can last thirty years.

One can answer boldly: No. It is impossible. Sooner or later, out of necessity, a disquiet must and will emerge amongst the peoples that will lead to that evil, which one currently fears. The desire to avoid it forever is thus futile.

Indeed, and most irritating—if every superstitious belief of weak minds and souls were fulfilled, if finally the point arrived, where a child, a weakling, became Napoleon's successor, and all people awakened to action—what else would occur other than a general battle, an unbridled imbroglio of all, a bloody feud amongst the parties, a time filled with misery and despair!

Is it thus not unbelievable folly to hope that everyone will recover the peaceful enjoyment of their property and their independence without a stroke of the sword?

Must not everyone acknowledge that this crisis will be more awful than the current; this battle of disunited forces against a tenfold enemy, even more

---

[†] **Note:** At this moment, and as long as the war with Russia has not broken out, as regards the policies of the Prussian Cabinet, it depends more on a decision than on action. Nobody demands that Prussia should initiate an offensive against France. Nobody demands that Prussia suddenly refuses to fulfill the demands required by existing conditions. But one should not be persuaded to relinquish that power which is still present for its defense. It should boldly declare to France: that it values its independence above all else; that it will never accept being deprived of the means to preserve this independence; and that it could agree to no other alignment with France than one that would guarantee absolutely its own security. One can make such declarations only if one has made a **firm decision** to go down with a fight. Everything depends on this decision.

It is very unlikely that such language will accelerate a breach of the peace, as the Emperor Napoleon will not be so foolish as to regard such language to be more important than the issue: to allow Prussia to complete its armament and then to be dragged into war by mere words. Should it come to pass, however, one would reach the point but a few months earlier. Failing to see what is unavoidable is to concentrate the entire folly of our frivolous policy on a single point.

lamentable than the battle of all those tightly aligned by duty, revenge, hate, self-interest, against a **single** enemy that is recognized by **all**?

The current opinion and mood of the people cannot truly be a consequence of rational deliberation. Rather, it is fear of the coming misfortune and short-sighted self-interest.

One cowers for fear before the danger, before the sacrifices one will have to bear, above all, before the improbability of success, of which one is convinced, and so one believes one behaves wisely by evading these dangers.

It is correct, that the **odds** of success are against us, but under what political conditions would they not be against us? How could we expect that the odds are for us, given that for many decades mistake after mistake, fault after fault has amassed, and we now see all the consequences thereof cumulating in the misfortune of our times?

Our misfortune resides in our facing precipices wherever we turn. Under such circumstances how can one hope for a chance of serendipitous success? It is enough that it is not **impossible**; whoever asks for more contradicts himself.

It would be futile to try to conceal the recognition of those true sources of public opinion, for it is impossible to further the argument, which unduly claims to be the **considered judgment**, without landing between the starkest of contradictions.

From everywhere one hears the call that **reason alone shall decide**. As if fear were not an expression of emotion, as if an independent reasoned judgment were possible. All that one can admit is that both creeds, for resistance as for submission, emerge in equal measure from emotions; but that one emotion is courage, the other is fear. Fear paralyzes reason, courage animates it.

These few general observations must lead to the conviction that however our situation may appear, the decision to gain our independence is indispensable. The formidable weight of current circumstances forces this decision upon us. It would be folly and weakness to try to avoid this pressure, which then with greater certainty would destroy us.

This truth requires no further evidence; it is not a function of whether we have more or less means for rescue. The resolve should emerge from the necessity of rescue, not from the ease of the same. There is no help apart from ourselves. There is no salvation apart from that which is found in our strength, in our reason and in our hearts.

Should a consideration of our political situation lead us to the decision to risk everything for our salvation and to regard this battle as indispensable, then an unbiased assessment of our available resources must reinvigorate our courage and cast away our faintheartedness, to which fears of a great danger and hopelessness have given rise.

We are rich in resources. Our situation is not desperate. Such is the conclusion of anyone, who, free of preconceived opinion, casts the eye of mature judgment on these circumstances. But the artisan spirit has cloistered this judgment behind a bulwark of false views, rules, maxims, and prejudices, so that only he who comes from the guild attempts to develop his own opinion.

In this spirit I add my third confession, in which I discuss our current status, as it appears from a military point of view.

THIRD CONFESSION

The resources of the Prussian state are:

People in General

A population of 4,600,000 people. Thereof comprise men

between 18 and 30 years of age		450,000
between 30 and 40 " " "		300,000
	Sum	750,000

This is a weapons-capable crew. If from them an army of 100,000 men were raised for a few years it certainly would not lead to the domestic ruin of the state. That is only one in 7 and if we include the elderly only one in 10 adult men.

100,000 men could be provided by the state without disrupting the usual social fabric.

Officers

The entire officer corps, which for the Prussian army once numbered 210,000 men, with the exception of roughly 1/5, is still available. If we are to commission officers experienced in service and the code of conduct, we can do so without difficulty. Otherwise we will produce officers the way we produce soldiers; that is, by selecting from the entire population those citizens who are suitable.

Weapons

Prussia has more than 120,000 ready firearms. Partly in the hands of the troops, partly in the depots.

Following the common ratio, these can be used to arm 160,000 combatants.

At any time and at reasonable price the state can purchase twenty to thirty thousand guns from Vienna. England is prepared at a moment's notice to set sail entire shiploads (fifty- to sixty-thousand armatures) for Prussia's needs. They are already mooring in the Baltic Sea, and the mere possibility that Prussia might once again take up the issue of its independence and honor has led the English government to offer these to Prussia's disposition.

Cannons

Prussia itself has a field artillery sufficient for 80,000 men following the common ratio. It has supplied all of its fortresses with artillery, following the same axioms according to which the French fortresses once were supplied.

England has shipped 30 to 40 artillery in case Prussia takes sides against France.

Thus without affecting the artillery for the fortresses, Prussia can equip an army of 100,000 field soldiers.

Munition

As with artillery, Prussia has supplied its fortresses with munition. In addition, the necessary munition for the entire campaign of an army of 100,000 men is in place. Much as England has offered generous support with regard to guns and artillery, it will not hesitate to send munition in superabundance; and since we ourselves have the essentials, we can regard as superabundant the extensive support that we can have at any moment.

Horses

In the entire Prussian state, according to the official registers, 725,000 horses are available. The actual number is probably closer to one million. Of those, 624,000 are on the right bank of the Oder and in Silesia. Is it not foolish to believe that there could be a shortage of horses? Yes, to muster one of 15 horses would amount to 40,000 horses just for the right bank of the Oder and for Silesia, which is more than an army of 100,000 men requires.

It would be a weak objection to assert that those horses were unfit for service in the cavalry. For one, Prussia already has a 10,000 man cavalry, which in any case is sufficient for its situation, since the infantry and not the cavalry is the main weapon in any war, especially in a war of defense. Second, if needed, every healthy horse that is not too old can be used for the cavalry.

Clothing

This is an issue that does not merit mention in such a general analysis. None of the 750,000 men is running around naked and the form of clothing is not important. Strictly speaking, there is hardly any urgency. Moreover, in a state such as Prussia, which has so many mills for raw fabric, the demand can be satisfied very quickly and under all circumstances.

Sure enough, packs, ammunition pockets, and boots seem to some of our generals to be so essential, that one cannot wage war without them. But the nature of circumstances sufficiently reveals this pedantry.

Foodstuffs

The Prussian fortresses are sufficiently, even over-supplied with all necessary items. Others have stores nearby, readily available at a moment's notice.

The field soldiers will not suffer from lack of foodstuffs as long as the enemy is fed. If food ever becomes a limiting condition for warfare, then this limitation must affect the French before us. In any case the entire argument is folly. The army lives as well now in the countryside as it would in the event of war, and the diminished production caused by war, will, as history teaches, be compensated with foreign imports.

Money

Formerly money was the nerve of war. This is no longer the case. Guibert[14] said prophetically:

> Assuming that in Europe a people arises, powerful through genius, potent means, and a good government, a people that combines with the strictest virtues and a good national militia a coherent plan of expansion, and never loses sight of this plan, a people that knew how to wage war with limited means and preserve itself through victory, and was not forced to lay down its arms because of lack of finances; such a people would subjugate its neighbors and destroy our weak constitution, much as the North wind blows the weak reed back and forth as it wishes.

This people has indeed existed, although armed with only half the attributes, with potent means and a good national militia, without virtue and a good government (France). This people courageously resisted as it was attacked

---

[14] Jacques-Antoine-Hippolyte, Comte de Guibert (1743–90), French general and military writer.

from all sides, became itself a conqueror, and cast aside the old weak constitutions. It was able to do so without money, for France had no treasure and twice has declared national bankruptcy.

Why can't we do the same? For what do we need money? To pay the army? The army must be fed, but doesn't need high pay. The state can provide what little is essential, which it would also have to provide in time of peace.

An army that fights on its own soil for its most vital interest cannot and must not be regarded as a bunch of mercenaries, who sell themselves to the highest bidder. The spirit of this army should be guided by the strongest renunciation of all luxury and affluence. Then the high salaries, which one believes reward the higher ranks for long service and retain talent, are not necessary. Fighting for the fatherland is the highest reward for service, the strongest attraction for talent. England will supply us with arms and munition, insofar as replacing spent material is of concern. It is unreasonable to call this into doubt, as England, not only now but also in the last war, has demonstrated a willingness to do so.

We thus should not look with greed upon Britain's treasures, uncertain whether millions in hard cash, which we have not earned, will flow from a minister's generosity. What does our freedom have to do with England's money? Should England purchase from us the courage necessary to achieve this freedom? No, once Guibert's prophecy has come true, the time will not return in which conceited money is the nerve of war and the nations. The history of our times demonstrates to us that the most forceful war can be waged with little money; but only with a great deal of courage and good will.

The Time

It is a common opinion, that France would not be so foolish as to leave Prussia much time for significant rearming; that the first steps in this direction would bring the French army, which would nip all such measures in the bud. Disorder, flight, and losses of all kinds would be the consequence, and the ruin would be just as inglorious as without any resistance.

This opinion holds up to scrutiny as poorly as many other dismal ideas.

The assumption that we must repeat the same mistake we have already made is an unworthy philosophy to which no one is entitled.

In fact, Prussia is now ten times as well prepared for war as in 1806, when nothing happened but the issuance of the so-called (laughable in our times) mobilization budgets. Everything has not been accomplished. Nevertheless, as was already pointed out, the most necessary has not been neglected.

Those measures that require time already have been taken. The fortifications (the most important of these measures) are ready to accommodate the, as of yet not fully organized, armed forces; the weapons-, clothing-, and munitions-depots are secured; the troops, by and large suitably deployed, already organized for war during the peace.

Under these conditions only two issues need to be settled.

First, the mustering of the men necessary to reinforce the army. This measure can be prepared so that it can be carried out in eight days. In eight days, however, the enemy is not likely to have advanced far into the country: At most one would lose those districts adjacent to him.

Second, the organization and training of the mustered troops. If necessary, this can be done in the fortified camps.

Thus we have reviewed those issues, which constitute the subject of war. We have seen that Prussia has everything in abundance for an army of 100,000 men. It thus follows directly, that with a little exertion, an army of 150,000 men can be raised.

Now we ask whether any of those assertions and the inferences we have drawn from them are exaggerated?

Any allegation of this sort would at once reveal itself as malicious intent and spiteful obstinacy.

After we have reached this conclusion, we wish to proceed to the analysis of the military situation and character of the Prussian state.

Under the current circumstances, the geographic position of the Prussian state, so ill reputed, is much more beneficial than detrimental.

The fact that the capital city is forwardly positioned and would have to be surrendered quickly, that an entire province, the *Kurmark*,[15] cannot be defended, is problematic, but not of highest priority. All the less so, as neither Berlin nor the *Kurmark* provide any extraordinary sources of help.

The benefits include a right flank that is covered by the sea to the outermost point of the Memel with three seaports (Memel, Pillau, Kolberg) for the link to England; the separation of Silesia from the remaining states, by which one gains a theater of war on the enemy's right flank; the alignment of this province with Austria and the position of the two poorest provinces (*Neumark* and Pomerania) in the middle of the theater of war, so that the enemy must extract his resources from them, while for the Prussian troops, the richest provinces of Lithuania, East Prussia, and Silesia remain.

The Prussian fortifications are tied precisely to these advantages.

Prussia has 8 fortifications manned by her troops in

Pillau, Kolberg, Graudenz in Prussia.
Glatz, Neisse, Silberberg, and **Cosel** in Silesia.
Spandau near **Berlin.**

---

[15] Western core region of Brandenburg.

The majority of these fortifications are amongst the strongest in the world. All are well maintained and supplied with every necessity.

Amongst these fortifications number the fortified camps of **Kolberg, Pillau, Neisse,** and **Glatz.**

There is space for 100 thousand men in these eight fortresses and three fortified camps; they therefore are invincible to every violent attack. These fortifications and camps can be defended adequately by 40 thousand men.

What then is to be feared under such circumstances, provided one does not reckon with extraordinary means?

Can Prussia lose her 8 fortresses with one stroke of the sword?

Are the examples of 1805, 1806, and 1809 applicable to Prussia?

Anyone who does not answer these questions with no must be out of his mind.

Assume that Prussia were to suffer the misfortune of being attacked with the full force of France before the war with Russia breaks out, because the Emperor **Napoleon** sought revenge for Prussia's rearmament on the spot.

Then the army would rush into the fortresses and fortified camps. All that the government would have to do is to name eight resolute commanders, and itself escape from hostile violence.

Finding these eight commanders is held by many to be an insurmountable difficulty. But this is a misjudgment. Amongst so many officers, the king will surely find eight, who combine resolve and insight. You don't have to be a Julius Caesar or Gustavus Adolphus to command a fortress or fortified camp. Even if with regard to his insights one of these commanders were to fall short of expectations, no great harm would result, as long as one had not erred with regard to his resolve; and that would be the government's own fault. Furthermore, it is mere hearsay, a simple prejudice, if one argues that 5 million people are not intelligent enough to produce extraordinary men for extraordinary ends. As long as the governments decide to create extraordinary men, even the smallest nation will not fail, for a hundred men tend to go down in dust before a single man overcomes the difficulties and hurdles that society has placed before him. France, over the course of the Seven Years' War,[16] had a shortage of first-rate generals such that one might come to believe that nature no longer begets Condés, Turennes, and Luxemburgs. In the Revolutionary War,[17] the French army was suddenly just as rich in excellent generals as was any other army. One could say much more, but these pathetic and truly absurd prejudices are not worthy of further rebuttal.

[16] The Seven Years' War, which actually lasted nine years, took place from 1754 to 1763 and involved all of the major European powers of the period.

[17] The Revolutionary War took place from 1792 to 1802 and pitted the French First Republic against several European monarchies.

How much more difficult it would be for the government to find, instead of those 8 commanders, one man, who combines the great qualities of a Commander-in-Chief (*OberFeldherr*), genius, knowledge of war, initiative, and constancy, in a serene greatness, and thereby unifies the tact of a gentleman and the energy of a Czar Peter. Indeed, one must regard it as impossible for the government to overcome its hesitation to place its entire trust in the hands of one man and to confer in him the highest authority. The daily history of our state has recognized no service, or exalted it high enough, such that it could be guarded from envy and defamation. No one could achieve so much for the state that his deeds could compel trust and respect. In order for a government to select among the more deserving the one man on whom it wishes to confer the highest authority, a self-confidence, achieved by means of open deliberation, is necessary. This, I must admit, is difficult to expect from the Prussian government, given the extreme consideration and little augustness with which the government proceeds in the appointment of its civil servants.

But precisely in this respect, it is a great advantage of our current situation that we do not need a Commander-in-Chief. And if, in the eight fortresses, men of resolve and ambition have the command, then the entire effect emerges by itself, without demanding the degree of conformity in measures and precision in the execution of orders that is necessary in every other war, but which we can hardly expect. This is not to say that one should not appoint a Commander-in-Chief in the various provinces, and that he would not be able to employ the armed forces with a certain coherence, but rather it merely follows that if those higher requirements of military organization are not fulfilled, nothing **essential** to the effect would be lost, and thus large setbacks are in no way to be feared.

This is a more decisive advantage than one might believe, because herein lies the main source of every skepticism that the people have in the government, and which, in turn, can be regarded as one of the main reasons for the widespread despondency.

We come back to our question: What could the enemy accomplish against these fortresses? To lay siege to them. Albeit France cannot lay siege to all 8 fortresses at·the same time, and there has never in history been an example of 8 well-defended sites being taken in one campaign. In addition, it can be evinced that in this case it is impossible. Indeed, more than one campaign will be necessary. It will require the sacrifice of 40 to 50 thousand men in order to conquer these 8 fortresses.

We cannot expect a better result. It is highly unlikely that Russia and Austria would allow the fall of 8 fortresses without starting the war against France. The political constellations of today allow such expectations.

So Prussia will not stand alone; not fall alone. It will be a strong rampart for its natural allies. It will cost the common enemy a considerable amount of time and blood and through its significant weight give the entire war a different direction.

It might be that the Russian army will be defeated; that Prussia's fortresses will fall after honorable resistance; that Austria remains neutral; that Russia abandons Prussia for the next peace. But all conceivable misfortunes are not **probable**, and we have already discussed elsewhere how little we should be deterred in the event they were indeed likely. In any event, one must admit that this impact of Prussia is more important than in the years 1806 and 1807, that the successes were seldom, perhaps even never, a matter of chance, and that one can boldly march into the decisive days of the future without demanding too much greatness from the government.

This is the result of the foregoing deliberations, if we leave things as simple as possible, and do not assume a greater exertion of energy, be it physical or intellectual. —

Without a doubt, however, one can imagine several degrees of higher potency, without approaching the border of impossibility.

First, in addition to the aforementioned straightforward analysis of Prussia's war preparedness, we can assume that in the most likely case, Russia will decide for war at the very moment in which Prussia is handled in a hostile manner by France. Thereupon, the Prussian troops do not need to seek shelter behind the walls of their fortified camps and fortresses. One no longer needs to fear that the army will be defeated and dispersed by a disproportionately superior enemy army.

Hence, in this case, while dispatching a corps of 30,000 men to the Russian army, Prussia can arrive on the scene as strongly in Silesia and with 20,000 men in Kolberg. The sum of 80,000 men will engage an equal number of enemy troops and thereby assure the Russian army a decisive predominance. For, without engaging in a debate about the opposing forces, which at this time in many respects would be very difficult, we can infer a more general and reliable measure of their relative strength from the wars of 1807 and 1809. The French did not significantly outnumber the Russians and by no means matched the Austrians in number. There is no reason why the French should now appear with far greater forces. Rather, one can imagine that the Russians will begin the campaign of 1812 better prepared than that of 1806. All reports justify this conclusion. If one thereby considers that the battles of Eylau, Friedland, Aspern, and Wagram were fought with armies of far fewer than 100,000 men, then the advantages offered the Russia armies by 80,000 Prussians in the field and 20,000 in the fortresses becomes apparent.

Under these circumstances the form of the Prussian theater of war is of decisive importance. Silesia lies on the right flank of the French operations. A decisive defeat of their corps in Silesia can call back the main army from the river Weichsel, or in any case will cripple their operation. With its four fortresses and mountain range, and its abundance of resources, Silesia is itself difficult to conquer; and without applying a decisive preponderance in Silesia, which would deprive the main army's operations of necessary power, France has no hope of conquering Silesia before Russia itself.

Kolberg, nearer to theater of war of the main armies on their left flank, strengthened by its link to England, will play a no less important role.

That these flank operations are of greater importance than a direct resistance and assault is an established truth, without thereby conceding the childishness of Herr v. Bülow[18] to be military wisdom. Whoever doubts this greater effectiveness lacks not only a clear conception of war, but also the judgment of common sense.

To completely discard these estimates of probability, which are based on physical advantages, in order to subordinate everything to the French advantage in morale, is a completely unreasonable view. War consists of the application of physical strength and morale; we could ignore the degree of one and yet hope to achieve the desired end result. Regardless of how superior the French morale may be, the aforementioned physical advantages will always animate our hopes.

With regard to the advantage in morale, we will have the opportunity to discuss this in more detail below.

The heretofore mentioned means exist under normal circumstances. Considering the shortness of time, they require no extraordinary efforts that might lead us to doubt that we could expect them from an undistinguished government.

One need not even count on great enthusiasm amongst the people. Everything will occur in standard fashion as required by the mediocre and narrow-minded. —

What then are the real sources of the accusations of exaggeration, gullibility, eccentricity, and carelessness, which one has spread behind the backs of those who believed in the possibility of resistance? Only ill will and a lack of insight can explain it. Whoever continues in this manner, after all that we said here, is such a pitiful person, that he should be ashamed of himself.

It is not impossible to suspend for a time the usual conditions; history teaches it. A nation is not ruined because it accepts for one or two years exertions that would be impossible to endure for ten or twenty years. If, however, the importance of the end requires and demands it, if we are speaking of the preservation of independence and honor, these exertions become a duty, and the government, which otherwise has the means to compel the people to fulfill its duties, can expect, demand, and coerce such exertions from them. This is how one behaves if one is strong, resolute, and able to conduct one's own affairs.

---

[18] Dietrich Adam Heinrich von Bülow (1757–1807), military writer, whose ideas Clausewitz had criticized publicly in 1805.

The exertions of which we are speaking consist of:

1st a considerable expansion of the army.
2nd the establishment of a *Landwehr* or of a *Landsturm*.[19]

The possibility of expanding the army to 150,000–200,000 men proceeds from the information above. There is no lack of the necessary *matériel*, if we give our utmost to achieve it. Through the most concerted action in the negotiations with England, through a firm indissoluble life and death alliance with this state, we could expect from this nation support, which would be adequate to our exceptional needs or even surpass them. The position and wealth of England, the truly noble disposition of this nation and of its government, confirm this in a way something in the political world never before has been confirmed.

Lacking time for its organization, one probably could not lead an army expanded in such a way against the enemy immediately. Nevertheless, it would be a decisive advantage in the event of a loss of a large number of the provinces, which the Prussian state would suffer at the outbreak of war, to be able to deploy disproportionately strong reserves behind the active army.

Wartime experience teaches that the rapid reinforcement of the army is of decisive advantage, because most armies are robbed of a third to a half of their men in action in the course of the campaign. Regardless of how well the French have organized their system of reinforcement, because they are unable to start conscription before January 1st, and their reserves must be positioned in the middle of their enormous warring state far removed from the northern theater of war, their reinforcement can be only as rapid as that of the Prussians, which is made possible through such a reserve. Toward the end of the campaign, the Prussian field army would have increased from 80,000 to 100,000 men. The corresponding number of French troops would have decreased from 80,000 to 60,000 men. The importance of this advantage can be appreciated only by those who have read many war histories.

Finally, we come to the *Landwehr* or to the *Landsturm*.

The first characteristic, if it is to be that which it was for the Austrians in 1809[20]—namely, a rich source for reinforcing the army and a defensive militia for remote spots of the war theater—seems to be inappropriate for our

[19] In German-speaking countries, the concepts of *Landwehr* and *Landsturm* were used in various ways for more or less regular militia or guerrilla forces. In Prussia, a *Landwehr* was finally formed by royal edict on March 17, 1813. It called all men between 17 and 40 years of age, capable of bearing arms and not serving in the regular army, to defend the country as part of a militia. On April 21, 1813 another edict made all men between 15 and 60, not serving in the regular forces or the *Landwehr*, members of the last national military reserve, the *Landsturm*.

[20] Clausewitz refers to various battles the Austrian army fought in alliance with the Tyrolean militia under the leadership of Andreas Hofer against Napoleon's forces.

situation, because a large number of our provinces will be cut off from the army.

Every general arming of the entire population for the immediate defense of a country can be called *Landsturm*.

Thus was the *Landsturm* in Tyrol.

Very few people have a clear understanding of the full extent of this fearsome, decisive measure, which throws the country into a state of dangerous crisis. They do not understand how individual citizens or communities, united into loose bands, can possess the daring courage to resist a large army or even just to enrage it through inflicting losses on its distant units.

The basic idea is the following. Every able-bodied man from 18 to 60 years, who does not serve in the standing forces, is armed and belongs to the *Landsturm*. Their arms and equipment include nothing more than a musket, if unavailable a pike or a scythe, a pack to carry a few days' worth of foodstuffs and some munition, a cap, outfitted with a straw wreath to protect against blows and on which a sign of the province and the commune is affixed.

This outfitting certainly does not demand too much. The farmers in the Vendée[21] have equipped themselves without any external support even more completely. (See Chambeau, *Geschichte des Vendeekrieges*.)[22]

Two to three communities come together and create a band or a company, however you wish to refer to it. The bands of a county constitute a column or a *Landsturm* and the *Landsturm* of an entire province a small army. At the head of this division stand leaders, who in large part are elected for and from the communities and counties, or are appointed by the king. The commander of the entire *Landsturm* of the province (*Landeshauptmann*) will be selected from the provincial population by the king. From the moment in which they assume their position, all these superiors of the *Landsturm* are official officers of the army.

This, in a few words, is the general outline of the organization. To achieve it, little time and preparation are required.

The task of the *Landsturm* is to mobilize quickly large numbers of troops everywhere in the country where the enemy **does not have his armies**. Even if they do not have the effect of standing armies, they can achieve the following objectives. **First:** To prevent deliveries and contributions of all kinds, which the enemy in far-off provinces extorts through means of tender or mere civil servants. **Second:** To fight enemy detachments, which show up in the province

---

[21] The war in the Vendée was a royalist insurrection against French revolutionary forces in western France from 1793 to 1796. Starting as peasant rebellion it quickly gathered counter-revolutionary momentum. After initial successes, the insurgency was finally defeated with utmost brutality by Republican forces.

[22] Clausewitz apparently erred when penning this parenthetical note. Werner Hahlweg (1966–90: vol. 1, 721, n. 134) suggests that rather than to someone named Chambeau the reference is to Alphonse Beauchamp (1806).

for similar reasons. **Third:** To secure the *matériel* that their own government wants to extract from the country, especially men and horses.

All of these objectives can be achieved with columns of one to two thousand men without extraordinary exertions and means of assistance.

The ringing of storm bells is the sign that the *Landsturm* of a village or county is to assemble. Assembly grounds are previously determined. Within a few hours, 2, 3, 5 thousand men are assembled where previously there was no hint of a war.

These are no flights of fancy. In the Vendée it happened so and exactly so; the practicality of a measure never was founded better historically.

If the enemy does not want to accept these disadvantages, if he wants to continue to rule all the distant provinces, he must maintain specific corps therein. It is easy to see that if, from an army of 200,000 men, 50,000 men are used for this purpose, this would already create a significant diversion in the central theater of war, for one must not forget that from the remaining 150,000 men, according to all historical experience, another 50,000 will be absent, either in the sick bay or left behind as occupying forces. Thus, the *Landsturm* deprives the main theater of war of 1/3 of its armed forces according to simple calculations. Whoever is not able to appreciate this great advantage is lacking in good judgment in this matter. For he knows nothing of how things develop in war.

But what can 50,000 men achieve against an armed mass of 500,000?

It is a matter of course that in a single district, where with 5000 inhabitants one is lord of the land, the enemy can only deploy 500 soldiers. One would have to have a ridiculous regard for saber, ammunition pocket, and lower tactics, if one were to fear that one could not master the enemy with a tenfold advantage. In this way, the enemy would hardly achieve its goal.

The enemy, therefore, will have to resolve himself to enter into a formal war with the *Landsturm*. In doing so, he generally will have to sacrifice a great deal of time and energy. Therefore, the true end of defense will be achieved, and this measure will not be futile; this much is entirely clear.

Of course there are some people who are not content with such an account and although they themselves do everything with common means, nevertheless wish to be certain of the most uncommon. They are not to be contented until one has proven with mathematical certainty that the destruction of the enemy army is at hand. This laughable demand was not met by the Romans at the height of their power and even less by the Greeks, as they fought against the Persians for their freedom.

We do not want to content ourselves with that general result, but rather to examine more closely the kind of war that will emerge between the *Landsturm* and the enemy army; remaining true to what we have already experienced in order not to be seduced by wishful thinking and false hopes.

To become more precise and to speak with more clarity, we wish to introduce an example and with it attempt to make clear our ideas. Therefore, we choose the example of a *Landsturm* employed against the French in the Mittelmark,[23] because sadly it is only too certain that the government, which does not have the courage to reach for this last means of rescue, is even less likely to employ it in a province that is so close to the enemy that it is almost too late for it.

Example of a *Landsturm* in the Mittelmark

Organization in General

The Mittelmark has 10 counties; every county establishes a *Landsturm* under the *Landsturm Obersten*.[24] All are subordinated to a *Landeshauptmann*.

1. The County Assembly Ground Ruppin

With 43 thousand souls can provide 7–8000 men.

Should the enemy advance into the province with might, the *Landsturm* withdraws either into the faults of Havelland County or into the woods in the north of Ruppin County itself.

2. The Havelland County

Assembly Ground the Island of Potsdam and Rathenow:

With 90,000 souls can provide 10–15,000 men.

Should the enemy appear with overwhelming force in the province, the Island of Potsdam will be defended; the other part withdraws into the Havelland fault.

3. The Counties Glien and Löwenbergsch

Population 13,000 people, can provide 2–3000 men.

Assembly Ground Cremmen.

It is unlikely that the enemy, regardless of the number of directions from which he advances into the Mittelmark, will appear strongly in this county, which lies out of the way of the direction of his march. The *Landsturm* there will thus be able to support the remaining counties.

4. The Niederbarmisch County

Assembly Grounds Berlin and Liebenwalde

A population of 190,000 including Berlin, and 30,000 excluding Berlin, results in a *Landsturm* of 10–15,000 men.

---

[23] Mittelmark refers to the core territory of the Margraviate of Brandenburg between the Oder and Elbe rivers.

[24] Clausewitz alternates between the terms *Obristen*, *Oberst*, and *Obersten*, all indicating the highest rank of a staff officer (e.g. Colonel).

Should the enemy appear with predominance in the county, the Berlin *Landsturm* withdraws to Spandau and the Island of Potsdam; that from the Liebenwalde withdraws to the woods and swamps.

5. The County of Upper-Barnim

Assembly Grounds Strausberg, Neustadt, Eberswalde

With a population of 40,000 souls can provide 7000 men. Should the enemy appear with predominance in the province, the woods along the Spree and in the north of the county provide security.

6. The County of Lebus

Assembly Grounds Fürstenwalde, Seelow

With 50 thousand souls can provide a *Landsturm* of 9000 men. Should the enemy appear with preponderance, it withdraws to the woods along the Spree.

7. The Counties of Beeskow and Storkow

Assembly Grounds Beeskow and Storkow
  With a population of 25,000 men, can provide 4000 men.
  The many woods and lakes provide sufficient security against a superior enemy.

8. The County of Teltow

Assembly Grounds Teltow and Zossen

With a population of 30 thousand souls can provide a *Landsturm* of 5000 men.
  The Island Köpenick and a number of other locations in this county rich with lakes and faults provide means to secure against a superior enemy.

9. The County of Luckenwalde

Assembly Ground Luckenwalde

Population 12,000. *Landsturm* 2500.
  If a superior enemy appears in the county, withdraws into the County of Teltow.

10. The County of Zauch

Assembly Ground Brandenburg

With 30,000 souls a *Landsturm* of 6000 men.
  Will find in the area of Plauen, and in addition on the Island of Potsdam, positions of security.
  With regard to the enemy, because every possibility cannot be considered, we will assume the following:
  He decamps with columns from Magdeburg, from Mecklenburg and the Lausitz, in order to unite with the corps from Stettin and Danzig and to deploy an army against the Russians, while a strong corps is deployed for the siege of Kolberg and another for Silesia. The enemy is aware of the arming of the

Landsturm in the Mark Brandenburg; he has decided first to destroy this general armament with his entire massed troops before he moves into Prussia, etc., so he wants to proceed carefully and secure his rear.

Thus, the troops from Mecklenburg receive orders, while marching with the main army against Stettin, to direct a corps (10–12,000 men) toward Berlin. 30,000 men are marching toward Berlin from Magdeburg, another 10,000 Saxons are marching toward Berlin. All of these diverse columns should fight and destroy any element of the *Landsturm* which crosses their path. After they unite in Berlin one shall detach strong corps to those regions, in which remnants of the *Landsturm* remain, in order to search out, to fight, and to destroy them. At the same time, the remaining troops besiege Spandau, to contain the capital city and to secure the route through Berlin and Frankfurt[25] for the follow-on troops.

We first observe the amount of time gained by the Russians and other powers through this mode of advancement, an effect of the *Landsturm*, which is by no means insignificant and which will never fail, even if everything else develops badly.

In view of these and other assumptions regarding the enemy, the following general provisions for the *Landsturm* are provided.

Instruction for the *Landsturm*

1. Every healthy man between 18 and 60 years of age is obliged at the ringing of the storm bell to assemble with arms in the community. Whoever avoids this will be subject to corporal punishment and fine.

2. The storm bell will be rung as soon as the enemy appears in the province or if the *Landsturm* of a neighboring province has assembled.

3. The *Landsturm Obristen* will decide on the assembly grounds.

4. They have complete freedom to do with the *Landsturm* of their county what they deem to be appropriate. They must only carry out an order if they receive it from the *Landeshauptmann*.

5. The task of the individual *Landsturm* bands is to attack with superior numbers weak parties and enemy posts, to take away and disperse supplies, etc.

6. The *Landsturm* band will retreat from a superior enemy; it will certainly avoid proximity to the great army.

---

[25] Clausewitz refers to Frankfurt on the Oder roughly 100 km east of Berlin.

7. If the enemy is not in the county, the *Landsturm Oberst* is required to rush to the assistance of the *Landsturm* of a neighboring county—**which one**, is left to him.

8. If the enemy endangers a *Landsturm* too much and there is no room for retreat, the *Landsturm Oberst* is permitted to disband it. The same applies if there is a grave shortage of foodstuffs. Nevertheless, a *Landsturm Oberst* should maintain a small group of determined individuals with whom he can dart into a neighboring province or rove about. A *Landsturm Oberst*, who cannot maintain any, is dismissed. Someone else is to be appointed in his place.

9. When attacking the enemy, one of the primary objectives is to seize artillery, mainly cannons, munition, foodstuffs, and from dead soldiers—money, and to equip oneself therewith. Prisoners can even be taken and sent to the rear as far back as space allows, where they are guarded in walled cities. In the event of disbandment, and if there is no opportunity to hand over the captives somewhere, they are to be set free.

10. The attacks occur mainly at night and it is essential for the *Landsturm* to determine a location for reassembly in case something goes wrong.

11. One or two positions, which are strong enough to be well defended, will be fortified in each province. The choice is left to the *Landsturm Oberst*, as is the decision whether or not to retreat to them.

12. The *Landeshauptmann* confines himself to locations where he is not in danger. He has the following responsibilities:

    1. to oversee the activities of the *Landsturm Obersten*,

    2. to meet the needs of the *Landsturm* as much as possible,

    3. in exceptional cases to unite the *Landsturm* of multiple counties in order to carry out large ventures. Yet, he leaves as much freedom of action to the *Landsturm Obersten* as possible.

The storm bell is rung as soon as the enemy advances. The *Landsturm* of every county assemble. Where they encounter enemy columns they withdraw a significant distance laterally into the woods without engaging in battle.

As soon as the bulk of the enemy columns has passed through, the *Landsturm* attacks the detachments and the wagon trains that follow, disperses them wherever possible, and withdraws as soon as the enemy returns with considerable force.

In this way the march of the columns toward the *rendezvous* in Berlin is impeded and the enemy soldiers receive a foretaste and preview of that which is to come: a Spanish civil war in Germany.

As soon as all columns have arrived in Berlin the actual defense plan is activated.

Depending on what previously, through thorough consideration, has been determined useful, Spandau—either alone, or Spandau and the Island of Potsdam—will be defended most tenaciously by the regular troops and *Landsturm* located there. On the Island of Potsdam one eventually would be defeated, but not without considerable enemy casualties. Spandau will not fall so quickly.

While this is happening near the capital city, the *Landsturm Obersten* attack those positions, which the enemy has left occupied in the rear, and where he can be attacked with superior force; for example Burg, Genthin, Fehrbellin etc.

In the vicinity of the army one is careful not to be seen. Because the *Landsturm* was not destroyed through the march of the individual columns, as indeed it could not have been, the enemy dispatches corps to attack individual counties.

How many such corps he will dispatch cannot be surmised, and is more or less irrelevant.

12,000 men have been ordered to advance into Havelland County. They march through Fehrbellin. Here, the *Landsturm* offers resistance. The defense of a dam with the length of 3000 paces is not difficult. The enemy circumvents the position and sends a strong column via Friesack. Here too, a strong defense is possible. But a new misfortune occurs. The enemy has decided to march simultaneously from Magdeburg against Habelberg, such that one would be attacked in the rear. One thing comes to another. The *Landsturm* of Havelland County withdraws into the woods of the northern county of Ruppin, unites with the *Landsturm* of this county and hopes to attack and defeat the enemy detachments with superior force in a territory that is to them unknown and unfavorable.

But the enemy corps is cautious; it realizes that it has 2 ways of dispersing the *Landsturm*.

The first is to assume a position between Fehrbellin and Ruppin, but to avoid sending detachments into the wooded areas where they inevitably would be destroyed. The enemy corps controls the fertile Havelland County and the best part of the County of Ruppin. The *Landsturm*, having been displaced from this area, is restricted to an arid region, poor of produce. It will be lacking in foodstuffs and far from home, will not remain together for long. The majority will disband of itself.

The second way is for the corps itself to advance methodically and carefully into the wooded areas, to pass through them while attacking and beating anything they encounter on their way and to drive to the Prignitz whatever is left of the *Landsturm*, namely that which has not disbanded itself or been captured. Assuming that success bears out these considerations and one of the two operational plans is carried out; then the enemy corps would assume position near Ruppin, occupy the northern areas through strong detachments, and hunt for anything that continues to appear in single squads of *Landsturm*.

Now an article appears in the newspapers, reporting that Havelland and the County of Ruppin are pacified. One would have to admit that we have not demanded of the *Landsturm* a miracle. Nonetheless, 4 weeks might pass before we arrive at this point. We have, for example, said nothing regarding the possibility, in the event foodstuffs were lacking, of withdrawing with the *Landsturm* beyond Lake Ruppin and the Bog of Kremmen, where one can find a fairly fertile area and sustain oneself for a long time; and nothing of the possibility of crossing the river Havel into the region of Magdeburg and even under these circumstances of maintaining a considerable corps—10,000–12,000 men.

We have admitted that little by little the *Landsturm* disbands, and the main leaders, with but a few committed men, withdraw into other provinces or rove about.

What is to happen next? First we ask, where have the *Landsturm* gone?

The true answer is: they are sitting calmly at home. For even if a good number of them are captured (although in relation to the whole this can only be a small part), it is nevertheless unlikely that many of them will be sent to France. The difficulties of transporting large numbers of prisoners are insurmountable. Of 150 thousand Prussians, which according to French accounts and according to the *Etats* of the Prussians themselves were said to have been captured in 1806, less than 20,000 were actually confined in France!

If the enemy corps remains in the County of Ruppin, it will, little by little, establish positions to secure its lines of communication, for the procurement of *matériel*, and to rule the country. But it is not that easy to control a country where everything directed against us enrages and leads to the idea of resistance. The inhabitants will recover from their initial fright. The enemies will enrage them through individual repressions and cruelties. One or the other will see that the affair is not so dangerous, that one can play a role in it. Some of those not yet disbanded bands will give cause. The storm bell will ring in some district; a *Landsturm* will reconstitute itself anew. One will raid individual weak posts, inflict considerable losses on them, cut off deliveries, capture money and munition and retreat from stronger detachments. In this way the enemy corps will have to overcome the most difficult defense and will lose strength daily in this most unfortunate of all wars.

Perhaps at the moment in which the enemy sustains itself with difficulty, encouraged by this example of national struggle, the whole of Northern Germany resorts to arms, so that in Hesse and Westphalia the enemy already is running out of those recruits, munition, weapons, foodstuffs, money, and intelligence, which one attempts to cut off in the *Mark*.

But can the enemy corps remain here?

Can the enemy patrol 70 square miles with 12,000 men, whereas the Prussian state comprises 2500 square miles of surface, of which those 70 miles thus are barely one 35th?

And are not the enemy armed forces primarily directed against an enemy of a different sort, against the standing armies?

What will the enemy be able to leave behind in the entire Mittelmark?

Maybe one division of 10–12,000 men. Can one division besiege Spandau and in addition keep the *Landsturm* of P[otsdam] County in check?

But assuming that Spandau has been conquered by a larger force, can one division keep Berlin, and in addition to Berlin, 250 square miles, which are littered with an armed people, at bay?

And if the enemy only had to devote 12,000 men to every 250 square miles of the Prussian monarchy to keep the country under control, what else would he be able to deploy against the Russians?

The scenario that we have played out here is founded on the history of the war in the Vendée;[26] that is, on historical evidence, through which it attains some cogency, even if one already has not been forced to admit that it is not inherently improbable.

How much force the enemy thus must employ in order to remain master in those rear and flank provinces, if only to such an extent that he can be certain of having secured the main routes, that his rule in the provinces is secure and the creation of a great army of insurgency is prevented!!

This is the case in Spain.[27] The French have half of their entire force in Spain, namely 300,000 men (of course not always at full strength, as this can never be the case) and they fight their main battles against Wellington[28] with armies of 40 and 50 thousand men. Anything remaining is used to keep the insurgent troops separated and to prevent the uniting of all forces of insurrection!

But who can promise that at some point the insurgents will not become masters of the enemy troops, led by some warrior, animated by fortune, inspired by rage? Then, larger incidents emerge from the individual setbacks and at some point it could happen that the insurgent army assumes the leading role. Then the tide of victory and of events is directed against the enemy. It no longer depends on individual happenstance and adroitness, from the dubious fortune of combat. A great general cause becomes dominant and the talent, strength, and greatness of the individual man are smashed to pieces like a light skiff on the waves of an angry sea.

There are a number of objections that one can raise against the *Landsturm*.

1st Above all, one believes that it will be difficult, without having prepared the means, to sustain the number of armed bands. But one only need consider

---

[26] See footnote 21.

[27] Clausewitz refers to the Spanish War of Independence (1808–14) against Napoleon which was fought both as a guerrilla war and in alliance with Portuguese and British regular forces under the Duke of Wellington.

[28] Field Marshal Arthur Wellesley, 1st Duke of Wellington (1769–1852).

that the enemy **also** has to live; that only there, where the presence of the enemy makes it necessary, are the armed bands concentrated; and that one is in possession of the fortifications, and in conjunction with the inhabitants, possesses ten times more sources of sustenance than the enemy.

This observation should remove every source of concern. Only a considerable army could give rise to the same, because only through a two- or threefold superiority, which one would have to have, could provision become more difficult for us than for the enemy.

However, such armies will be sustained from the fortifications of the country or otherwise assembled stockpiles; or they will be allowed to disband, in order to reinforce the bands reconstituted in the rear as described above.

2nd It is commonly held that the enemy can deprive us of the necessary courage through cruel treatment of captured insurgents, through the death penalty, etc. But what an unnecessary concern! As if we could not be as cruel as the enemy, as if the enemy would not consist of flesh and blood! The enemy will indeed try to use such means, and the war will rapidly acquire a barbarous quality. But to whose disadvantage? Obviously to the disadvantage of those who can put fewer lives on the line, who fight with standing armies! So let us take our chances and answer cruelty with cruelty, respond to atrocities with atrocity. It will be easy for us to exceed the enemy and to force him back into the bounds of moderation and humanity.

Wasn't it the case that the tiger, that ruled France in the years 93 and 94 under the name of a republican government, had to stop drinking thirstily the blood of the Vendée?—In the competition of atrocities the Republicans were the first to give in. The Vendée was not defeated after one had fought against her with considerable luck for one-and-a-half years, more than once marched across her with the sword of devastation, with death and destruction—only humane principles, pardon, respect, peace, could soothe the enraged nature of man. Only this balsam could heal the cancerous wound, which *Barère*[29] wished in vain to destroy with the knife and red-hot iron.

But these extremes, of which one hears from Spain, will not necessarily occur everywhere, and perhaps may be avoided if the government takes every armed man of its population under the protection of its authority, and threatens to take out reprisals on the captives for every atrocity that is contrary to the law of war and custom and directed against the true defenders of the fatherland. How many executions will the enemy venture? And should we not accept that a few dozen men die in this manner for the fatherland given the many casualties that war claims every day? —

Truly, the fears one has had of this danger, which is no more a danger than any other in war, have been far too great and completely exaggerated. Even the

---

[29] Bertrand Barère de Vieuzac (1755–1841), French politician and member of the National Convention during the French Revolution.

situation in Spain is not as grave as one thinks and the enemy readily would concede, after the warning shots of its military police, to treat the insurgent troops as any other.

3rd The claim is often repeated that our regions are not mountainous and inaccessible enough for such a people's war. But the Vendée, that is the areas of Poitou and Anjou, which waged the famous war of the Vendée, and which consist only of some hundred square miles, are nothing other than a hilly woodland. They are as far removed from inaccessible mountains as are the principalities of Schweidnitz and Jauer and the County Glatz in Silesia; by far not as inaccessible as the woody and faulty regions of the Mittelmark, the boggy forests of Pomerania, East Prussia, West Prussia, and Silesia.

The other objections that are raised against the *Landsturm* concern the courage, the skill and the intelligence of the nation, the good will and patriotic enthusiasm that it requires, of which it is believed our people in comparison to other nations, specifically the French, have less. Let me take this opportunity to share some observations, which flow from my innermost convictions.

It is outright **absurd** to rank the German nation behind the French in terms of true intelligence. Neither in the history nor the literature of the two nations, nor in the arts and crafts, which flourish in both, is there any rational reason for that—and to put it bluntly, it is nothing less than the language and idle talk of the French, which has given rise to such a rash judgment. If it is generally disagreeable to rank a whole nation in terms of intelligence ahead of another, it is childish to be misled by mere talk and esprit. Is the talkative man, the wordy, the rattler, yes even the eloquent, always the man of reason? Isn't the latter here, at least in most cases, more introverted and silent? Shouldn't this give us ground for thought?

It is quite clear to me how the spirits of both nations relate to one another, and I see no advantage for the French. Adam Smith[30] has remarked that if the occupation of the lower classes is indicative of the true development of their minds, then one must grant the peasant a higher stage of intelligence than the city dweller. His affairs constitute an organic whole of manifold variety, which necessitates the continuous use of his capacity of judgment and makes possible a certain degree of freedom of action. It is different for the city dweller, whose entire life and occupation often consist of a neverending repetition of skilled movements of his hand.

Nevertheless, when they meet, the city dweller appears to be infinitely superior to the peasant, because of the liveliness of his presentation and the wealth of expressions he has acquired.

The same applies to the Germans and French, and even if I do not assume the superiority of the former, I cannot concede the opposing argument.

---

[30] Adam Smith (1723–90), Scottish philosopher and pioneer of political economy.

The French language, rich in phrases, that is, in ready-made thoughts, which of course are a dime a dozen, and which everyone uses without shame, cannot provide the true sign of genius and intelligence. But it can conceal defects in nature. I consider a person who speaks French to be a woman in a farthingale. The natural activities of the mind, as in this example the body, are concealed through rigid forms. The German language is a wide garment, in which every movement of the body is perceived, including the clumsy and the blundering movements of those natures not privileged by fate.

But even if the German is not at all to be ranked behind the French in terms of intelligence, it is still possible that the French is superior to the German in terms of liveliness and esprit. Yet it is not clear, and seems to me to be very unlikely, that these qualities are essential for the war, the battlegrounds or the vaulting stable. Fearlessness, courage, and good judgment are such essential qualities of a good soldier, that if they are present, the others no longer are decisive.

These qualities, however, cannot be denied the Germans; and one need only look beyond our present circumstances into more distant times in order to be convinced of the small-mindedness with which we cling to the agility of the French *tirailleurs*.[31] Everything in the world has its measure, nothing should be overrated, and one should not overlook the more important for the less important.

It would be easy, through an extended refutation, to expose this admiration for the French spirit as laughable, if this were the appropriate place and if we did not have more important things to say. Another matter that concerns the nation is the courage for such undertakings, the enthusiasm, the patriotic allegiance. One tries to avoid seeing these amongst the Germans and regards the mood amongst the people, especially here, with a sort of consternation.

Granted, the mood is not propitious, if one limits oneself to superficial appearances. I myself must admit, that a despondence is amongst us, a lack of confidence that increasingly is spreading itself from top to bottom. But mood, what is it? What, in the entire sphere of moral phenomena, could be more ephemeral, more superficial, more governed by unworthy, unimportant chance? The mood of the Prussian army before the battle of Auerstedt[32] was splendid, after the battle most miserable, the mood of the people is also so.

It is, however, different when it comes to the public's opinion of itself and of the government, to allegiance to the constitution, to the depravity of customs, to the enervation, and all that is more deeply established in a nation and

---

[31] *Tirailleurs* are sharpshooters.
[32] The battle of Auerstedt on October 14, 1806 was one of two simultaneous French victories over the Prussian army. Marshal Davout defeated the larger part of the Prussian forces with a single corps, while Napoleon with the bulk of the *Grande Armée* overwhelmed Prussian flank guards at Jena.

previously brought about. These qualities admittedly do not change with insignificant events. But even if we were to grant that these things weighed against the prospect of a forceful resistance, that the people were weak and discouraged, could this be a reason for the government to act in the same way? Should not the government be better than the people? A nation does not become suddenly as weak and discouraged and immoral as can be imagined, the path thereto is long. It is the responsibility of the government to stop it on that path, at whatever point it may find itself. If the French are stronger than we, it is thanks to similar exertions.

Why didn't the government want to force the nation? Why didn't it want to coerce the people to do and to be what it deemed prudent?

The government often enough has used coercive means against the people for much narrower aims and insignificant purposes. Thus shall a fatherly government, as is the Prussian (and it is in no danger of being misunderstood in this respect), use all means of coercion at its disposal to energetically compel the people to observe their most sacred duty. There is coercion, and even the most fearsome coercion, which is not tyranny. Who can doubt for a moment that this energy and these reasonable measures of the government will quickly bring back the confidence of the subjects; that the powerful spirit itself will flow back into the people? Nothing is so certain as the fact that extraordinary cases of misfortune, once men resolve to confront them with extraordinary means and to direct all their energies against them, serve to elevate them above themselves and inspire within them powers of mind and reason of which they never dreamt. One may be assured that a people which is subjected to the utmost danger, that is, not lacking in necessity, will not light-headedly leave behind the narrow existence and calm of private life and be seized by an enthusiasm, spurred by hate and rage, which are falsely attributed only to religious fervor. Everything can develop in man, given the proper circumstances.

The German peoples have demonstrated in more than one way the ability to move toward such a state, which in the beginning one might term tense, but which calls forth a new vigorous life. If they decline, if they completely decay, it is the fault of the governments, which out of a concern for their own safety, let pass the moment at which they could have been saved. A concern, which if looked at more closely, is nothing more than the fear of not being up to the task, as the meager worry not to compromise oneself. If the first step already has been taken, additional steps require less motivation, for nothing is truer than that man loves those things most and pursues most passionately those things for which he already has sacrificed most.

Therefore, one need not fear that the misfortune that befalls the people will destroy the people; far more will it thirst for vengeance.

Only if it has placed its entire confidence in a salaried army and is an idle spectator to the great disaster of defeat, only then is the maximum despondence to be feared.

There are others who do not deny the possibility of a *Landsturm*, but warn against the danger to the existing order of things, to the governments themselves, that could result from the application of this means. However, this is in fact an advantage of our present condition: the government, which itself arouses this storm, remains its master. It is in general able to provide the *Landsturm* with the proper direction and to direct all forces toward one aim. Even the discordance in opinions and actions, that we saw destroy a large degree of effect in Spain, and that once split the forces of the Vendée, can and will be prevented by a government, which relates to its people as Prussia does. Every danger predicted by the know-alls, is based on a single historical example.

Finally, there are those who tremble before the idea of a people's war, because it is bloodier than any other, seldom remains free of dreadful scenes, and will escalate all tragedy and ruin.

But who is to blame for that? Is not he who drives others to the height of despair to blame? The people's war is here. You condemn its ruinous effects—well condemn those who forced it upon us. If you pose as judges of human behavior, then do not condemn the oppressed because he is weak, but be just. Hurl your allegations at those who have made this evil necessary.[‡]

ADDENDUM

On the Nature of Defense

Traditionally a state regards itself as being already halfway on the road to defeat if it awaits the enemy within its borders and has to secure its independence through a defensive war.

This customary view in government and people generates a dulled sense of fear that soon will be transformed into despondency. Therefore, it is worth the effort to clarify the concepts of offense and defense. What once was timidity might then become the source of courage.

———

Since war no longer consists of a single battle, as was the case with barbarous peoples, the art of war decomposes into two parts, distinguished by ends and means.

[‡] **Note:** You wish peace, direct yourselves to those who can give it to the world. These are, however, people whose minds are full of lofty projects; they wish to be independent arbiters of the rulers, and people who think as I do are ill disposed to like that. I love peace; but no other than a good, stable, and honorable peace. Socrates and Plato would have thought as I do if they had stood in the unfortunate position that I assume in this world.
Frederick II in his posthumously published papers.

The first is the art of battle. (Tactics)

The second is the art of combining individual battles (for the end of the campaign, of the war) into a whole. (Strategy)

The difference between offensive and defensive war runs through both parts, and even extends into policy.

Defense, therefore, can be tactical, strategic, or political.

Political defense, which consists in a nation fighting for its survival rather than for conquest (by the way, regardless by which manner) has nothing to do with proper warfare, although it has an important influence on the spirit of the army and may in that way become significant.

Tactical and strategic defense have their own properties, some common, some specific, thus we will discuss both.

First, what is defense? Evidently not the mere repelling of enemy thrusts, not an entirely passive behavior; that would be nonsense. One can be active in defense and thereby combine it with an attack. It remains defense as long as the intention and the advantage, which one enjoys in the defense, are not suspended through the procedure.

These intentions and advantages are:

1. To await the attack. One should fight only if it is unavoidable. This is impossible if one attacks.

2. To enjoy the assistance of the locality.

3. To be close to sources of support.

We wish to apply these three points to tactics and strategy and ask ourselves whether the offense offers any advantages over them.

1. Tactical

1. If I am in a position from which I wish to await an enemy attack, my behavior is tactically defensive. The strategic advantage accrues to me, insofar as I engage in battle only when it is unavoidable. In the event that the enemy neglects to attack me, the time that elapses without incident is lost to him and not to me, for I am only interested in maintaining the *status quo*. This calculus would be wrong if I were not allowed to assume that the enemy will make mistakes. If the enemy behaves exactly as he should, I will not escape the battle, but then it might have been advantageous to at least choose the moment that is most beneficial to me, that is, to become tactically the attacker.

It would be foolish, however, to always count on the perfect behavior of one's enemy in war. It would even be a contradiction, and whoever believes that in general everything happens in war that can possibly happen, can never have read any war history. The rule is rather that less happens.

Frederick II counted on the inactivity of Field Marshal Daun[33] and the Russians during the four final years of the Seven Years' War rather than his own talent. He spared himself thereby many a battle, and one can say that this patience from 1758 onward was the main component of his defense and saved his state.

But it is unreasonable in war to count on improbable mistakes. It follows, of course, that one cannot expect to reap from the advantage of the defense a large harvest when faced with a very active enemy.

2. If I await the enemy attack in a certain position, it means nothing more than that I do not engage in battle before the enemy, which advancing for attack, enters the territory that I have chosen to be the battlefield. Whether or not I am in this position; or whether I have it in front of me, and wait for the moment of his advance to enter, or behind me, in order to withdraw thereto; whether it is to my right or my left; whether I attack the enemy only with a part of my army; remain passive with others, or conduct the attack with all; none of this changes the essence of the matter. My conduct remains defensive and I enjoy the support of the locality.

From this it is clear that through defense one can accomplish results as decisive as through the offense, for in this respect the active defense is in no way different from the offense. It is self-evident that the enemy will be pursued after he has been overcome, and therefore, the tactical defense ends; for one only made use of it to achieve victory.

But what does support of the locality mean? It consists not only in every advantage offered by the ground, which in itself is a huge source of predominance, but also primarily in the preparatory arrangements that one can complete for the battle.

One can use the entrenchments, one can deploy one's troops in advance, one can familiarize them with the *terrain*; all advantages that are essential for an army, but especially for one that has little training for war.

It would be possible to say much more about these things, but shortness of time limits us to the essentials.

2. Strategic

1. If I behave in a theater of war in such fashion as to only fight the enemy that advances into this theater of war, whether fighting defensively or offensively, my behavior is strategically defensive.

---

[33] Count Leopold Joseph von Daun (1705–66) was an Austrian field marshal and commander in the Seven Years' War (1756–63).

As in the previous case regarding tactics, here the advantage emerges in that I might not need to defend a theater of war that the enemy refrains from attacking, his opposing forces remaining idle.

Usually those theaters of war remain defensive in which forces weaker than those of the enemy are deployed, while in all others the war is waged offensively (Saxony in the Seven Years' War). Moreover, it is possible that a state, having more than one theater of war, conducts itself defensively in all of them at the same time.

2. The support of the locality is much more decisive for strategic defense than for the tactical, more important for the theater of war than for a particular position. This is mainly the case because of the fortresses. A theater of war that is strong owing to its fortresses and fortifications is able to double the effect of its armed forces as the history of war teaches. It is self-evident that the strategic defense does not necessarily imply a tactical defense. Within the theater of war that one has committed to defend, the enemy can be attacked wherever and whenever one pleases. Hence, one thereby has a means to completely destroy an enemy army as good as that offered by any offense: yes, it is easier in our own theater of war for us than for the enemy.

Obviously, one can pursue a defeated enemy beyond the borders of his own theater of war and thus proceed to the strategic offense, as was the case in tactics above. Indeed, one will have to do it, if one does not want to use the superiority provided by victory in other locations and transfer part of the armed forces to other theaters of war.

3. For the defender, the proximity of his supplies is of strategic importance in order to replace the loss of men and other forces faster than the enemy, who requires far more time for this, not only because of the great distance, but also because he has to employ part of his army to secure his long lines of operation.

On the other hand, what advantages are offered by the offense?

First, it determines time and place.

The measures of the defender must have a certain general character and are therefore weak when compared to the measures of the attacker, as these can be adjusted to circumstances and be concentrated in time and space.

Tactically, this was a very decisive advantage, as long as defenses were largely passive, as was formerly the case.

Every point along a defensive position, from which one only seeks to repel the enemy attack, must be equally advantageous if complete victory is the desired result. In order to secure a decisive victory the attacker only needs to break through a single point. What an incredible advantage for the attacker! A second, equally important, was that the attacker had learned about the defender's measures through reconnaissance and other means, so that he could adjust his own and appear with overwhelming force at specific positions. In one word, he appeared to dictate the terms and the defender either had to adjust his measures accordingly or to settle for weaker measures altogether.

But since the idea has emerged to defend oneself actively—to lure the enemy into a region chosen by ourselves as into an ambush, to mass one's troops as little as possible, to hide them as much as possible—since then, the extreme advantage of the tactical offensive has vanished and perhaps the advantage in this respect is on the side of the defense.

At least nothing is more certain than that ignorance of the *terrain* calls for generals and officers with war experience and remains a disadvantage for the attacker for which there is no compensation.

Strategically the advantage of which we here speak, namely knowledge of time and place, and the ability therein to make concentrated use of his armed forces, never could have been more important.

In most cases, one realizes the direction of the enemy attack and the general distribution of his forces at the initiation of the campaign, early enough to adjust one's countermeasures.

More important are the surprises with which the attacker, through quick marches during the campaign, can direct overwhelming armed forces on a single point where we have not expected them.

Then, in most cases, it would be impossible and detrimental if the strategic defense were willing and coerced to accept the rules of the enemy offensive.

But because the strategic defense by no means excludes the tactical offense inside one's own theater of war, where one has superior forces, one easily proceeds to the tactical offense, attacks the enemy and destroys him. Hence, the aforementioned disadvantage is not at all restricted to strategic defense. For the strategic defense it is only important to know toward which theater of war the enemy has directed the bulk of his forces, and as previously mentioned, this will not be difficult to surmise. For one cannot transfer troops during a campaign from one theater to another quickly enough to surprise the defender.

From this we conclude with great conviction that the aforementioned advantage of the offense is not as decisive as it used to be and as one commonly believes.

2. The attacker carries the war into the countryside of the attacked, destroys a part of his forces from the first moment of war onward, where the battle is already decided. Sending his forces toward the attacker, the defender's sources of sustenance run dry.

This advantage is so decisive that in all times men of great insight were able to choose offensive war for the purpose of defense.

However, time and circumstances also can change this point of view dramatically. If the army already has been withdrawn from the countryside, and if the forces required for defense have been segregated from the state's forces for the campaign, then the loss of a part of the countryside is far less decisive for the initial campaign than for whole war.

Of course a war that is to be waged defensively for several years can hardly be shouldered by a small state that has developed completely into a theater of war.

But it can be expected that the defensive of the first year, if it becomes as decisive as it can be, will transform the war into an offensive war.

The example of Prussia during the Seven Years' War, by the way, proves how long a state of modest size nevertheless can sustain a defensive war. Holland and Switzerland provide further evidence.[34]

Be that as it may, we should not overlook that this disadvantage of the defense is actually more of a political than of a military nature.

Victory and the destruction of the enemy army are the military aims, and these are more likely to be achieved through defense than through offense, so that one can say: the defense as such is stronger than the offense.

A defense that over the course of many years cannot proceed to offense is a war that is waged for several years unhappily. But it would also be unhappy if it were waged offensively, for as we have just demonstrated, the defense itself is stronger than the offense. Yet, an unhappy offensive war will throw us back to the defense, and we will not be in a better position than the state that began with the defense.

Therefore, it could be advantageous to start with the defense, in order with more assurance to finish with the offense, rather than to run the risk of taking the opposite course.

From this one can draw the conclusion that for the political end of the defense, the opening of a war with an offense is only appropriate if, like Frederick II during the Seven Years' War, one can assault an unprepared enemy.

We have thus far not discussed the sentiment of moral advantage, which tends to accrue to the offense.

Moral qualities must be included in the calculus of war. But is the sense of defending one's own hearth, which the common man experiences only by actually defending, worth nothing? Nothing indeed, if one treats humans like machines and does not try to influence their hearts and minds; otherwise just as much as that sense of advantage.

Apropos, this sense of advantage by no means will belong exclusively to the attacker during an active defense, as is self-evident.

So far we have not said a single word about the truly great defense, which by means of a *Landsturm* is mounted by a whole nation.

---

[34] Hahlweg (1966–90: vol. 1, 747) points to the Franco-Dutch War (1672–78) and the idea of a Swiss National Redoubt.

It is not necessary to mention or further expand on the enormous amount of strength, both physical and mental, which thereby is thrown into the balance of the defender.

This will be decisive. Posterity will recognize it. The preservation of all constitutions and states will depend on this great means. Peace in Europe will be restored solely by it.

If we want to confirm our reasoning regarding defensive war through history, a single glance from the paper to the real world, from theory to the realm of action, is sufficient.

Wasn't it always the case that one of two belligerents deliberately chose the role of the defender? Must not defense possess particular advantages?

Since it always has been the weaker who traditionally assumed the role of the defender, doesn't one have to conclude that with regard to the effectiveness of the armed forces, the defensive form is stronger than the offensive? Or should one believe that from the beginning of the time, ignorance and prejudice have created such principles?

What would one think of a commander, who uses weaker forces where he attacks and stronger forces where he defends himself?

I believe that all these questions answer themselves and demonstrate what we hope to have learned thus far: that only a complete conceptual confusion in conjunction with many false perspectives has created the idea of the advantage of the offense that now tends to rob the courage of the defender who is fighting for his legitimate cause.

It is to be excused, if one had this opinion with regard to earlier political circumstances and the nature of war; since both have changed, it is only a prejudice and conventional wisdom.

Formerly, that is especially during the last centuries, one waged war as two duelists waged their petty conflict. One fought with moderation and caution according to traditional conventions. This knocking about began and ended depending on whether or not the petty interests of a prince weighed in favor of keeping the machine running. The entire end of the war was to assert a diplomatic whim, and its spirit could scarcely be elevated above the aim of the military *point d'honneur*. A contemporary author has quite rightly and nicely said: honor is not the fruit but the blossom of human education.

It was not the citizens who took up arms and fought one another, but the armies. It was not the hearts of armies, but rather of the rulers that inspired them to battle.

The citizen took part in such a war only to the extent that he was pressed into the service of its interests; and then it was quite important, whether this common war was waged at the expense of one state or the other, that is, whether through offense one should carry the whole ruin of war into the country of the other, or await the same in one's own. There was nothing in the world that could have compensated the defender for this disadvantage.

Moreover, in a war in which the entirety of the moral forces resided in the pure *point d'honneur* of the commander and his army, the proud or haughty sentiment necessarily generated a substantial superiority.

Finally, the attacker could, through a sudden move, create a small disadvantage for the defender; the loss of a position, a depot, even a so-called *bataille*; and given the short supply of war resources, this was a decisive loss. One no longer speaks of this kind of war. One would have to be blind not to see the difference between our wars; that is, the wars that our times and our conditions require and for which there is more than one example. The war of the current era is a war of all against all. Kings no longer wage war against kings, nor armies against each other, but one nation against the other, the nation encompassing the king and army.

It is unlikely that this character of war will change again, and it truly is not to be wished that the old bloody and the too often boring chess-game of struggling soldiers will ever return.

This is not to say that the national uprising *en Masse*, as we have twice witnessed in great examples (France and Spain), will be the only way in which nations will wage war against each other in the future, heaven help us. This phenomenon belongs alone to the present and its fateful hours.

As certain as this great remedy results from a natural expression of suppressed national energies and not some individual intrigues, so certain will it cease to be necessary, once, through it, the European peoples out of their chaos, and following the laws of nature, will have formed organic states.

If there are ever again to be centuries in which no nation will be compelled to take refuge in the last desperate means of a national uprising, in these centuries every war will be regarded nevertheless as a national affair and waged in this spirit, according to the degree of effort that the national character and the government determine.

4

On the political advantages and disadvantages of the Prussian institution of the *Landwehr*

The institution of the *Landwehr*[1]—insofar as it assembles a significant share of the population in regular regiments, namely about 1/3 of all men eligible for war, provides officers from its midst, and stores its weapons in open arsenals—obviously places the weapons into the hands of the people.

The people, like all people, are difficult to satisfy completely. One could even say that in the strictest sense this is quite impossible. But the present moment is characterized by a vague aspiration and by a spirit of discontent with governments, and thus it is now twice as dangerous to lay the weapons into the hands of the people.

In times of internal turmoil and of resistance of the lower classes, every government must be ready, after every means of persuasion and advice has been exhausted, to regard the sword as a last prop of its laws and affairs. This sword, however, is no longer a prop if the government does not wield it alone, if the most recalcitrant part of the population is just as well outfitted.

We do not intend to challenge the inner truth of the sequence of these propositions and conclusions. Rather, we only want to find the counterweight that is present and balances its effect on the scale of truth and wisdom, as if the propositions themselves were destroyed.

The arming of the people, that is the institution of the *Landwehr*, provides an outward resistance that cannot be achieved through a standing army. Whatever measures are adopted, one will never be able to enhance the fighting power of a standing army to the same extent as the *Landwehr* system, with the

---

[1] This handwritten memorandum was sent by Clausewitz to his superior and friend August Neidhardt von Gneisenau (1760–1831) in December 1819. In it he reflects on the arguments, emphasized by conservatives in the Prussian government, that making the *Landwehr* militia a regular feature of the Prussian Army and, consequently, arming the people would greatly enhance the danger of revolution. The translation is based on Hahlweg (1966–90: vol. 2.1, 367–72).

same financial means, and with the same devotion on the part of the subjects. Whoever denies this completely needs to be convinced by arguments of a different kind than we are able to supply here. We only want to continue speaking with those who accept this proposition, at least for the time being; for whom, leaving aside the internal proof, the experience of the years 1806 and 1813 taken together provides strong evidence.[2]

The *Landwehr* increased the danger of revolution. The disarming of the *Landwehr* increases the danger of an invasion and subjugation. Which of the two according to historical evidence is the greater? Where in Germany should one look for revolutionary incidents, which have appeared so often in Italy, France, and England? In which century, in which province? I should think that Doubt would feel ashamed by these questions. Was it perhaps in the Prussian lands that the otherwise calm and bloodless Germany was most restless and violent? Could it have been mainly in the 18th century?

We know nothing of a revolution, of a true rebellion. Do we also know nothing of an invasion?

If then in this regard it may be risky to rule an armed people, is it not in another regard much more risky to rule an unarmed people?

We would recommend a conscientious answer to this first question to those who are swept away by the inconvenient requirements of the moment.

The second point we wish to clarify is the relationship between the disarming of the people and the internal order and security of the government in order to determine the measure of advantage provided in this regard by the disarmament, and thereby compare it to the counterargument.

Does it depend only or primarily on the weapons? Were the Tyroleans[3] inferior subjects because they were armed?

Was the French population armed in 1789?[4]

Furthermore, are the *Landwehr* and a standing army, politically speaking, truly opposed to one another, as some suggest?

Is it so easy to exclude from the standing army the spirit of the people when it starts to deteriorate? Was this not the case to the highest degree with the standing army of Louis XVI? And was it not destroyed by the spirit of

---

[2] 1806 and 1813 are important dates for the Prussian Army in general and the idea of the *Landwehr* in particular. In 1806 Napoleon's forces defeated the outdated Prussian army in the Battle of Jena and Auerstedt. In the years after, Gerhard von Scharnhorst with the support of Gneisenau, Clausewitz, and others, introduced wide-ranging military reforms, including universal military conscription. In 1812, when Napoleon retreated from Moscow, Karl Freiherr vom und zum Stein created a *Landwehr* which was later instrumental in the victory over Napoleon in the Battle of Leipzig in 1813.

[3] The Tyrolean uprising in 1809 was a peasant rebellion against French and Bavarian occupying troops. Temporarily victorious in several battles, the insurgents under Andreas Hofer (1767–1810) were finally defeated in November 1819 and Hofer executed in 1810.

[4] The French Revolution started with the storming of the Bastille in 1789 where the insurgents found large amounts of weapons and munitions.

revolution, melted away like the snow in springtime? Can we really regard the dissolution of the *Landwehr* and the enlargement of the standing army as a Talisman against the fire of revolution if the necessary sparks already are present? Obviously, nothing would be more pernicious than this belief. The sword on which a government, attacked by a people who have been seduced by a drunken spirit, ultimately relies must be the martial personality of the ruler and his family in conjunction with a virtuous will. For these two things there will always be a group of men who, permeated by a sense of right, will closely attach themselves to the throne.

This extreme situation is only touched upon in order to suggest that we are not of the opinion that an ever-accelerating process of concession, an unfailing meekness, a martyrdom of sufferance, are the only or true means of remedy. Otherwise it strikes us as rather futile to talk about this extreme situation as long as there is not yet any fighting.

Thus, the formula of a standing army is not what could prevent such a mishap if it were brewing. It is not the arming of the *Landwehr* that constitutes the focus of danger.

Only an honest and prudent treatment of the army, the *Landwehr*, and the people can keep and enhance the elements of loyalty and allegiance in all three. Otherwise, there is nowhere security and the danger of the *Landwehr* cannot surpass their power.

The third point we wish to touch upon relates to the source of all these concerns. What else is the source other than the government's feeling of standing alone? It sees the arousing spirit of dissatisfaction and the spirit of open resistance. It fears this element will sooner or later ignite, and with what could it then respond? The strength of an armed power will be destroyed by a much more numerous *Landwehr*. Thus, one advises disbanding the latter and reliance on the former. That this prop is illusory we believe to have demonstrated. Rather, the government should assemble around itself the representatives of the people, chosen from men who share the true interests of the government and are not alien to the people. They would be its first prop, its friend and advisor, as has been the parliament to the King of England for 100 years. With this instrument it should guide the lofty forces of a stalwart people against its external enemies and rivals. With this instrument it should shackle reckless forces, when in the rage of fermenting spirits they seek to turn the sword on themselves. From our point of view, there is no other way, and the goal cannot be reached comfortably or at a lower price. Whoever promises to achieve this through palliatives is to be regarded as a charlatan who only exacerbates the malady.

And would not the impression made on the people by their disarming be the first sign of this exacerbation? If there is a tension, will it not be amplified and would not the last measure of trust in the government perish?

This argument is of course secondary in the entire reasoning with respect to its philosophical position, but not with regard to its practical importance.

And this disarming of the people, the benefit of which has to be regarded as minor when seen in relation to the danger of internal ferment, is perhaps more rightly regarded as a means of promoting the same. How does it increase the dangers that threaten us from abroad?

We don't even want to mention the current situation and leave untouched the issue of whether it is advantageous or disadvantageous. Rather, we only want to consider the general condition of Prussia since its elevation to the great powers, its relation to the others, and to think about what has constituted its particular existence.

It is everywhere surrounded by powerful enemies. Both its acquisitions and its internal constitution have given rise to hate and envy in others. Most of all, the splendor of its armor has aroused in small and large alike, a secret resentment, a malicious intention to inflict harm upon it in Germany. It is said that Prussia has an inflated military system, by which is meant that Prussia has inflated it more than the others and thereby maintains a balance with the first powers despite its lesser resources. What will happen if Prussia eases this so-called inflation? It will fall back considerably from its position and importance and once in decline, it will not be difficult to put it down completely, or it will only persist at the mercy of others. This prospect must be too attractive for other self-interested powers not to encourage the first voluntary steps through all means of solicitation. Out of a ghostly fear of the sword, we do it ourselves, and let ourselves be led away in chains.

Only great institutions of real forces, permeated by a vital spirit, can maintain our position; not empty forms such as we had prior to 1806, not the echo of glory which becomes weaker year by year. Our own recent history has made it abundantly clear, such that we cannot ignore it as long as we are guided by the slightest desire for the truth.

Thus may the men of 1806, who looked for salvation in the obsolete forms of that time, honestly submit all the questions that we have posed here to their conscience and then feel the tremendous responsibility for destroying with a wanton recklessness that was perhaps only the work of a dilettante, that building on which our great fortune in the years 1813, 1814, and 1815 rested like a goddess of victory on her war chariot.

5

The arming of the people

Volksbewaffnung

In cultivated Europe, people's war is a phenomenon of the nineteenth century.[1] It has its proponents and its opponents, the latter either for political reasons, because they regard it as a revolutionary means, that is, a legally declared state of anarchy, which is as dangerous internally for the social order as it is externally for the enemy; or, for military reasons, because they believe that the success does not correspond to the expended effort. The first argument is of no consequence to us here, as we will treat people's war merely as a means of combat; that is, in its relationship to the enemy. The latter point, however, leads us to the observation that people's war in general is to be regarded as a consequence of the breaching of old artificial barriers by the warlike element in our times; as an extension and reinforcement of the entire process of fermentation, which we call war. The system of recruitment and general conscription that enabled the surge of the army to enormous size and the use of the *Landwehr* are all matters, which, from the perspective of the traditional circumscribed military system, point in the same direction. In this direction also lies the appeal for the *Landsturm*, that is, the arming of the people.[2] If the first of these new means is a natural and necessary consequence of the discarded restraints, and if it has increased the power of the one who

---

[1] This text consists of Chapter 26 of Book VI of Clausewitz's main work *On War*, which was published posthumously by his wife Marie in 1832. Clausewitz had started writing *On War* in 1816 but had not finished his work when he died of cholera in 1831. In *On War*, Clausewitz integrates his ideas about people's war and the *Landwehr* and *Landsturm* militia into his larger theory of war and identifies the arming of the people as only one measure of the defense among others. He thus takes back some of his earlier enthusiasm evident e.g. in his "*Bekenntnisdenk-schrift*" of 1812. The translation is based on Clausewitz (1980: 799–806).

[2] According to a royal edict of March 17, 1813, the Prussian *Landwehr* consisted of all men older than 18 and younger than 45 who were able to carry weapons and did not serve in the regular army. By contrast, the edict of April 21, 1813, called all men older than 17 and younger than 60 to serve in the *Landsturm*, if they were not already drafted into the regular forces or the *Landwehr*.

used it first to such an extent that the other has been forced to follow suit and adopt it as well, then such will also be the case with regard to people's war. In most cases, those who resort to people's war in a rational manner will gain relative dominance over those who scorn it. If this is the case, then the only question is whether or not this new intensification of the warlike element is altogether beneficial for humanity. The question probably is to be answered in similar fashion to the question of war itself. We leave both to the philosophers. One could argue, however, that the energy, which is consumed by people's war, could be used with greater success when applied to other means of combat. Yet no great investigation is required to convince oneself that these energies for the most part are not freely available and do not lend themselves to arbitrary usage. An important part, namely the element of morale, first comes into being through this practice. We therefore no longer ask: What is the price of resistance for a people if the entire population takes up arms? Rather we ask: What effect can this resistance have, what are its preconditions, and how can it be used?

It is in the nature of things that a resistance dispersed in this fashion is not suited to achieve the temporally and spatially concentrated effect of large strikes. Its effect directs itself, as in the process of evaporation, toward the outer surface. The larger the surface area and the contact between it and the enemy army, that is, the more the latter is diffused, the more effective is the arming of the people. The arming of the people destroys the foundations of the enemy army like quietly smoldering embers. Requiring time to achieve their successes, while both elements interact, a state of tension emerges that either gradually eases, if in some locations the people's war is smothered and in other locations slowly burns out, or leads to a crisis, if the flames of this general fire envelop the enemy army and compel it to leave the country before it is totally destroyed. Inducing this crisis through people's war alone, either requires a surface area of conquered territory such as only Russia and no other European state possesses, or a mismatch between the invading army and the surface area of the country, which in reality does not occur. If one does not wish to chase an illusion, one must conceive of people's war in combination with war waged by a standing army and both united through an all-encompassing plan. The conditions under which people's war alone can be effective are the following:

1. that the war is waged within the borders of the country;
2. that it not be decided by a single catastrophe;
3. that the theater of war comprises a considerable track of territory;
4. that the national character is conducive to the measure;
5. that the country is rough and inaccessible, either through mountains or through woods and swamps or through the nature of the agriculture.

Whether the population is large or small is not decisive, for a lack of people is of least concern. Whether or not the inhabitants are poor or rich is also not particularly decisive, or at least shouldn't be, for it cannot be denied that the poorer classes, accustomed to hard work and exertion, usually prove to be more belligerent and strong.

A particular characteristic of the countryside, which promotes tremendously the potency of the people's war, is the scattered pattern of settlement that can be found in many German provinces. The countryside is thereby more dissected and concealed, the roads are made worse, although more numerous, the quartering of troops entails endless difficulties, and above all, the singularity that characterizes people's war in general repeats itself in particular: namely, the principal of resistance exists everywhere and nowhere. If the inhabitants live together in villages, the most restless will be occupied by troops or ransacked as punishment, burned down, etc., which, however, is not easily carried out against a Westphalian peasantry.

The employment of the **Landsturm** and of armed crowds cannot and should not be directed against the main body of the enemy, not even against sizeable corps; it should not quash the center. Rather, it should only gnaw at the surface and the boundaries. It should rise up in the provinces that flank the theater of war and into which the attacker cannot project power, in order to deprive him entirely of influence in these provinces. These storm clouds, surging at his side, should pursue him to the extent that he advances. Where the enemy has not yet appeared, courage to get ready for him is not lacking, and bit by bit the bulk of the neighboring population will follow this example. In this way, the flame will spread like a fire in the heath and in the end will reach the territory on which the attacker is based. It spreads to his supply lines and saps the lifeline of his existence. Even if one does not have an exaggerated conception of the omnipotence of a people's war and does not regard it as an inexhaustible and invincible element, which is as unstoppable by brute armed force as are the wind and rain by man, in short, if one does not base one's judgment on polemic pamphlets, one nevertheless has to concede that armed peasants cannot be pushed back in the same way as a division of soldiers. These cling together like a herd and in general keep moving straight along, whereas those dispersed [armed peasants] scatter themselves in every direction needing no artificial plan. Hence every march of small units through the mountains, in a forest, or other varied terrain, becomes a dangerous endeavor. For at any moment the march can turn into a battle. And though there had long been no mention of belligerent enemy population, at any time the same peasants can appear at the rear of the column, which had already been dispersed by its front. When it comes to the destruction of routes and the barricading of narrow streets, the means employed by army outposts or reconnaissance teams, and those used by enraged crowds of peasants, are about as similar as are the movements of a machine to those of a human being. The enemy has no means against the activities of the *Landsturm* other than the deployment of many units to escort its supplies, the manning of military stations, passes, bridges, etc. As minimal as will be the first attempts of the *Landsturm*, so weak will be the deployed units, because one fears a large dispersion of the forces. But the fire of the people's war tends to ignite all the more amidst these weak units. If in some places one overwhelms them through numbers, courage and passion grows and the intensity of the struggle increases until it reaches the point of culmination that will decide the outcome.

According to our understanding, people's war should resemble fog or clouds. It should nowhere consolidate into a concrete entity, otherwise the enemy can direct an appropriate force against this core, destroy it, and take a large number of prisoners. Consequently courage is lost, everyone believes the main issue has been decided, further efforts are futile, and the people drop their weapons. On the other hand, it is nonetheless necessary that at certain locations the fog concentrates into a dense mass, creating threatening clouds from which at some point a lightning bolt can strike. As mentioned earlier, these locations are mainly along the flanks of the enemy theater of war. Then, the armed people must unite into larger and more orderly entities, with modest reinforcements from the standing army so that it achieves the appearance of an organized force and is enabled to undertake larger activities. From these locations the intensity of the *Landsturm* is removed to the enemy's rear which is exposed to the strongest blows. These denser masses are intended for ambushing the more sizeable garrisons sent back by the enemy. Moreover, they inspire fear and unease, increasing the entire impact on morale. Without them, the whole effect would not be strong enough and the entire situation not troubling enough for the enemy.

The commander achieves the intended configuration of the arming of the people with greatest ease through small units of the standing army with which he supports the *Landsturm*. Without such encouraging support from some troops of the standing army most of the population will lack the confidence and drive to take up arms. Hence, the greater the units which are created for this purpose, the greater will be their force of attraction and the greater the avalanche, which they are intended to trigger. But there are limits. On the one hand, it would be ruinous for this subordinated end to disperse the entire army, in a sense dissolving it into the *Landsturm* and thus creating a widespread yet everywhere weak defensive line. One could be certain that both the army and the *Landsturm* would be thoroughly destroyed. On the other hand, experience seems to teach that when too many regular troops are deployed in the province, people's war tends to decrease in energy and effectiveness. The cause of this is first, that too many enemy troops are drawn into the province; second, the population wants now to rely on their own regular troops; third, the existence of large numbers of troops consumes the strength of the population in a different way, namely through quartering, consignments, deliveries, etc.

Another means of preventing too strong an enemy reaction against people's war is at the same time a chief principle of its use. It is the principle that in using this great means of strategic defense one should rarely or never allow oneself to be drawn into tactical defense. The character of a *Landsturm* battle (*Gefecht*) is that of all battles with inferior troops: great force and heat in the run-up, but little cold blood and persistence.[3] Furthermore, it is not very important whether the bulk of the *Landsturm* is defeated and dispersed. For this it is prepared. But it should not be entirely destroyed by myriad fatalities, wounded and prisoners. Such defeats would smother the embers. These two particularities contradict the nature of tactical defense. The defensive battle requires a sustainable, slow, well-planned proceeding and decisive action. A mere attempt, from which one can withdraw as soon as one wants, can never lead to a successful defense. If the *Landsturm* is to defend a certain terrain it must never come to a decisive defensive battle; then it would be eliminated, regardless how beneficial the circumstances. The *Landsturm* can and should defend mountain approaches, swamp embankments, river crossings, as long as it can. But if they are overrun, it should disperse and continue the defense with surprise assaults rather than concentrating in a formal defensive posture and letting itself become encircled. No matter how courageous a people may be, how belligerent its culture, how great its hatred of the enemy, how favorable its terrain: it is undeniable that people's war cannot sustain itself in an atmosphere that is too dense with danger. If its combustible material is somewhere to burst into flames, it must occur at remote locations where there is enough oxygen and where it cannot be beaten back with a decisive blow.

After these considerations, which are more an effort to gain a sense of the truth than an objective analysis, because the phenomenon is simply too rare and has not been thoroughly described by those who for long have observed it with their own eyes, all that remains to be said is that the plan of strategic defense can incorporate the contribution made by the arming of the people in two different ways: namely, either as a last resource after a lost battle (*Schlacht*), or as a natural support in the run-up to a decisive battle (*Schlacht*). The latter requires withdrawal into the heart of the country and the sort of indirect response of which we spoke in chapters eight[4] and twenty-four[5] of this book.[6] We therefore have but a few words to say about the employment of the *Landsturm* after a lost battle (*Schlacht*).

---

[3] Because the German-language terms "*Gefecht*" and "*Schlacht*" usually are both translated into the English term "battle" in this text we have indicated in parenthesis which term is found in the German original. In this passage, Clausewitz is speaking of single encounters in the context of a larger campaign.

[4] Chapter 8 of Book VI is entitled "Types of Resistance." See Clausewitz (1984).

[5] Chapter 24 of Book VI is entitled "Operations on a Flank." See Clausewitz (1984).

[6] Book VI: *On Defense*. See Clausewitz (1984).

No state should believe that its fate, that is its entire existence, is dependent on a single battle (*Schlacht*), even the most decisive. If it is defeated, the mobilization of inherent new energies in conjunction with the natural weakening which every attack suffers over time, can lead to a reversal of fortunes, or the state can receive help from abroad. There is always enough time left to die, and just as it is a natural instinct for the drowning to grab at straws, it is the natural order in the realm of morale, that a people grasps at the last means of salvation if it is pushed to the outermost edge of the abyss.

No matter how small and feeble a state may be in relation to its enemy, it should not eschew these last exertions of energy, lest one should say there is no longer a soul left in it. This does not preclude the possibility of saving oneself from complete ruin through a bitter peace, but such an intention does not exclude on its side the utility of new defensive measures; the peace is made thereby neither harder nor worse, rather easier and better. They are even more necessary if help is expected from those who have an interest in our preservation. Hence, a government having lost a battle can think of nothing other than dragging the population to the comforts of peace and is overwhelmed by a sense of some grand failure of hope, no longer feels the courage and passion to mobilize its entire energies, and for reasons of weakness, lacks consequence and demonstrates that it was not worthy, and for this very reason perhaps was not even capable of victory.

Regardless of how decisive the defeat suffered by the state may be, the retreat of the army into the heartland of the country must call forth the activity of the fortresses and the arming of the people. In this regard it is advantageous if the flanks of the main field of battle are bordered by mountains or other difficult terrain, which now emerge as bastions from which the advancing force is subjected to strategic barrage.

If the victor is in the midst of laying siege, he will have left behind strong garrisons along the way to establish conduits, or even sent corps to make room for maneuver and to keep the neighboring provinces under control. If he already is weakened through manifold losses of men and materiel, then the point has come for the defensive army to once again assume its battle position and to topple the attacker in his precarious condition through a well-placed blow.

Bibliography

Adelung, Johann C., Soltau, Dietrich W., and Schönberger, Franz X. (1808). *Grammatisch kritisches Wörterbuch der hochdeutschen Mundart.* 4 volumes. Wien: Pichler.

Bassford, Christopher (1999). *Chris Bassford's Latest Attempt at an Accurate Translation of Clausewitz's "Trinity" Discussion* [online]. Available at <http://www.clausewitz.com/readings/Bassford/Trinity/NewVers1.htm>, accessed October 28, 2013.

Beauchamp, Alphonse (1806). *Histoire de la guerre de la Vendée et des Chouans, depuis son origine jusqu'à la pacification de 1800.* 3 volumes. Paris: Giguet et Michaud.

Brodie, Bernard (1973). *War and Politics.* New York: Macmillan.

Brodie, Bernard (1984). "The Continuing Relevance of *On War*," in Carl von Clausewitz, *On War*, trans. Michael Howard and Peter Paret. Princeton: Princeton University Press, 45–58.

Camon, Hubert (1911). *Clausewitz.* Paris: R. Chapelot.

Clausewitz, Carl von (*c.*1810). *Meine Vorlesungen über den kleinen Krieg gehalten auf der Kriegs-Schule 1810 u. 1811.* Handwritten manuscript, N. Clausewitz 4,001, in possession of the Universitäts- und Landesbibliothek Münster.

Clausewitz, Carl von (1835). *On War*, trans. and ed. unknown. *The Military and Naval Magazine of the United States*, 5 and 6 (August and September issues).

Clausewitz, Carl von (1873). *On War*, trans. Colonel James J. Graham. London: N. Trubner.

Clausewitz, Carl von (1908). *On War*, trans. Colonel James J. Graham. New and revised edn by Colonel Frederik N. Maude. 3 volumes. London: K. Paul, Trench, Trubner, & Co.

Clausewitz, Carl von (1909). *General Carl von Clausewitz on War*, trans. Miss [A. M. E.] Maguire, with notes by Thomas M. Maguire. London: William Clowes and Sons, Limited.

Clausewitz, Carl von (1943). *On War*, trans. Otto J. M. Jolles. New York: Random House.

Clausewitz, Carl von (1980). *Vom Kriege*, ed. Werner Hahlweg. 19th edn. Bonn: Dümmler.

Clausewitz, Carl von (1984). *On War*, trans. and ed. Michael Howard and Peter Paret. Revised edn. Princeton: Princeton University Press.

Clausewitz, Carl von (2010). *Vom Kriege.* Köln: Anaconda.

Cohen, Eliot A. (2002). *Supreme Command: Soldiers, Statesmen, and Leadership in Wartime.* New York: Simon and Schuster.

Creveld, Martin van (1991). *On Future War.* London: Brassey's.

Creveld, Martin van (2002). "The Transformation of War Revisited," *Small Wars and Insurgencies*, 13 (2): 3–15.

Croix, Armand-François de la (1759) [1752]. *Traité de la Petite Guerre pour les Compagnies Franches.* Paris: Antoin Boudet.

Daase, Christopher (2007). "Clausewitz and Small Wars," in Hew Strachan and Andreas Herberg-Rothe (eds.), Clausewitz in the Twenty-First Century. Oxford: Oxford University Press, 182–95.

Daase, Christopher and Schindler, Sebastian (2009). "Clausewitz, Guerillakrieg und Terrorismus: Zur Aktualität einer missverstandenen Kriegstheorie," *Politische Vierteljahresschrift*, 50 (4): 701–31.

Echevarria II, Antullio J. (1996). "War and Politics: The Revolution in Military Affairs and the Continued Relevance of Clausewitz," *Joint Forces Quarterly*, 10: 76–82.

Echevarria II, Antullio J. (2004). "Center of Gravity: Recommendations for Joint Doctrine," *Joint Forces Quarterly*, 35 (October): 10–17.

Echevarria II, Antullio J. (2007). *Clausewitz and Contemporary War*. Oxford: Oxford University Press.

Eikmeier, Dale C. (2013). "Give Carl von Clausewitz and the Center of Gravity a Divorce," *Small Wars Journal*, 9 (7) [online]. Available at <http://smallwarsjournal.com/jrnl/art/give-carl-von-clausewitz-and-the-center-of-gravity-a-divorce>, accessed November 21, 2013.

Emmerich, Andreas (1789). *The Partisan in War or the Use of a Corps of Light Troops to an Army*. London: H. Reynell for J. Debrett.

Emmerich, Andreas (1791). *Der Partheygänger im Kriege, oder der Nutzen eines Corps leichter Truppen für eine Armee*. Berlin: Vossische Buchhandlung.

Ewald, Johann von (1774). *Gedanken eines Hessischen Officiers über das, was man bey Führung eines Detaschements im Felde zu thun hat*. Cassel: Cramer.

Ewald, Johann von (1979). *Diary of the American War: A Hessian Journal*, trans. and ed. Joseph P. Tustin. New Haven: Yale University Press.

Ewald, Johann von (1790). *Abhandlung von dem Dienst der leichten Truppe*. Flensburg: Kortensche Buchhandlung and R. J. Boie.

Ewald, Johann von (1798). *Belehrungen über den Krieg, besonders über den kleinen Krieg, durch Beispiele grosser Helden und kluger und tapfere Männer*. 2 volumes. Schleswig: Rohß.

Gat, Azar (2001). *A History of Military Thought: From the Enlightenment to the Cold War*. Oxford: Oxford University Press.

Goltz, Colmar von der (1887). *The Nation in Arms*, trans. Philip A. Ashworth. London: W. H. Allen.

Hahlweg, Werner (1962). *Preußische Reformzeit und revolutionärer Krieg*. Frankfurt: Mittler & Sohn.

Hahlweg, Werner (ed.) (1966–90). *Carl von Clausewitz: Schriften, Aufsätze, Studien, Briefe*. 2 volumes, with vol. 2 comprising two separately bound parts. Göttingen: Vandenhoeck & Ruprecht.

Hahlweg, Werner (1986). "Clausewitz and Guerrilla Warfare," in Michael I. Handel (ed.), *Clausewitz and Modern Strategy*. London: Frank Cass, 127–33.

Hart, B. H. Liddell (1932). *Foch, Man of Orleans*. Boston: Little Brown.

Heuser, Beatrice (2010a). "Small Wars in the Age of Clausewitz: The Watershed between Partisan War and Peoples' War," *Journal of Strategic Studies*, 33 (1): 137–60.

Heuser, Beatrice (2010b). *The Evolution of Strategy: Thinking War from Antiquity to the Present*. Cambridge: Cambridge University Press.

Howard, Michael (1984). "The Influence of Clausewitz," in Carl von Clausewitz, *On War*, trans. Michael Howard and Peter Paret. Princeton: Princeton University Press, 27–44.

Huntington, Samuel P. (1957). *The Soldier and the State: The Theory and Politics of Civil–Military Relations*. Cambridge: Harvard University Press.

Jeney, Louis Michel de (1759). *Le partisan, ou l'art de faire la petite-guerre avec succès selon e génie de nos jours*. Den Haag: Constapel.

Kaldor, Mary (2010). "Inconclusive Wars: Is Clausewitz Still Relevant in these Global Times?" *Global Policy*, 1 (3): 271–81.

Kaldor, Mary (2012). *New and Old Wars: Violence in a Global Era*. 3rd edn. Stanford: Stanford University Press.

Keegan, John (1994). *A History of Warfare*. New York: Vintage.

Keen, David (2000). "Incentives and Disincentives for Violence," in Mats Berdal and David M. Malone (eds), *Greed and Grievance: Economic Agendas in Civil Wars*. Boulder: Lynne Rienner, 19–41.

Kinross, Stuart (2004). "Clausewitz and Low-Intensity Conflict," *Journal of Strategic Studies*, 27 (1): 35–58.

Luttwak, Edward (1995). "Toward Post-Heroic Warfare," *Foreign Affairs*, 74 (3): 109–22.

Marshall, Monty (1997). "Systems at Risk: Violence, Diffusion, and Disintegration in the Middle East," in David Carment and Patrick James (eds), *Wars in the Midst of Peace: The International Politics of Ethnic Conflict*. Pittsburgh: University of Pittsburgh Press, 82–115.

Melton, Stephen L. (2009). *The Clausewitzian Delusion: How the American Army Screwed Up the Wars in Iraq and Afghanistan*. Minneapolis: Zenith Press.

Mertsalov, Andrei N. (2004). "Jomini versus Clausewitz," in Ljubica Erickson and Mark Erickson (eds), *Russia: War, Peace and Diplomacy*. London: Weidenfeld & Nicolson, 11–19.

Moody, Peter R. Jr. (1979). "Clausewitz and the Fading Dialectic of War," *World Politics*, 31 (3): 417–33.

Moran, Daniel (1989). "Clausewitz and the Revolution," *Central European History*, 22 (2): 183–99.

Münkler, Herfried (2003). *Clausewitz' Theorie des Krieges: Würzburger Vorträge zur Rechtsphilosophie, Rechtstheorie und Rechtssoziologie*. Baden-Baden: Nomos.

Münkler, Herfried (2004). "Clausewitz und die neuen Kriege: Über Terrorismus, Partisanenkrieg und die Ökonomie der Gewalt," in Wilhelm Heitmeyer and Hans-Georg Soeffner (eds), *Gewalt*. Frankfurt: Suhrkamp, 362–80.

Münkler, Herfried (2008). "Krieg," *Erwägen-Wissen-Ethik*, 19 (1): 27–43.

Österreich, Erzherzog Karl von (1816). *Exercier-Reglement für die kaiserlich-königliche Infanterie*. Wien: Kaiserlich-königlich Hof- und Staats-Druckerei.

Paret, Peter (2010). "Clausewitz' Vorlesungen über den Kleinen Krieg an der neuen Kriegsschule in Berlin, 1810–1812," in Clausewitz Gesellschaft e.V. (ed.), *Jahrbuch 2010: Eine Zusammenfassung von Beiträgen aus der Arbeit der Gesellschaf 2010*. Hamburg: Deutsche Bibliothek, 34–45.

Pertz, Georg Heinrich (1865). *Das Leben des Feldmarschalls Grafen Neithardt von Gneisenau*. 2 volumes. Berlin: Reimer.

Rink, Martin (1999). *Vom "Partheygänger" zum Partisanen: Die Konzeption des kleinen Krieges in Preußen 1740–1813*. Frankfurt am Main: Peter Lang.

Rink, Martin (2006). "Der kleine Krieg: Entwicklung und Trends asymmetrischer Gewalt 1740 bis 1815," *Militärgeschichtliche Zeitschrift*, 65 (2): 355–88.

Roche, Compte de la (1770). *Essai sur la petite guerre; ou méthode de diriger les différentes opération d'un corps de 2500 hommes de troupes légères*. Paris: Saillant & Nyon.

Rothfels, Hans (1943). "Clausewitz," in Edward M. Earle (ed.), *Makers of Modern Strategy*. Princeton: Princeton University Press, 93–113.

Scharnhorst, Gerhard (1980) [1794]. *Militairisches Taschenbuch zum Gebrauch im Felde. Mit einem Vorwort von Ulrich Marwedel*. Reprint of the 3rd edn. Osnabrück: Biblio Verlag. (First edn 1792.)

Shepherd, John E. Jr. (1990). "*On War*: Is Clausewitz Still Relevant?" *Parameters*, 20 (3): 85–99.

Showalter, Dennis E. (1971). "The Prussian Landwehr and its Critics, 1813–1819," *Central European History* 4 (1): 3–33.

Snow, Donald M. (1997). *Distant Thunder: Patterns of Conflict in the Developing World*. 2nd edn. London: M. E. Sharpe.

Strachan, Hew (2001). "Clausewitz and the First World War," *Journal of Military History*, 75 (2): 367–91.

Strachan, Hew (2011). *Carl von Clausewitz's On War: A Biography*. Bhopal: Manjul.

Strange, Joseph L. and Iron, Richard (2004). "Center of Gravity: What Clausewitz Actually Meant," *Joint Forces Quarterly*, 35: 20–7.

Summers, Harry G. Jr. (1984). *On Strategy: A Critical Analysis of the Vietnam War*. New York: Dell.

Sumida, Jon T. (2001). "The Relationship of History and Theory in *On War*: The Clausewitzian Ideal and its Implications," *Journal of Military History*, 65 (2): 333–54.

Sumida, Jon T. (2008). *Decoding Clausewitz: A New Approach to On War*. Lawrence: University Press of Kansas.

[Süßmilch] (1805). *Versuch eines zweckmäßigen Vorpostendienstes bei den deutschen Armeen nach neuen auf die Erfahrung des letztern Krieges gebaueten Grundsätzen von einem deutschen Kavallerieoffizier*. Leipzig: Baumgärtnerische Buchhandlung.

Toffler, Alvin and Toffler, Heidi (1994). *War and Anti-War: Survival at the Dawn of the 21st Century*. London: Little & Brown.

Tse-Tung, Mao (1961). *On Guerrilla Warfare*, trans. Samuel B. Griffiths. Chicago: University of Illinois Press.

Valentini, Georg W. Freiherr von (1802). *Abhandlungen über den kleinen Krieg und über den Gebrauch der leichten Truppen mit Rücksicht auf den französischen Krieg, von einem preuß. Offizier*. Berlin: Himburgische Buchhandlung.

Villacres, Edward J. and Bassford, Christopher (1995). "Reclaiming the Clausewitzian Trinity," *Parameters*, 25 (3): 9–19.

Wilkinson, Philip (2003). "The Changing Nature of War: New Wine in Old Bottles—A New Paradigm or Paradigm Shift?" *The Royal Swedish Academy of War Sciences: Proceedings and Journal*, 207 (1): 25–35.

Index

advantageous 146
appropriate 97
barrier of 75
defense of the 36
difficult 226
extend of the 36
flat 38
irregular 83
mountainous 74
obstacles of (the) 74, 85
open 113
remote 37
rough(ness of) 82, 108
uneven 81
unsuitable 91
varied 30, 33–5, 38, 80, 94, 107–8, 113, 120,
 136, 146, 149, 156, 223
wide 25
terror(ism/ist) 1, 10, 18, 131, 133–6, 139,
 158, 163
Teupitz 123
theater of war 14, 16, 20, 64, 181, 190, 193–5,
 197, 211–14, 222–4
theory 7, 18, 22, 144, 166, 215
 abstract 4
 of insurgency 16
 of Small War 168
 of war(fare) 1, 4–5, 7, 221
Tiedemann, Major Karl Ludwig Heinrich
 v. 19, 24
Tiergarten 106, 119
timid(ity) 51, 143–4, 181, 209, *see also*
 intimidate(d)
tirailleurs 12, 207, *see also* units, specialized;
 Jäger
trade 22, 174–5
 blockades of 175
traditional(ly) 209, 215
 circumscribed military system 221
 conventions 215
 rule 168
 views 21
trap 61, 118, 133, 177
treasure(s) 189
Treaty of Paris 174
trench(es) 37, 75, 80, 85–7, 106, *see also*
 entrenchment
Treptow 119
Trinitarian
 conception 9
 framework 17
trinity 6–8
troop(s) 20, 23, 26–30, 32–4, 37, 39, 43, 46–7,
 50–3, 57–8, 60, 66, 68–72, 74–5, 79, 82,
 88, 91, 94–5, 100, 104–5, 108, 111,
 124–31, 133, 135–6, 138, 140, 143, 146,

148, 157–60, 165, 174, 186, 190, 196, 200,
 211, 213, 223–4
 assembly of 52
 Austrian 88, 102, 138
 auxiliary 26
 Bavarian 70, 218
 British 88
 cavalry 29, 45
 closed 36
 corps of 44
 decampment of the 133
 detached 117
 dispersion of the 127
 Dutch 88
 enemy('s) 70, 131, 133, 159, 193,
 204, 224
 English 77
 follow-on 200
 forward post 50, 96
 French 39, 70, 78, 138, 174, 182,
 195, 218
 German 51
 Hessian 39
 infantry 45
 inferior 225
 insurgent 204, 206
 irregular 12
 large masses (of) 31, 35, 37
 large numbers of 224
 light 41, 43–4, 52, 59–60, 62, 83, 100, 109,
 160, 167
 loss of 130
 marching of 93
 occupying 74, 218
 Prussian 39, 160, 174, 177, 190, 193
 quartering of 174, 223
 rations 54
 regular 12, 202, 224
 remaining 136, 138, 200
 retreating 158–9
 returning 133
 Russian 174
 side 116, 118–19
 small 81, 118
 soutiens 98
 Spanish 138
 steadfastness of 146
 subordinate 46
 supporting 30, 42, 56
 units 35
 weary 43
 withdrawing 93
Tugendbund 172
tyranny 169, 177, 184, 208
tyrant 173, 180
Tyrol(ean/s) 70, 131, 196, 218

Printed in the USA/Agawam, MA
November 7, 2017

662044.069